MONOGRAPHS OF THE
SOCIETY FOR RESEARCH IN
CHILD DEVELOPMENT

Serial No. 254, Vol. 63, Nos. 2–3, 1998

INDIVIDUAL DIFFERENCES AND THE DEVELOPMENT OF PERCEIVED CONTROL

Ellen A. Skinner
Melanie J. Zimmer-Gembeck
James P. Connell

WITH COMMENTARY BY
Jacquelynne S. Eccles

MONOGRAPHS OF THE SOCIETY FOR RESEARCH IN CHILD DEVELOPMENT
Serial No. 254, Vol. 63, Nos. 2–3, 1998

CONTENTS

ABSTRACT

SKINNER, ELLEN A.; ZIMMER-GEMBECK, MELANIE J.; and CONNELL, JAMES P. Individual Differences and the Development of Perceived Control. *Monographs of the Society for Research in Child Development*, 1998, **63**(2–3, Serial No. 254).

Research on individual differences demonstrates that children's perceived control exerts a strong effect on their academic achievement and that, in turn, children's actual school performance influences their sense of control. At the same time, developmental research shows systematic age-graded changes in the processes that children use to regulate and interpret control experiences. Drawing on both these perspectives, the current study examines (1) age differences in the operation of beliefs-performance cycles and (2) the effects of these cycles on the development of children's perceived control and classroom engagement from the third to the seventh grade.

Longitudinal data on about 1,600 children were collected six times (every fall and spring) over 3 consecutive school years, including children's reports of their perceived control and individual interactions with teachers; teachers' reports of each student's engagement in class; and, for a subset of students, grades and achievement tests. Analyses of individual differences and individual growth curves (estimated using hierarchical linear modeling procedures) were consistent, not only with a cyclic model of context, self, action, and outcomes, but also with predictors of individual development over 5 years from grade 3 to grade 7. Children who experienced teachers as warm and contingent were more likely to develop optimal profiles of control; these beliefs supported more active engagement in the classroom, resulting in better academic performance; success in turn predicted the maintenance of optimistic beliefs about the effectiveness of effort. In contrast, children who experienced teachers as unsupportive were more likely to develop beliefs that emphasized external causes; these profiles of control predicted escalating classroom disaffection and lower scholastic achievement; in turn, these poor performances led children to increasingly doubt their own capacities and to believe even more strongly in the power of luck and unknown causes.

Systematic age differences in analyses suggested that the aspects of control around which these cycles are organized change with development. The beliefs that regulated engagement shifted from effort to ability and from beliefs about the causes of school performance (strategy beliefs) to beliefs about the self's capacities. The feedback loop from individual performance to subsequent perceived control also became more pronounced and more focused on ability. These relatively linear developmental changes may have contributed to an abrupt decline in children's classroom engagement as they negotiated the transition to middle school and experienced losses in teacher support. Implications are discussed for future study of individual differences and development, especially the role of changing school contexts, mechanisms of influence, and developmentally appropriate interventions to optimize children's perceived control and engagement.

I. INTRODUCTION AND OVERVIEW

One of the strongest predictors of children's performance in school is individual differences in their perceived control. Reviews of hundreds of studies document robust relations between children's cognitive performance and different aspects of their perceived control, including locus of control (Findley & Cooper, 1983; Stipek, 1980; Stipek & Weisz, 1981), mastery versus helplessness (Dweck & Elliott, 1983; Nolen-Hoeksema, Girgus, & Seligman, 1986), causal attributions for success and failure (Graham, 1991; Marsh, 1984; Weiner, 1985a, 1986), and self-efficacy (Bandura, 1986; Berry & West, 1993; Schunk, 1989, 1991; Zimmerman, 1995).

Experimental and intervention studies have demonstrated that the relation between control beliefs and academic functioning is a reciprocal one. Experimental studies show that changes in children's perceptions of efficacy, contingency, and control do in fact produce changes in quality and persistence of problem solving and performance on academic tasks (e.g., Diener & Dweck, 1978; Dweck, 1991; Schunk, 1991; Seligman, 1975). At the same time, intervention studies also reveal that, when children's actual academic performance is improved (e.g., through direct tuition of metacognitive skills), these changes in level of performance have a direct effect on children's self-efficacy judgments, sense of control, ability estimates, and perceived competence (e.g., Bouffard-Bouchard, 1989; Redlich, Debus, & Walker, 1986; Schunk, 1981; Schunk & Swartz, 1991).

Control experts have argued that the reciprocal relations between control beliefs and level of actual performance can set up self-confirming cycles in which "the rich get richer and the poor get poorer" (Seligman, 1975). Children who hold high perceptions of control are likely to produce performances that confirm their initial expectations, whereas children who initially have a low sense of control are likely to generate experiences for themselves that confirm their pessimistic beliefs. Nowhere should a self-confirming cycle be more evident than in the academic domain. In school, learning materials are geared to be challenging, to require effort for success, and to be based on cumulative mastery. If children begin to fail, their self-doubt and deteriorating performance may create a downward spiral (Skinner, 1991).

Because of its strong effects on performance, perceived control has been the target of much research on children's functioning in the academic domain. For the most part, this work focuses on the mechanisms by which perceived control can exert an influence on children's actual cognitive performance. To some extent, however, researchers have also attempted to identify, among the many constructs of control, the specific sets of beliefs that have the strongest effect on children's academic achievement. An overview of this work is provided, followed by a description of the current research program and how it aims to build on and extend previous research.

INDIVIDUAL DIFFERENCES IN PERCEIVED CONTROL

In general, *perceived control* refers to a whole set of beliefs about how effective the self can be in producing desired and preventing undesired outcomes. Included in the concept are convictions about the self as capable and efficacious as well as about the environment as structured and responsive. The history of research on the role of perceived control in children's academic performance is a long one, involving many different general theoretical frameworks and a host of specific constructs, including locus of control, causal attributions, learned helplessness, and self-efficacy (H. Heckhausen, 1991; Weiner, 1986; for a review of definitions and related constructs, see Skinner, 1996). As is common, the earliest work with children was derived quite directly from research with adults. However, subsequent work refined and reconceptualized the nature of perceived control in children.

Locus of Control

From Rotter's general social learning theory, itself an exemplar from the class of expectancy-value models, came the construct *internal versus external locus of control* (Rotter, 1966, 1975, 1990). Initially, the construct was defined as follows:

> When a reinforcement is perceived by the subject as following some action of his own but not being entirely contingent upon his action, then in our culture, it is typically perceived as the result of luck, chance, fate, as under the control of powerful others, or as unpredictable because of the great complexity of forces surrounding him. When the event is interpreted in this way by an individual, we have labeled this a belief in external control. If the person perceives that the event is contingent

upon his own behavior or relatively permanent characteristics, we have termed this a belief in internal control. (Rotter, 1966, p. 1)

Adapted for use with children by Nowicki, Strickland, Bialer, and others in the form of general measures (e.g., Bialer, 1961; Mischel, Zeiss, & Zeiss, 1974; Nowicki & Strickland, 1973), the link between children's locus of control and their school performance was established early and often. In a review by Findley and Cooper in 1983, 98 studies were cited that demonstrated correlations between locus of control and children's school grades and achievement test scores (for a review, see also Stipek & Weisz, 1981).

The work of the Crandalls marked the beginning of domain-specific assessment of locus of control in children with the construction of the Intellectual Achievement Responsibility Questionnaire, a forced-choice measure that focuses on effort as the internal cause and teachers as the external cause of school success and failure (Crandall, Katkovsky, & Crandall, 1965). This research compared both motivational and behavioral characteristics of children classified as showing an internal versus an external locus of control (Crandall, 1967; Crandall, Katkovsky, & Preston, 1962; Crandall & Rabson, 1960) and the antecedents of locus of control in parent-child interactions (Carton & Nowicki, 1994; Crandall & Crandall, 1983; Schneewind, 1995).

Attribution Theory

Almost as soon as research on locus of control was published, theorists pointed out that the two causal categories used to demonstrate the effects of locus of control (i.e., tasks of skill and tasks of chance) differed not only on the dimension of internality but also on stability (Weiner, Heckhausen, Meyer, & Cook, 1972; Weiner, Nierenberg, & Goldstein, 1976). From this analysis, a theory of causal attribution was constructed (Weiner, 1985a, 1986) according to which people spontaneously attempt to interpret the causes of important successes and failures (especially failures; Weiner, 1985b). From this perspective, the subsequent effects of causal interpretations are determined by the dimensions underlying the causes, specifically, the dimensions of internality, stability, and controllability. For example, a causal attribution of failure to effort has a marked positive effect on subsequent task persistence because the cause is typically perceived to be internal, controllable, and unstable. Subsequent research has examined the consequences of different attributional patterns, which seem to have their biggest effects on differentiated emotional reactions to success and failure and on subsequent expectations of performance (Weiner, 1986).

Causal attribution theory has been broadly applied to children's academic behavior, emotion, motivation, performance, and achievement (for re-

3

views, see Graham, 1991; Marsh, 1984; Mullen & Riordan, 1988; Weiner, 1979; Whitley & Frieze, 1985). Research has also examined the antecedents of different patterns of attributions, most notably, the kinds of performance profiles that lead to certain attributions. For example, failure is most likely to be attributed to ability when a person repeatedly fails on a normatively easy task despite great effort. In addition, attributional researchers have examined the kinds of social cues that communicate different causal interpretations of children's school performance. For example, research shows that, when a teacher displays anger following a student's failure, this communicates to the student that a controllable cause is responsible and the child is more likely to attribute the failure to inadequate effort; however, when a teacher reacts with sympathy to a student's poor performance, she communicates that an uncontrollable cause is responsible, and the child is more likely to attribute the failure to insufficient ability (Graham, 1984; for a review, see Graham, 1990).

Researchers have also examined different attributional patterns in children's and parents' understandings of the causes of school performance as a factor in cross-cultural differences in school achievement. For example, Stevenson and Lee (1990) have shown that Chinese and Japanese parents accord a more prominent role to children's effort than to their innate ability as causes of school achievement, whereas American parents view effort and ability as of about equal importance. In addition, Chinese and Japanese children were less likely than American children to emphasize factors associated with innate ability. In all three cultures, children who attributed failure to lack of effort also showed the highest achievement in math and reading.

Based on decades of support for an attributional model of behavior and emotion, interventions have aimed to improve children's academic performance by means of attributional retraining (Foersterling, 1985). The basic goal is to move children away from attributions of failure to stable and uncontrollable causes, such as ability, and toward an understanding of performance in terms of causes that are unstable and potentially controllable, such as effort, interest, or specific strategies (e.g., Dweck, Davidson, Nelson, & Enna, 1978).

Learned Helplessness

The classic work on learned helplessness provided a breakthrough in the understanding of the effects of loss of control on human behavior, emotion, and motivation. Early experiments (initially conducted with infrahuman species) demonstrated that noncontingency, defined as a lack of connection between actions and outcomes ($p[O|A] = p[O|\text{not } A]$), undermined subsequent performance even on contingent tasks. Prolonged exposure to noncontingency produced a syndrome of helplessness effects, including lowered response initiation, difficulty detecting actual contingencies, passivity, apathy, depressed affect, and sometimes even death (Seligman, 1975).

Different explanations for the severe and pervasive effects of exposure to noncontingency have been offered. From the original work on helplessness, it was widely assumed that performance deficits were a motivational problem: individuals formed expectations of noncontingency during exposure to actual noncontingency and generalized those expectations to subsequent contingent tasks. However, researchers were forced to reconsider when studies produced findings inconsistent with these explanations. First, studies found that noncontingency caused performance deficits even when it was *not* perceived (e.g., when noncontingent outcomes were positive; Tennen, Drum, Gillen, & Stanton, 1982). Second, despite the fact that noncontingent failure (i.e., low-probability outcome) produced higher expectations of noncontingency, experiments showed that noncontingency with *high* outcome probability caused worse performance deficits (Kofta & Sedek, 1989). Supplementing motivational explanations have been functional explanations, proposed by action theorists, who argue that prolonged exposure to noncontingency interferes directly with action implementation (Brunstein, 1994; Brunstein & Olbrich, 1985; Gollwitzer, 1990; Heckhausen & Gollwitzer, 1987; Kofta, 1993; Kuhl, 1981, 1984; Kuhl & Beckman, 1985; Kuhl & Weiss, 1994; Sedek & Kofta, 1990; Sedek, Kofta, & Tyszka, 1993).

Seligman and his colleagues (Abramson, Seligman, & Teasdale, 1978) offered a reformulated version of learned helplessness, positing that expectations of noncontingency were a sufficient (but not a necessary) cause of helplessness deficits, and proposing as a central predictor of these expectations a pattern of interpretations, referred to as an *explanatory style,* that construed the causes of negative outcomes to be internal, global, and stable. Research on explanatory style has demonstrated the negative effects of this pattern of explanations on a wide range of emotional and behavioral outcomes, especially in times of challenge or failure (Peterson, Maier, & Seligman, 1993; Peterson & Seligman, 1984).

Failure in school seemed to provide an apt, ecologically valid analogy to experimentally created experiences of noncontingency, and several research programs were conducted using different operationalizations of noncontingency and a range of different cognitive and academic outcomes (Fincham, Hokoda, & Sanders, 1989; Nolen-Hoeksema, Girgus, & Seligman, 1986, 1992; for a review, see Fincham & Cain, 1986). The earliest and most comprehensive program of research to examine and elaborate on helplessness as a factor in children's cognitive and school performances was initiated by Dweck and her colleagues (for reviews, see Burhans & Dweck, 1995; Dweck, 1991; Dweck & Elliott, 1983; Dweck & Leggett, 1988; Dweck & Licht, 1980). These studies examined the mechanisms through which helplessness interfered with children's performance (Diener & Dweck, 1978, 1980; Dweck, 1975; Dweck &

Gillard, 1975; Licht & Dweck, 1984) as well as exploring the social antecedents of helplessness in interactions with teachers in the classroom (Dweck, 1976; Dweck & Bush, 1976; Dweck et al., 1978) and parents at home (Hokoda & Fincham, 1995; Nolen-Hoeksema, Wolfson, Mumme, & Guskin, 1995).

Self-Efficacy

When the first major theoretical article on self-efficacy (Bandura, 1977) appeared, the field was dominated by theories of locus of control and learned helplessness. Bandura pointed out that these theories focused exclusively on what he termed *response-outcome expectations,* or, in general, "a person's estimate that a given behavior will lead to certain outcomes." He argued, however, that, no matter how strong people's convictions are that a particular course of action will produce a desired outcome, people will nevertheless refrain from acting unless they are convinced that they "can successfully execute the behavior required to produce the outcome" (Bandura, 1977, p. 193). These convictions were referred to as *efficacy expectations* or, later, simply as *self-efficacy.* Bandura's seminal article introduced into psychology a distinction that had been present in sociological thinking for several decades (for a review, see Gurin & Brim, 1984) and had also appeared in some expectancy-value models (e.g., Vroom, 1964) and action-theory models of achievement motivation (Heckhausen, 1977).

Work on children's school performance figures prominently among the many different domains and age groups in which the effects of self-efficacy have been examined. Research by Bandura himself and by his colleagues, most notably Schunk and Zimmerman, has examined the multiple pathways by which self-efficacy can promote or interfere with children's self-regulated learning, motivation, affect, performance, and achievement in many different academic subjects (Bandura, 1991; Bandura, Barbaranelli, Caprara, & Pastorelli, 1996; Bandura & Schunk, 1981; Bouffard-Bouchard, Parent, & Larivee, 1991; Pintrich & De Groot, 1990; Schunk & Swartz, 1991; Zimmerman, Bandura, & Martinez-Pons, 1992), especially mathematics (e.g., Pajares & Miller, 1994) (for reviews, see Bandura, 1989, 1996; Multon, Brown, & Lent, 1991; Schunk, 1989, 1991; Zimmerman, 1995).

Based on accumulating evidence, interventions have been constructed to bolster children's estimates of their academic efficacy, using a variety of creative methods, including modeling (Schunk & Hanson, 1985; Zimmerman & Ringle, 1981), positive performance feedback, attributional retraining (Schunk & Cox, 1986), and tutoring of effective strategies. These interventions have been among the most effective in improving children's sense of control and their subsequent motivation for and engagement in academic activities.

Subjective Probability of Success, Ability Estimates, and Perceived Competence

Children's perceptions of their own ability or competence constitute another set of constructs that has been studied both as a product of prior and as a predictor of future school performance. These self-perceptions, not necessarily conceptualized as related to children's perceived control, have been examined in isolation as predictors of children's academic success (Helmke & van Aken, 1995; Marsh, 1984; Phillips, 1984) and in combination with other constructs from expectancy-value theories (Blumenfeld, Pintrich, Meece, & Wessels, 1982; Eccles et al., 1983; Eccles, Lord, Roeser, Barber, & Jozefowicz, in press; Eccles, Midgley, & Adler, 1984; Eccles, Wigfield, Harold, & Blumenfeld, 1993; Meece, Wigfield, & Eccles, 1990; Roeser, Midgley, & Urdan, 1996) and theories of effectance motivation (Harter, 1978, 1982; Harter & Connell, 1984; Harter, Whitesell, & Kowalski, 1992).

Children's perceptions that they are incompetent have been shown to exert a detrimental effect on their school performance, even among high-achieving children (Miserandino, 1996; Phillips, 1984, 1987; Phillips & Zimmerman, 1990). For example, objectively competent third and fourth graders who doubted their own abilities (relative to more confident children) reported feeling less curiosity and enjoyment and more anxiety, anger, and boredom in school and reported that they ignored, avoided, and faked more schoolwork; in addition, they performed more poorly in math and social studies (Miserandino, 1996). In a similar vein, and consistent with theories of achievement motivation, children's estimates of the probability that they will succeed on academic tasks, in combination with the value that they place on those tasks, have been found to predict many aspects of their academic functioning, including goal setting, task choice, involvement, and persistence (for reviews, see Eccles et al., 1983; Eccles, Wigfield, & Schiefele, 1998).

Multidimensional Conceptualizations of Perceived Control

Multidimensional conceptions of perceived control attempted to differentiate and integrate major theories of control (including locus of control, causal attributions, learned helplessness, and self-efficacy), preserving their unique constructs while at the same time combining them within an integrative framework (Connell, 1985; J. Heckhausen, 1991; Little, Oettingen, Stetsenko, & Baltes, 1995; Skinner, Chapman, & Baltes, 1988b; Skinner, Wellborn, & Connell, 1990; Weisz, 1983, 1986; Weisz & Stipek, 1982). Pivotal in this regard was the distinction between beliefs about the causal structure and responsiveness of the environment (which were central to theories of locus of control and attributional theories) and beliefs about the self's access to potentially effective means (which were central to theories of self-efficacy, perceived competence, and ability estimates) (for an overview, see Skinner,

1996). These two sets of beliefs are sometimes referred to, respectively, as *contingency* and *competence* (Weisz, 1986; Weisz & Stipek, 1982), *strategy* and *capacity* (Wellborn, Connell, & Skinner, 1989), or *means-ends* and *agency* (Little et al., 1995).

As researchers integrated theories focusing on causal dimensions (e.g., attribution theory) with theories focusing on the resources of the self (e.g., self-efficacy theory), they also realized that it would be necessary to broaden the range of causal categories considered. In addition to the prototypical cause associated with control, namely, an individual's own responses or efforts, causal categories include *powerful others* (Crandall et al., 1965) and *chance* or *luck* (Levenson, 1973). In the area of school performance, an additional important causal category, identified by both attribution theory and learned helplessness researchers, has been *ability* (Dweck, 1991). Taken together, these categories map onto the important causal dimensions of *internality, stability,* and *controllability* (Weiner, 1985a).

Developmental researchers also identified causal categories that may be unique to children's beliefs. The most important was the causal category *unknown source of control* (Connell, 1985). Discovered in open-ended interviews with children about the causes of success and failure, *unknown control* was designed to capture children's perceptions that they simply had no idea about the causes of desired and undesired outcomes in a particular domain. Individual differences in unknown source of control were among the strongest predictors of poor school performance during childhood (Connell, 1985).

Studies that used these multidimensional assessments to sort out the aspects of perceived control that predict school performance have both confirmed and extended research findings based on other frameworks. For example, in an earlier study of the predictors of elementary school children's engagement in classroom activities, their school grades, and their achievement test scores (Skinner et al., 1990), we found a pattern of multiple predictors. Consistent with theories of perceived competence and success expectancies, control beliefs were strong predictors of academic success. Consistent with reformulated learned helplessness and self-efficacy theories, children's beliefs about their ability and their capacity to exert effort were also closely related to good school performance. Consistent with attribution and locus of control theories, however, additional strong predictors of (impaired) academic performance included children's beliefs that school success and failure were caused by external (e.g., powerful others), uncontrollable (e.g., luck), or unknown factors. Extending this work, multidimensional measures also allowed us to examine unique and interactive effects of beliefs about capacities and strategies. For example, school performance was lowest for children who believed that ability was an important cause (high strategy beliefs) *and* that they themselves were not very smart (low capacity beliefs).

Multidimensional measures also allow for the study of how different as-

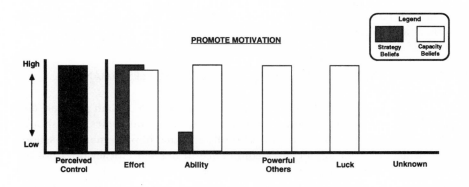

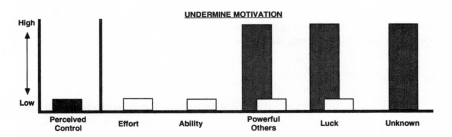

FIGURE 1.—Profiles of perceived control hypothesized to promote and undermine engagement. (From Skinner, 1995, reprinted with permission from Sage Publications.)

pects of perceived control function in the action sequence (H. Heckhausen, 1991; Heckhausen & Gollwitzer, 1987; Skinner, 1991, 1995, 1996). For example, beliefs about capacities and control (akin to self-efficacy beliefs) seem to have their effects in the *regulation* of action and so most strongly predict goal setting, outcome choice, initiation and implementation of action, and persistence. In contrast, beliefs about the causes of performance (e.g., attributional processes) seem to have their effects on the *interpretation* of action and so most strongly influence emotional reactions to action sequences and expectations about future control.

From this research, it has been possible to identify *profiles* of perceived control, or combinations of beliefs, that promote and undermine children's school performance (see Figure 1). For example, the profile of beliefs most likely to undermine academic engagement and school performance would be the combination of beliefs that one has little control (low control beliefs), that the causes of school success and failure are unknown (high unknown strategy beliefs), that one's ability and one's capacity to exert effort are low (low capacity beliefs for effort and ability), and that, although external and uncontrollable factors like powerful others and luck are critical to school success, one has access to neither (high strategy and low capacity for powerful others and luck).

PROCESSES OF PERCEIVED CONTROL AND ACADEMIC PERFORMANCE

A goal central to all theories of control has been to explain precisely *how* children's perceptions of control affect their academic outcomes. Why should the simple *belief* that one has control result in actual improvements in school performance? After all, a child's confidence in her self-efficacy does not increase her innate ability. Over several decades of intense scrutiny, initial motivational explanations (in which it was assumed that, when children realize that their actions are futile, they rationally decide not to exert any effort) have given way to explanations that invoke multiple mechanisms, including motivation, but also involving emotion, coping, volition, self-regulation, metacognition, and "other even more mysterious mechanisms" (Brown, 1984).

Mechanisms

Decades of research with the constructs described previously have used a wide range of designs, including process-oriented descriptive studies analyzing children's talk-aloud protocols as they succeed and fail (Diener & Dweck, 1978), experimental studies with finely grained outcomes (Kuhl, 1984), and naturalistic studies with a broad range of mediating variables (Bandura et al., 1996). This research converges on a picture in which loss of control undermines almost every aspect of the action sequence and in which the effects of high and low control are opposite but not symmetrical (for reviews, see Bandura, 1989; Skinner, 1995). The effects of control are pronounced under conditions of stress or challenge and in difficult tasks that place great demands on cognitive capacities (Boggiano, Main, & Katz, 1988; Licht & Dweck, 1984), the very conditions that are likely to characterize much of children's performance in school.

Compared to children who have high perceived control, children who doubt their competence select and prefer easier tasks and set lower and less concrete goals. They fail to impose structure on the problem space or to sequence their proposed action steps; their plans are less detailed and contain fewer fallback strategies. On demanding tasks, they show impaired information structuring in different phases of processing, such as truncated information search, forming impoverished mental representations of decision alternatives, or applying less complex decision rules and strategies. In the face of challenges or failure, children who question their efficacy become confused; they lose concentration and focus; they are more likely to ruminate about the causes of difficulty and to begin making attributions that involve their own ability. Over time, their effort decreases, they experience cognitive demobilization and inhibited generation of ideas, they initiate fewer responses, and they become discouraged, despondent, and passive. They tend to explain failures in terms of their own shortcomings and to attribute any successes to luck or unknown causes. They hold a pessimistic view of subsequent encounters, reduce their expectations of future control, and do not plan action steps to prevent the reoccurrence of aversive events.

In contrast, compared to children with low perceived control, children who believe that they are competent are likely to select challenging tasks, set high and concrete goals, and form well-structured sequential plans. They initiate action, exert effort, and persist. Even in the face of obstacles and resistance, they are able to implement their intentions fully. Challenges actually improve their concentration and attention. They focus on the task at hand and do not ruminate about the causes of failure, even in a self-enhancing way. They remain able to generate and monitor strategies flexibly and to test alternative hypotheses systematically. In general, they maintain or improve access to their entire cognitive and problem-solving repertoires, actually learning and acquiring more skills during taxing interactions. Even if all efforts are unsuccessful, they maintain an optimistic outlook and do not doubt their efficacy or their potential for future control. They actively take steps to prevent subsequent failure by making and carrying out plans to obtain help or information and to study and learn more.

Self-Confirming Cycles

It is no wonder, then, that control theorists have argued that these patterns of action contribute to a self-confirming cycle. If children with low perceived control approach and respond to difficult tasks in ways that undermine their chances for actual success, then their deteriorating performances should confirm their already low perceptions of control. In contrast, if children with initially high perceived control actually initiate and implement actions more effectively, then difficult interactions are likely to be resolved more successfully, consolidating or enhancing initial feelings of competence and control.

In one of the few empirical tests to date, a time-series study directly examined the unfolding of cycles of beliefs, action, and outcomes in naturally existing school classrooms over real time (Schmitz & Skinner, 1993). The design of this study was organized around children's academic performances, operationalized as all graded assignments (homework and tests). Following completion of an assignment, and again directly after an assignment was returned, children filled out short questionnaires that assessed their expected control, engagement, actual performance, subjective performance evaluation, and attributions about the causes of their correct answers and their mistakes.

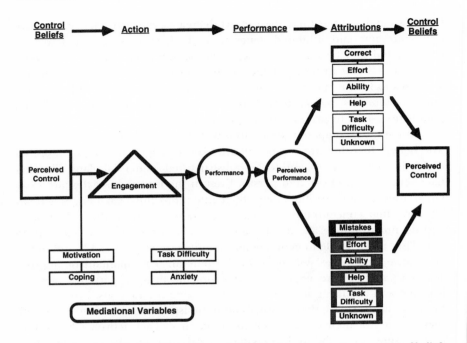

FIGURE 2.—Overview of a time-series study designed to examine the processes of beliefs-performance cycles across real time in the classroom (Schmitz & Skinner, 1993). (Adapted from Skinner, 1995, with permission from Sage Publications.)

Specifically, when an assignment was completed, each child reported his or her behavioral engagement in completing the work (time spent and effort exertion) and the difficulty of the task. Directly after the graded assignments were returned, children completed another assessment in which they reported their actual performance (number correct and incorrect), their subjective estimate of the performance, their attributions of the causes of their right and wrong answers (ratings for effort, ability, task difficulty, help, and unknown causes), and their estimates of future control. The 152 fourth and sixth graders who participated reported on 20–25 cycles during the 3–4-month study. An overview of the study is provided in Figure 2.

Data were arranged sequentially, and interindividual correlations were calculated in order to examine (1) the effects of expected control on subsequent engagement, (2) the effects of engagement on subsequent actual performance, (3) the effects of performance on subsequent causal attributions, and (4) the effects of attributions on subsequent expectations of control. At the interindividual level, the findings were consistent with each link in a cyclic model. Children with higher expected control exerted more effort in the preparation and implementation of their academic tasks (relative to children who expected less control). Children who tried harder and persisted longer were more likely to achieve better actual performances (than children who were less engaged).

Compared to children who performed more poorly, children who succeeded at academic tasks were more likely to take credit for their successes, by attributing their correct answers to effort, ability, concentration on tests, ease of homework, and help with homework, and to attribute their wrong answers to unknown causes. In contrast, children who performed more poorly were more likely to blame themselves, by attributing correct answers to unknown causes and errors to lack of effort and difficult tests. Finally, children's attributions predicted their subsequent performance expectations. The strongest predictors of high subsequent control expectations were attributions of correct answers to effort, ability, and concentration; and the strongest predictors of lower subsequent perceived control were attributions of errors to effort, ability, and unknown causes.

These results are consistent with experimental and correlational studies that confirm both a strong contribution of perceived control to academic performance and a strong feedback effect of academic performance on subsequent perceived control (effects that are found in other domains and for other age groups as well). The results of the time-series study, taken together with decades of interindividual studies, document the self-fulfilling nature of beliefs-performance relations. If these cycles are allowed to unfold across time, they could result in magnification of initial individual differences in control and academic performance and eventually in actual differences in cognitive competencies. This possibility is depicted graphically in Figure 3.

OVERVIEW OF THE RESEARCH PROJECT

From the beginning of research examining how individual differences in perceived control influence children's academic performance and achievement, developmentalists and developmental sensibilities were present. Measures of perceived control were developmentally appropriate; that is, they were geared to the language and concrete causal categories used by children (see esp. Connell, 1985; Crandall et al., 1965; Harter, 1983). Likewise, the dependent measures of cognitive functioning and performance were appropriately age graded, with such concrete tasks as puzzles or building blocks used with preschoolers and more advanced activities, such as concept formation tasks and mazes, used with elementary school children.

Development and Individual Differences

However, just as there is no single correct definition of development, there is no single developmental perspective; in fact, the conceptions of devel-

13

SKINNER ET AL.

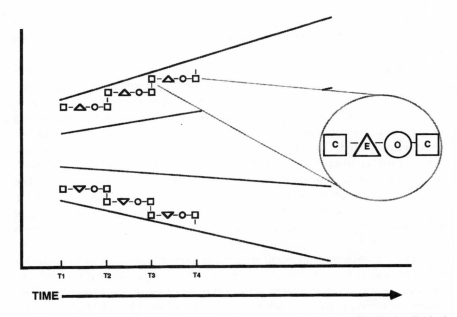

FIGURE 3.—A depiction of how beliefs-performance cycles can magnify initial individual differences and shape trajectories of control and engagement over time. C = perceived control; E = engagement; O = outcomes. (Adapted from Skinner, 1991, with permission from the University of Chicago Press.)

opment that guide the field change over time. In the 1960s, when work on children's perceived control was initially flourishing, conceptions of and research on individual differences were, for the most part, distinct from those involving development. Although children were considered a unique subpopulation within which to examine the functioning of individual differences, few attempts were made to integrate individual and developmental conceptions. If developmental perspectives were employed at all, they were usually used to explore questions about the origins of individual differences, that is, to examine the early developmental conditions (usually of child rearing) that shaped later individual differences in perceptions of control (for a review, see Carton & Nowicki, 1994).

In general, the only work considered to be "purely" developmental focused on *normative* patterns of change. This work examined, for instance, the ages at which children are first able to detect contingencies between their actions and desired outcomes accurately, the cognitive prerequisites for understanding the role of task difficulty as a performance factor, whether internal locus of control increases or decreases across childhood, or the earliest ages at which children can compare their own abilities to those of their agemates (for reviews, see Flammer, 1995; Harter, 1983; Heckhausen, 1982, 1984;

14

Skinner, 1995; Weisz, 1983). Compared to the enormous volume of research on individual differences, the literature on normative development was small and, for the most part, typically considered peripheral to an understanding of the functioning of individual differences. Recently, however, researchers have begun to focus explicitly on the intersection of individual differences and the development of perceived control (Baltes & Baltes, 1986; Brandt-staedter, 1984, 1989; Brandtstaedter, Wentura, & Greve, 1993; Connell, 1985; Fincham & Cain, 1986; Flammer, 1995; Gatz & Karel, 1993; Lachman, 1986; Skinner, 1991, 1995; Skinner & Connell, 1986; Steitz, 1982).

Primary Goals

The program of research described here was an attempt to build on previous work both on individual differences and on the development of perceived control and to explicitly integrate those two bodies of work. It was grounded in life span conceptions of development (Baltes, 1987; Baltes, Lindenberger, & Staudinger, 1998) and guided by the overarching notion that the target of developmental study is the pattern of an individual's change across time and the explanation of interindividual differences in these trajectories of change (Baltes, Reese, & Nesselroade, 1977). Hence, the primary contribution of this program of research is the description of individual differences in developmental trajectories of children's control and engagement in the classroom from the beginning of the third to the end of the seventh grade and the examination of systematic predictors of different trajectories.

The second major contribution of this research is the examination of whether normative developments in the ways children perceive and interpret control experiences have an effect on the functioning of individual differences in perceived control. For example, given that children's beliefs that the causes of their school success and failure are unknown decline during the elementary school years, do these normative declines produce changes in the effects of individual differences in unknown control beliefs, with the result that these beliefs are more powerful predictors of engagement and school performance at younger rather than older ages? In this program of research, we examined how two normative developmental shifts, one at about grade 4 and another at about grade 6, might produce changes in the aspects of perceived control that predict and are influenced by children's school performance.

The research program involved about 1,600 children aged 8–13 who were assessed six times (each fall and spring) over 3 years. Children reported their perceived control and their experiences with the social context—in this case, with teachers. Teachers reported on each student's engagement and disaffection in the classroom. For a subset of children, information on actual performance was obtained from school records.

15

In Chapter II, we describe the developmental work that provided the basis for the present study, including work on the origins of perceived control, on developmental assessments of control, and on the normative development of some of the cognitive processes that children use to perceive and interpret control experiences. This chapter ends with a brief introduction to the potential contributions of the present program of research (highlighting the motivational model of cyclic relations between children's beliefs and their performance), suggestions about the ways in which normative development shapes the particulars of how individual differences function within that model, and a discussion of different ways to examine the antecedents and consequences of children's individual trajectories of engagement and perceived control.

Chapter III describes the sample and measures and presents descriptive statistics. In this chapter, we highlight the sequential design of the study and describe the rationale for the linked decisions that we made about how to divide up the cross-sectional and longitudinal samples for different analyses. Chapter IV presents detailed hypotheses and results of the analyses designed to examine issues of developmental change in the functioning of individual differences—including tests of the cyclic model across a school year, an examination of age differences in the functioning of the model, and more finely grained analyses of age differences in the aspects of perceived control that predict and are predicted by school performance.

Chapter V deals with the estimation, description, and examination of individual differences in children's trajectories of engagement and perceived control from the third to the seventh grade. We provide an overview of the statistical procedures used to estimate individual growth curves and their parameters and show step by step how these were determined and calculated for the variables in this sample. Detailed hypotheses and results are presented for both the antecedents and the consequences of individual differences in children's trajectories of control. Finally, we report a set of exploratory analyses designed to detect whether the antecedents and consequences of individual trajectories differ depending on the developmental phase encompassed by the trajectory. For example, do the predictors of individual differences in children's engagement trajectories differ when the target is that portion of the engagement trajectory that is normatively stable compared to that portion that is normatively declining?

At the end of each results chapter, we provide a summary. We then use Chapter VI to integrate the findings and highlight their implications. These include discussion of conceptual and empirical issues directly related to children's perceived control in the academic domain but also explore the more general challenges of integrating individual differences and developmental phenomena as well as the potential and limitations of growth curve methodologies for capturing patterns of individual development.

II. DEVELOPMENT AND THE STUDY OF PERCEIVED CONTROL

In some of the first developmental work in this area, researchers examined the early antecedents of individual differences in perceived control, especially their construction in interactions with caregivers. On the basis of the then dominant notion that a sense of control was akin to a personality characteristic, it was assumed that, once formed, these individual differences were relatively stable and enduring. Parallel to this work, normative research was conducted that examined the age-graded sequence of developments through which children's understanding of causality and control proceeds during childhood. Each of these strands of research will be reviewed briefly, as a basis for the present program of research, followed by a more detailed discussion of the conceptual features of the present framework, including the cyclic model and the developmental conception and measurement of perceived control.

ORIGINS OF INDIVIDUAL DIFFERENCES IN PERCEIVED CONTROL

Many theories of perceived control are based on the metatheoretical assumption that all children (and, in fact, all people) have an innate need to experience themselves as effective in their interactions with the physical and social environment. This need has been described as a desire for effectance (White, 1959), mastery (Harter, 1978), or competence (Connell, 1990; Connell & Wellborn, 1991; Koestner & McClelland, 1990; Skinner, 1991, 1995). According to this perspective, which we explicitly adopt in our motivational model, the fundamental need for competence is built into human psychophysiology and is manifest in the infant's ability to detect contingencies between the self and desired and undesired events (Watson, 1966), in the infant's joy at contingent stimulation (Finkelstein & Ramey, 1977), in the disruptive effects of noncontingency (Seligman, 1975), and in the centrality of control across the life span (Baltes & Baltes, 1986). Experiences of efficacy are one source of children's active engagement with the social and physical

17

context, just as experiences of helplessness can be a source of passivity, distress, and disaffection.

As evidence accumulates about the neuropsychophysiological mechanisms that regulate contingency experiences (Gunnar, 1986), it is becoming clear that individual differences in mastery motivation exist at birth. Research has documented inborn differences in interest in creating effects, sensitivity to and detection of contingencies, focus of attention, and intensity of responsiveness to contingent stimulation (Morgan & Harmon, 1984). During the first year of life, markers of individual differences include differential span and focus of attention, exploration and curiosity, persistence of engagement with objects, and practicing of effects; in addition, children show individual differences in task pleasure, that is, expressions of positive affect both during task interaction and after successful effect production (Frodi, Bridges, & Grolnick, 1985; Grolnick, Frodi, & Bridges, 1984; Jennings, Harmon, Morgan, Gaiter, & Yarrow, 1979; Morgan, Harmon, & Maslin-Cole, 1990; Morgan, Maslin-Cole, Biringen, & Harmon, 1991).

Role of Social Context

Research on familial antecedents of children's perceived control has for the most part focused on children's locus of control, but a number of studies have also targeted children's mastery, learned helplessness, perceived competence, or self-efficacy. Most of this work examines the connection between children's or adolescents' perceived control and cross-sectional or retrospective information about parenting practices or styles, usually measured through parents' or children's reports (for reviews, see Beyer, 1995; Carton & Nowicki, 1994; Grolnick & Ryan, 1992; Krampen, 1994; and Schneewind, 1995).

In general, children with a greater sense of control and mastery have parents who related to the child in a benevolent, warm, caring, and emotionally supportive way (Estrada, Arsenio, Hess, & Holloway, 1987; Hokoda & Fincham, 1995; Krampen, 1989; MacDonald, 1971; Nolen-Hoeksema et al., 1995; Nowicki & Segal, 1974; Schaffer & Blatt, 1990; Wagner & Phillips, 1992) and showed more educational and noneducational involvement (Gordon, Nowicki, & Wichern, 1981; Grolnick, Ryan, & Deci, 1991; Grolnick & Slowiaczek, 1994; Orr, Assor, & Priel, 1989).

In addition, parents provided a more stimulating family environment (Bradley & Caldwell, 1979; Nowicki & Schneewind, 1982), were more consistent and contingently responsive to children's behavior (Davis & Phares, 1969; Diethelm, 1991; Hokoda & Fincham, 1995; Skinner, 1986; Yates, Kennelly, & Cox, 1975), showed more encouragement and better teaching during problem-solving tasks, especially difficult ones (Hokoda & Fincham, 1995;

Nolen-Hoeksema et al., 1995; Sigel, Stinson, & Flaugher, 1989), and employed more inductive disciplinary techniques (Davis & Phares, 1969; Krampen, 1989; Whitbeck, 1987). Finally, parents emphasized independence training (Chance, 1972; Chandler, Wolf, Cook, & Dugovics, 1980; Wichern & Nowicki, 1976), granted more autonomy, and were less intrusive, critical, and punitive (Gordon et al., 1981; Grolnick & Ryan, 1987, 1989, 1992; Grolnick et al., 1991; Loeb, 1975; Nolen-Hoeksema et al., 1995).

Reviewers have correctly criticized this research for its focus on concurrent self-report data and have suggested that additional longitudinal and observational studies are needed (Carton & Nowicki, 1994; Krampen, 1989). In studies that rely solely on data from children's reports, it is possible that children's perceived control may color their concurrent or retrospective interpretations of parents' practices. Cross-sectional data also make causal interpretations problematic. It is at least possible that parents treat children differently depending on differences among children in their perceived control.

In addition, few of these studies examined either the role of parenting practices in shaping the *development* of children's perceived control or the effects of parenting practices on different aspects of perceived control. One of the few studies that did so (Krampen 1989) found that different aspects of child-rearing practices predicted changes in different aspects of adolescents' perceived control. Specifically, improvements over a 10-month period in children's internal locus of control were predicted by parents' approval of and attention to children's positive behavior; increases in powerful-others control were predicted by parents' reinforcement that emphasized downward social comparison of the child's behavior and achievements; and increases in children's chance control orientations were predicted by parents' general disparagement of the child—without attention to his or her specific behavior. This study suggests that a promising avenue for future research would be the examination of the effects of social context on the development of different aspects of children's perceived control.

Structure as a Dimension of Social Contexts

Theoretical discussions of the role that social context plays in shaping children's perceived control focus on *why* certain parental practices (such as warmth or punitiveness) should have an effect on children's sense of control (Carton & Nowicki, 1994; Krampen, 1989). One general notion is that social contexts differ in the extent to which they provide children with opportunities to fulfill the need for competence (Connell & Wellborn, 1991). Although, according to the motivational model, children come with the desire to be effective in interactions with the environment, nevertheless, the social context itself is hypothesized to play a critical role in whether children have opportunities to experience such interactions. On the basis of this assumption, it is possible to analyze the factors in social interactions that promote or undermine children's experiences of themselves as effective and of the world as structured and responsive.

Two factors emerge. The first originated in theories of infant cognition (Watson, 1966, 1979) and motivational theories of helplessness (Alloy & Abramson, 1979; Seligman, 1975). These suggest that environments characterized by *contingency* provide children with opportunities for control. Both correlational studies (Diethelm, 1991; Finkelstein & Ramey, 1977; Watson & Ramey, 1972) and intervention efforts (Riksen-Walraven, 1978) demonstrate that, starting in earliest infancy, parental practices that are contingent and responsive are critical to the emergence of a sense of agency and control in children. Parents who provide their infants with more contingent stimulation have children who show greater "contingency awareness" (Watson, 1966) in detecting experimentally induced behavior-outcome contingencies and who also explore their social and physical environments more intensely and positively (for a review, see Gunnar, 1980). Highly contingent environments are ones in which an individual's actions are consistently and discriminately followed by events. In noncontingent environments, the probability of the outcome can be high or low, but outcomes do not consistently follow from the individual's actions.

In our motivational model, contingency is one aspect of the more general construct *structure,* which refers to the extent to which social and physical contexts provide individuals with both information about the pathways to achieving desired and avoiding undesired outcomes and support and guidance for following those pathways (Connell & Wellborn, 1991; Grolnick & Ryan, 1989; Skinner, 1991, 1995). Structure includes contingency, both contingent social stimulation and the provision of materials that respond contingently to the actions of which the child is currently capable.

However, structure can also be seen in everyday parent-child interactions as caregivers model, explain, coach, and directly teach metacognitive skills and strategies that allow children to place structure on challenging tasks, such as planning, strategy generation, or problem solving. For example, structure can be provided in comforting interactions as parents suggest and support children's use of active strategies to regulate their emotions and then encourage active attempts to repair or prevent negative events. Structure can be seen in play activities as parents read instructions, explain strategies for solving problems, and discuss the consequences of actions. Structure in limit setting includes, not only providing clear expectations and rules with contingent follow-through, but also providing cause-effect rationales for rules and prohibitions (inductive disciplinary techniques). The opposite of structure is *chaos,* which refers to social practices that are noncontingent, inconsistent, or arbitrary or, in general, interfere with or obscure the pathways from means to ends.

Involvement as a Dimension of Social Contexts

Theories focusing on perceived control have often assumed that contingency (or structure) is the single most important social factor influencing children's experiences of control. However, attachment theorists point out that the notion of contingency specifies only the relation between a child's actions and outcomes; it is mute with respect to the nature of the outcome (Krampen, 1989). These theorists argue that social contexts (e.g., parents) must be both contingent and *appropriate* in their responses to children. To describe this combination, they coined the term *sensitivity* (Ainsworth, 1979; see also Dix, 1991).

In our motivational model, the distinction is maintained between contingency or structure, on the one hand, and the dimension of appropriateness or warmth, on the other hand, which we refer to as *involvement*. In addition to appropriateness, involvement includes the expression of caring, enjoyment, and affection, the actual dedication of resources, and physical and emotional availability and accessibility. The opposite of involvement is hostility, which ranges from inaccessibility and lack of involvement to the communication of criticism and rejection.

The importance of involvement to children's perceptions of control is underscored by the research on the parental antecedents of children's locus of control. Reviewers of this work argue that parental warmth is the one dimension that consistently predicts children's locus of control (see Carton & Nowicki, 1994; Lefcourt, 1977; cf. Crandall & Crandall, 1983). In the motivational model, involvement is distinguished from structure in order to examine the individual effects of each on different self-systems (see Connell & Wellborn, 1991; Skinner, 1991, 1995), but both are hypothesized to contribute to the experience of control (Grolnick & Ryan, 1987, 1989; Krampen, 1989; Skinner, 1986). Involvement may be an especially important contributor to children's control experiences at younger ages (Skinner, 1986).

Teacher Context

Most of the work on the effects of social context on perceived control has focused on the role of parents. However, in the academic domain, it is reasonable to assume that an additional important source of involvement and structure in the classroom should be the teacher. Teachers are important sources of warmth and affection for children. In addition, they can provide contingencies—either directly, through their own responses to children, or indirectly, by the way they teach and structure learning activities. Children's experiences of teachers as involved and providing structure (or as neglectful and chaotic) should contribute to their feelings of academic competence and control.

In the few studies of this connection, the expected relations have been found (Barker & Graham, 1987; Birch & Ladd, 1997; Blumenfeld et al., 1982; Dweck et al., 1978; Pintrich & Blumenfeld, 1985; Roeser et al., 1996; Skinner et al., 1990; Stipek, Feiler, Daniels, & Milburn, 1995; Wentzel, 1997). In addition, some studies have shown that the connection between teachers' behavior and children's perceived control differs among children of different ages (Graham, 1990) and genders (Dweck et al., 1978) and that different aspects of interactions between children and teachers influence different aspects of children's perceived control. For example, in an observational study of second- and sixth-grade children's interactions with teachers, Pintrich and Blumenfeld (1985) found that teachers' praise of children's work heightened children's perceptions of their effort and ability, whereas teachers' criticism of work had a detrimental effect only on children's self-perceptions of effort.

Teacher Context in the Current Research

Building on earlier work, the current program of research offers two possible extensions. First, we examined whether there are age changes in the effects of the social context on perceived control. For example, it is possible that involvement or structure are differentially important to the construction of control beliefs at different ages, with involvement likely more important at younger ages. Second, we investigated whether social context factors influence individual differences in the development of perceived control, shaping the level and direction of children's individual trajectories across successive school years. Specific hypotheses and their rationales are presented in subsequent chapters.

Academic Performance as an Antecedent of Perceived Control

According to many theories, a factor that is central to the development of children's perceived control is the contingency that they experience in interactions with the physical environment and the level of performance that they actually achieve. For example, Bandura explicitly lists *performance enactments* or *mastery experiences* as strong influences on estimates of self-efficacy (Bandura, 1986). In fact, all theories that discuss the cyclic nature of beliefs and performance include a reciprocal link from level of performance to sub-sequent perceptions of control.

In the academic domain, the materials with which children interact are learning activities, including classroom presentations, in-class examples, readings, homework, and tests, and one marker of an individual's cumulative achievement is his or her school grades. Hence, an important predictor of children's perceptions of control in the academic domain should be their actual performance and grades in school (Lopez, Little, Oettingen, & Baltes, 1997; Nolen-Hoeksema et al., 1986; Schmitz & Skinner, 1993; Stipek, 1980).

Differences as a function of both age and culture have been found in the correlations between children's school grades and their perceived control, locus of control, and ability estimates. Some of the most comprehensive findings on cultural differences come from a program of research (which includes 14 countries so far) designed to examine the links between control and cognition (for an overview, see Grob, Little, Wanner, Wearing, & Euronet, 1996; see also Little, in press). Stronger relations between beliefs and performance are found in such cultures as the former East Germany (compared to the former West Germany), in which school systems provided performance feedback that was public, realistic, honest, and performance based as well as a unitary curriculum in which all children's performances were judged on the same tasks and by the same standards (for an overview, see Oettingen, 1995).

These differences were replicated even in longitudinal studies in which the "feedforward" effect of control on performance could be separated from the feedback effect of performance on control (Lopez et al., 1997). Perhaps the most convincing evidence was found in a study that capitalized on a naturally occurring "experiment" in which, following reunification, the curriculum used in schools in the former West Germany was introduced in schools in the former East Germany; researchers were able to document a corresponding shift in several characteristics of students' perceived control, including a reduction in the correlations between actual performance and ability estimates (Oettingen, Little, Lindenberger, & Baltes, 1994).

Age differences in the feedback effects of academic performance on ability estimates and perceived competence have been examined most systematically by researchers interested in self-evaluation and perceived competence (Phillips, 1984; Phillips & Zimmerman, 1990; Stipek, 1984a, 1984b; Stipek & Hoffman, 1980; Weisz, 1983, 1986). This work suggests that, as children progress through the school system, their estimates of their own ability come to correspond more closely to the grades that they receive. At younger ages, children tend to overestimate their competence relative to their actual school grades, whereas, by grade 3, children's ability estimates decline and become more closely associated with their actual school performance (Paris & Oka, 1986; Stipek, 1984b).

Academic Performance in the Current Research

The current research program attempts to expand the consideration of how academic performance influences the development of control by building on these efforts in two ways. The first innovation is to examine whether the effect of actual performance on perceived control changes with age; specifically, does school performance become a more central predictor of perceived control across middle childhood? The second is to examine whether school performance can exert an effect, not just on level of subsequent control, but on the entire trajectory of perceived control across multiple school years. Specific hypotheses are presented in subsequent chapters.

NORMATIVE DEVELOPMENTS IN THE PROCESSES UNDERLYING PERCEIVED CONTROL

Although it is no surprise to individual difference theorists, the consistency with which control has been found to regulate cognitive performance across childhood may seem almost paradoxical to developmentalists. Beginning with studies of infancy, and continuing in studies of early and middle childhood and adolescence, researchers have discovered regular developmental changes in almost every constituent process that children use to perceive and interpret their control experiences (for reviews, see Bullock, Gelman, & Baillargeon, 1982; Flammer, 1995; Heckhausen, 1982, 1984; Krampen, 1987; Skinner, 1995; Stipek, 1984a; Stipek & MacIver, 1989; Stipek, Recchia, & McClintic, 1992). Although infants can detect and respond to social and physical contingencies from the earliest ages at which our methods can assess these competencies, children do not even develop a "categorical self" to which they can attribute effects until they are about 18 months old (Lewis & Brooks-Gunn, 1979). In addition, regular changes have been detected in the processes of self-evaluation and its links with emotion (Stipek et al., 1992). Moreover, children show age-graded progression in the strategies by which they estimate covariation (Shaklee & Mims, 1981) and in their use of causal schema (e.g., Shultz, Butkowsky, Pearce, & Shanfield, 1975).

Middle Childhood

In middle childhood and adolescence, two of the most significant changes revolve around the processing of information about the causes of desired and undesired events (Flammer, 1995; Skinner, 1995). In the preschool years, children have a global, undifferentiated concept of competence,

or what Heider called *personal force* (Heckhausen, 1982), which is an amal-
gam of effort, ability, desire, and will, and which is inferred from exertion,
level of outcome, and objective and social feedback (Nicholls, 1978). The
multiple facets of this concept are slowly distinguished, in that concepts such
as intentions and goals, task difficulty, chance, ability, and effort come to be
successively differentiated.

During the first few years of schooling, children's conceptions of competence come to be distinguished from wishes and intentions (Stipek, 1984a)
and from level of task difficulty (Nicholls, 1978, 1980; Nicholls & Miller,
1985a). However, they are still organized around global conceptions of effort.
Then, at about ages 9–10 (the fourth grade), children are first able to distinguish tasks depending on skill from those governed by chance (Nicholls &
Miller, 1985b; Weisz, 1980, 1981, 1986). Prior to this shift, children imbue
performance on chance-determined tasks with the properties of tasks that
are contingent on effort. Children believe that performance on chance-
determined tasks will be superior for people who are older, have more practice, try harder, and are more familiar with the tasks. Only as mature conceptions of chance develop do children begin to view outcomes as unaffected
by these aspects of performance. This opens the way for beliefs about powerful others and luck to be distinguished from effort.

Finally, in early adolescence, children have the cognitive capacities to
distinguish effort from conceptions of ability as a fixed, stable entity (Blumenfeld, Pintrich, & Hamilton, 1986; Karabenick & Heller, 1976; Kun, 1977; Kun,
Parsons, & Ruble, 1974; Nicholls, 1984; Nicholls & Miller, 1985a). Prior to
this shift, children do not separate ability from effort. Instead, they imbue
ability with all the properties of effort: they see ability as voluntary, controllable, and mutable. In fact, they view effort and ability as *positively* correlated,
perhaps because, in their classroom experiences, smarter children do try
harder. At this developmental phase, children assume that, when two students
receive *equal* academic outcomes, the child who tried harder is also the one
with more ability.

After a mature conception of ability is achieved, children are able to
grasp the conception held by our culture of an inverse compensatory relation
between effort and ability. They understand that children who are smart do
not need to try as hard to achieve the same outcomes as children who are
not. They see that, when two children achieve the same academic outcomes,
the one who exerted *less* effort to accomplish it is probably smarter. They
recognize that poor performance on easy tasks despite great exertion implies
low ability. At this point, children can shift their conceptions of ability to
match ones held by adults in our culture: they may see ability as less open
to voluntary deployment, as uncontrollable, and as fixed (Dweck, 1991). This
is also the age at which great exertion becomes a "double-edged sword" in

that high effort, even when accompanied by success, may imply lower ability (Covington & Omelich, 1979, 1985).

Interaction of Normative Development and Individual Differences

From a developmentalist's point of view, it may seem surprising to discover how little the work on individual differences has been informed by research on developmental changes in children's perceived control. Some studies do exist that look at age differences in the correlations between aspects of perceived control and academic performance (Fincham et al., 1989; Findley & Cooper, 1983; Rholes, Blackwell, Jordan, & Walters, 1980; Shell, Colvin, & Bruning, 1995). However, only a small body of research has directly examined how normative developmental changes in conceptions of causes may interact with individual differences in children's perceived control.

These studies suggest that the emergence of new conceptions in children's reasoning about causes may influence the functioning of individual differences in perceived control. For example, Miller (1985) found that children who had not yet attained a mature conception of ability showed no helplessness effects when they failed on tasks that were supposedly easy for age-mates. Children needed to understand the relations between effort and ability before poor performance on normatively easy tasks despite great effort implied low ability, thus undermining subsequent performance. In a similar vein, Chapman and Skinner (1989) found that preexisting individual differences in children's ability estimates increased in their relation to cognitive performance as children became more sophisticated in their conceptions of ability. As they differentiated effort from ability, children's estimations of their own ability played a successively more prominent role in their academic performance.

Normative Development in the Current Research

The central notion is that normative changes in how children construct control experiences may set the stage for changes in how individual differences in children's control perceptions regulate performance. In the few studies examining this issue, children's beliefs about the causes of success and failure show normative changes in factor-analytic structure consistent with changes in children's conceptions of causes (Skinner, 1990). At the same time, there have been suggestions that, as a result of these normative changes, different causal beliefs may be more central in regulating and interpreting performances at some ages than at others (Shell et al., 1995; Skinner, 1990, 1991; Skinner & Connell, 1986; Stipek, 1993). Testing some of these ideas is a central focus of the current program of research.

DEVELOPMENTAL ASSESSMENT OF PERCEIVED CONTROL

Using prior research on the antecedents and consequences of perceived control, we derived hypotheses about developmental changes in the aspects of children's perceived control that are influenced by the social context and by their own academic performance. In addition, we formulated hypotheses about developmental changes in the aspects of children's perceived control that regulate their engagement in the classroom and their cumulative academic performance. An essential first step in testing these general propositions was the use of a developmental conception and measure of perceived control.

Developmental Conceptions and Assessments of Control

A new assessment was needed because, with the exception of attributions and explanatory style, most conceptualizations and measures of perceived control have focused on a single set of beliefs, such as estimates of efficacy, expectations of contingency, or locus of control. These measures were not designed to examine, and cannot detect, whether the beliefs that regulate and interpret performance change with age. For example, measures of locus of control that assess it as a bipolar internal versus external dimension cannot be used to examine whether beliefs in the power of external causes are better (negative) predictors of children's school performance at younger ages whereas beliefs about the effectiveness of internal causes are stronger (positive) influences on engagement in school as children become older. However, recent conceptualizations of perceived control, originating from a developmental perspective, are more differentiated (Connell, 1985; J. Heckhausen, 1991; Little et al., 1995; Skinner et al., 1988b; Skinner et al., 1990; Weisz, 1983, 1986; Weisz & Stipek, 1982) and so allow an examination of age differences in the aspects of control that predict and are influenced by school performance.

Differentiation of Perceived Control in the Current Research

In the present program of research, we used a differentiated assessment of perceived control in the academic domain (Wellborn et al., 1989). Children reported on (1) their overall control beliefs, or generalized expectations about the extent to which they can produce desired and prevent undesired events in school; (2) their strategy beliefs, or generalized expectations about "what it takes" to do well in school; and (3) their capacity beliefs, or generalized expectations about their access to these strategies, that is, whether they "have what it takes" (Skinner, Chapman, & Baltes, 1983, 1988b; Skinner et

27

al., 1990; Wellborn et al., 1989). Children reported on their beliefs about the effectiveness of strategies and about their capacities for four causes, namely, effort, ability, powerful others, and luck. In addition, they reported on their unknown strategy beliefs, or their beliefs that they simply had no idea what causes success and failure in school.

A multidimensional conceptualization made it possible to empirically test questions about the effects of development on the functioning of individual differences in perceived control. In terms of consequences, it was possible to examine whether the kinds of beliefs that influence academic performance change with age. For example, it seems that unknown control is a more central predictor of performance in young (relative to older) children (Skinner, 1991). In terms of antecedents, it could be determined whether the kinds of control beliefs that are influenced by teacher context and by individual performance differ at different ages. On the one hand, the aspects of control beliefs that are influenced by the social context may change as children develop, with the result that, for example, at younger ages involvement and structure shape beliefs about the effectiveness of effort or the role of powerful others in children's academic success, whereas, as children become older, social context factors begin to affect children's beliefs about their own ability. On the other hand, it was possible to examine whether the aspects of perceived control that are shaped by level of performance change with age. For example, it is possible that, when younger children do not do well in school, this strengthens their conviction that the causes of school success and failure are unknown, whereas, by the sixth grade, the same pattern of academic failure leads children to doubt their own ability.

Finally, a more differentiated conception and measure allowed empirical inquiry into whether different aspects of perceived control show distinct developmental trajectories (for a review in childhood, see Weisz, 1986; for a review across adulthood, see Gurin & Brim, 1984). For example, it is possible that children's beliefs about their own capacities remain relatively high and stable across middle childhood but that, owing to normative changes in children's conceptions of causes, their beliefs about the strategies responsible for school success and failure change dramatically across the same developmental period (Little & Lopez, 1997; Skinner, Chapman, & Baltes, 1988a). Specific hypotheses are described in later sections.

INDIVIDUAL DIFFERENCES IN DEVELOPMENTAL TRAJECTORIES OF PERCEIVED CONTROL AND ENGAGEMENT

Taken together, the work on individual differences can be used as the basis for a model of the functioning of perceived control that specifies both the social contextual and individual antecedents of perceptions of control

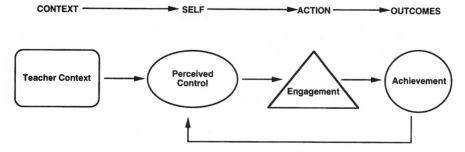

FIGURE 4.—A model of cyclic relations between perceived control and achievement

and the consequences of control that influence school performance. We refer to this as a model of *context, self, action, and outcomes*. As depicted in Figure 4, this model holds that children's experiences of their teachers as involved and structured influence their perceived control, which in turn has an effect on the extent to which the children actively engage in classroom activities. This engagement has a direct effect on the level of children's actual academic performance, which in turn feeds back on their sense of control.

Each of these links in the model, from social context to control, from control to engagement and academic performance, and from performance to subsequent control, has been demonstrated in "real process" time; that is, they have been found in the time span within which the hypothesized causal process takes place (Turkewitz & Devenny, 1993). For example, control has been found to influence subsequent effort on graded assignments (Schmitz & Skinner, 1993). However, we were also interested in how this model operated across developmental time, that is, whether and how its effects unfolded across seasons of a school year, for example, whether children's control in the fall would influence their level of engagement in the spring.

Further, if cycles of context, self, action, and outcomes do unfold across developmental time, and if, as predicted by individual differences theorists, they operate as self-confirming cycles of beliefs and performance, then they should eventually come to shape, not just individual differences at a single point in time, but individual differences in entire developmental trajectories. For example, good academic performance in the early grades should not just contribute to a strong sense of control at the time but should also initiate a pattern of engagement that leads to the continuing development of control. Likewise, poor performance in the early years should not just undermine control at the time but should also contribute to patterns of disengagement that lead to deterioration of perceived control over the coming years.

From this perspective, the targets of inquiry are individual trajectories of perceived control and engagement over time, and at issue are systematic

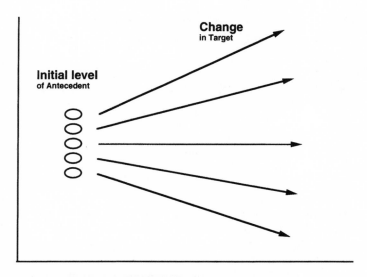

LAUNCH MODEL

FIGURE 5.—The launch model of development, in which individual differences in the development of a target outcome are a function of individual differences in initial level of an antecedent.

individual differences in these patterns of individual change. For example, what are the factors that produce increasingly optimistic as opposed to increasingly pessimistic perceptions of control? What influences whether children's engagement rises or falls over the elementary school years? Hence, a major contribution of the present program of research was to examine the predictors of individual differences in children's trajectories of control and engagement from grade 3 to grade 7.

The Launch Model of Developmental Change

Individual differences theories suggest a particular perspective on these issues, reflecting their assumption that individual differences tend to remain stable over time. They suggest that these trajectories are set by early experiences, such as parental child-rearing style, and that, once these differences are established, they continue over time (Carton & Nowicki, 1994). We refer to this model of individual differences in development as a *launch* model because children's trajectories are hypothesized to be a function of their initial differential starting levels on some other construct (Connell & Skinner, 1990). This model is depicted in Figure 5. Perhaps surprisingly, even developmentalists have tended to favor a launch model, in which early influences set

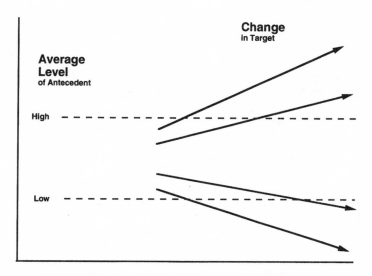

AMBIENT LEVEL MODEL

FIGURE 6.—The ambient-level model of development, in which individual differences in the development of a target outcome are a function of individual differences in the average level of an antecedent while the target trajectory is unfolding.

the stage for the unfolding of later development. The preference for this perspective stems, in part, from assumptions about the primacy of early experience, about the stability of social contexts, and about continuity in development (Baltes, 1987; Kindermann & Skinner, 1992).

Ambient-Level and Change-to-Change Models of Development

In addition to the launch model, we have suggested two other models as predictors of individual differences in developmental change (Connell & Skinner, 1990). The first is the *ambient-level* model, in which trajectories are determined by the average level of support provided while the trajectory is unfolding. This model is depicted in Figure 6. Ambient-level models may be especially useful as accounts of the influence of social contexts or social context transitions on individual development. These models assume, for example, that a favorable early environment is not sufficient to support a positive trajectory over time unless the environment continues to provide at least a threshold level of subsequent support. However, according to this model, the environment does not need to improve continuously in order to support a continuously improving developmental trajectory from the child. Work on the "continuity of caregiving," in which good early parenting is usually ac-

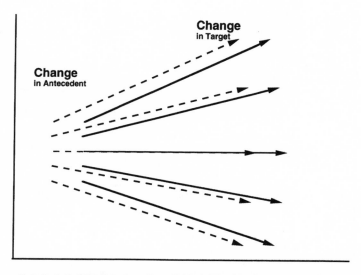

CHANGE-TO-CHANGE MODEL

FIGURE 7.—The change-to-change model of development, in which individual differences in the development of a target outcome are a function of individual differences in change of an antecedent.

companied by good subsequent parenting, suggests that some research that is usually interpreted as supporting a launch model may be more consistent with an ambient-level model.

A second alternative to the launch model is referred to as the *change-to-change* model, which looks at changes in one trajectory as a function of changes in another. According to this perspective, increments or decrements in a target developmental trajectory would be influenced, not simply by the average level of another variable, but by the pattern of change in that variable. This model is depicted in Figure 7. For example, the number of coping strategies in a child's repertoire would have to increase over time in order for perceived competence to increase.

Because ambient-level and change-to-change models are consistent with implicit metatheoretical and explicit theoretical views on how contexts shape individual development, it is easy to overestimate their representation in empirical studies. Few empirical studies directly assess the proposed antecedent variable (e.g., parental contingency) repeatedly over the period of development of the target variable (e.g., the child's sense of control). Fewer still examine the development of the target variables as a function of *changes* in the antecedent variable over time. Even studies that posit transitions as the explicit cause of individual development do not usually look at the *extent* of change in proposed causal variables. For example, although divorce is hypothesized as a transition that may produce decreases in children's internal locus of control, studies have not directly measured the extent of the changes in proposed antecedent variables (e.g., changes in parental consistency or warmth over time) and examined their relation to individual differences in change in locus of control.

A notable exception can be found in the work on transitions in early adolescence (Hirsch & DuBois, 1991), especially school transitions (e.g., Eccles et al., in press; Harter et al., 1992; Lord, Eccles, & McCarthy, 1994; Wigfield, Eccles, MacIver, Reuman, & Midgley, 1991). This research explicitly targets changes in children's self-perceptions and motivation over the transition to middle or junior high school, using individual differences in transitions on one variable sometimes to predict transitions in other variables (Harter et al., 1992; Lord et al., 1994) and sometimes to predict individual differences at a later point in school (Eccles et al., in press). The explication and empirical use of different developmental models are explicit goals of the present research program.

Models of Change in the Current Research

In considering their relevance to perceived control, we expected that different models would provide better accounts of different predictors of developmental change. For example, the launch model might provide a good description of the effects of early academic performance on subsequent trajectories of control. Children who perform well in school initially may develop more adaptive beliefs about control over the subsequent years, whereas children who perform poorly in school initially may develop more maladaptive trajectories of control over their elementary school years.

In contrast, a change-to-change model might provide a better account of the effects of perceived control on individual differences in the development of engagement. A launch model would not provide a good account of these relations because it would imply that early optimistic perceived control would predict the development of engagement (and early pessimistic beliefs the development of disaffection) regardless of subsequent changes in children's perceived control. In contrast, a change-to-change model is more consistent with the notion that children's beliefs and performance form self-confirming cycles, implying that *changes* in perceived control would be more likely predictors of changes in children's engagement in the classroom.

Finally, we hypothesized that ambient-level models would provide a good description of the effects of the social context on the development of children's control. A launch model was not expected to provide a good fit; we did not expect that a child who had a good teacher in the fall of third grade would automatically develop optimal profiles of control regardless of his or her subsequent teachers. However, we also did not expect that a change-to-change model would be a good account of the relations between teacher context and the development of perceived control; we did not expect that teachers would have to be better and better each year for children to develop adaptive profiles of control. An ambient-level model was hypothesized to provide a good account because it holds that, for optimal development of perceived control, teacher support must remain above a certain threshold during the entire time that perceived control is developing.

As with the functional model, we were also interested in whether normative development colors the effects of the development of perceived control on engagement. As with hypotheses that the aspects of perceived control that predict engagement might differ at different ages, we explored whether the relations between *trajectories* of different aspects of perceived control and *trajectories* of engagement change with age. For example, perhaps it is the decline of unknown control that predicts increases in engagement in the third grade, whereas it is increases in perceived ability that predict increases in engagement during junior high. Specific predictions are described in subsequent chapters.

OVERVIEW OF THE RESULTS CHAPTERS

Chapter III presents the methods, including a description of the sample, design, and measures, as well as the initial descriptive analyses. The substantive results are presented in Chapters IV and V. Chapter IV contains hypotheses and the results of analyses designed to test predictions about *interindividual differences in perceived control* across middle childhood (from age 8 to age 13), their consequences for children's engagement and school performance, and their antecedents in teacher context. We tested alternative functional models of these individual differences. We looked at how they operated across the school year, and we examined similarities and variations in these models for children of different ages. An overview of the hypotheses tested in Chapter IV is provided in the portion of Figure 8 headed *functional model.* This figure shows the general organizational scheme of the data analyses.

Chapter V contains the results of analyses examining the *development of perceived control.* It describes the normative trajectories of context, self, and action across this age range, testing predictions about the differential patterns of change shown by different aspects of perceived control. We estimated individual trajectories of self and action and then tested three kinds of models, launch, ambient level, and change to change, as accounts of the predictors of individual differences in developmental trajectories. Finally, we explored whether changes in engagement over 2 years were a function of different

Functional Model				
	Teacher Context to Control	**Control to Engagement**	**Engagement to Performance**	**Performance to Control**
Mediational	Control mediates effects of context on engagement.	Engagement mediates effects of control on performance.		
Causal	Teacher context influences control.	Control influences engagement.	Engagement influences performance.	Performance influences control.
Differentiated Predictors		+ Control beliefs + Capacities - External strategies		Performance especially influences capacity ability.
Age Differences	Teacher involvement stronger influence for youngest children.	Strategy Beliefs Youngest: Effort and Unknown Middle: Others and Luck Oldest: Ability		Performance a stronger influence for oldest children.

Developmental Model				
	Teacher Context to Control	**Control to Engagement**	**Engagement to Performance**	**Performance to Control**
Normative Change	Teacher context stable, perhaps decline starting in grade 6.	Control and capacity beliefs stable. Strategy beliefs more differentiated with age.	Engagement declines over entire age range.	
Causal	Ambient Level Model Average teacher context influences development of control.	Change-to-change Model Changes in control influence changes in engagement.		Launch Model Early performance influences development of control.
Differentiated Predictors		+ Control beliefs + Capacities - External strategies		Especially the development of ability capacity.
Age Differences	Teacher involvement stronger influence on development of control for youngest children.	Strategy Beliefs Youngest: Effort and Unknown Oldest: Ability		Performanment of control for oldest children.

FIGURE 8.—Summary of hypotheses about individual differences and development

aspects of perceived control at different points during middle childhood, for example, when engagement was normatively stable as opposed to when it was normatively declining. The hypotheses tested in Chapter V are listed at the bottom of Figure 8 under the heading "developmental model."

Both results chapters are divided into subsections organized around specific sets of hypotheses. At the beginning of each subsection, the specific hypotheses and rationales are detailed; then the results of the corresponding analyses are presented, followed by a brief summary. The results from both chapters are integrated in the initial sections of Chapter VI.

III. METHODS AND RESULTS OF DESCRIPTIVE ANALYSES

PARTICIPANTS AND STUDY DESIGN

Sample

Participants were 1,608 students, aged 8–13, in grades 3–7, approximately equally divided by sex, in a rural-suburban school district in upstate New York, and 53 of their teachers. Students' socioeconomic status was lower middle to middle class, as measured by parents' occupation and educational attainment, and most were Caucasian. The most prominent minority group (fewer than 3%) was Hispanic. Data collection was conducted as part of a districtwide assessment.

Design

As part of a larger cohort sequential study, data were collected every fall (October) and spring (May) for 3 consecutive years. In year 1, the first cross section of children was in grades 3–5. In year 2, we followed these children, who at that time were in grades 4–6. However, we also recruited a second wave of third graders and additional fourth and fifth graders whose teachers became willing to participate in the study during its second year. In year 3, we followed both waves, who at that time were in grades 4–7. The design is presented in Figure 9. In this school district, children started middle school in grade 6, at about age 12.

The number of children in each grade who were assessed at each time of measurement is presented in Table 1. Since children were tested on the basis of their attendance at the times of measurement, the sample at each measurement point contained children who had not previously been tested as well as children who had been tested at some or all of the previous sessions. The cumulative size of the sample, broken down by number of times tested previously (none, some, or all), for each measurement point, is presented in Figure 10. Also shown in the figure is the number of children who had been

Time of Measurement		Year One		Year Two		Year Three	
		Fall	Spring	Fall	Spring	Fall	Spring
		Time 1	Time 2	Time 3	Time 4	Time 5	Time 6
Wave	Longitudinal Sequences	Cross-section One					
Wave 1	Longitudinal grades 3 - 5	Grade 3--->	Grade 3--->	Grade 4--->	Grade 4--->	Grade 5--->	Grade 5
	Longitudinal grades 4 - 6	Grade 4--->	Grade 4--->	Grade 5--->	Grade 5--->	Grade 6--->	Grade 6
	Longitudinal grades 5 - 7	Grade 5--->	Grade 5--->	Grade 6--->	Grade 6--->	Grade 7--->	Grade 7
Wave	Longitudinal Sequences			Cross-section Two			
Wave 2	Longitudinal grades 3 - 4			Grade 3--->	Grade 3--->	Grade 4--->	Grade 4
	Longitudinal grades 4 - 5			Grade 4--->	Grade 4--->	Grade 5--->	Grade 5
	Longitudinal grades 5 - 6			Grade 5--->	Grade 5--->	Grade 6--->	Grade 6

FIGURE 9.—The cohort sequential design of the study

tested previously but were not present at the current measurement point. As a result of this design, each child in the sample could have participated in from one to six assessments. The number of children who completed one, two, three, four, five, and six assessments was 157, 489, 128, 445, 88, and 222, respectively. In addition, 104 children had teachers' assessments only. The average number of assessments per child was 3.1.

Procedure

Questionnaires were administered to students in their normal classroom settings by pairs of trained interviewers in three 40-minute sessions. All questionnaire items were read aloud by one interviewer, and a second interviewer

TABLE 1

NUMBER OF CHILDREN ASSESSED AT EACH GRADE LEVEL AT EACH TIME OF MEASUREMENT

STUDENT GRADE	YEAR 1		YEAR 2		YEAR 3		TOTAL
	Fall	Spring	Fall	Spring	Fall	Spring	
3	220	216	132	118	· · ·	· · ·	686
4	126	129	333	318	300	285	1,491
5	162	141	161	148	218	215	1,045
6	· · ·	· · ·	342	312	321	315	1,290
7	· · ·	· · ·	· · ·	· · ·	324	234	558
Total	508	486	968	896	1,163	1,049	5,070

NOTE.—Totals are the number of assessments completed at that measurement point.

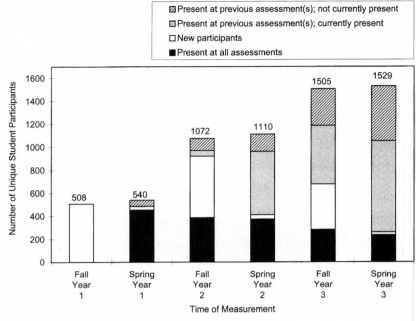

Note. 104 students were excluded as only teacher ratings were available.

Figure 10.—Frequencies of children who were assessed at each measurement point, broken down by their participation at previous points.

monitored understanding and answered individual questions. Teachers were not present in the classroom during assessments, and they usually completed their questionnaires while students were being tested.

MEASURES

Teachers reported on each child's engagement/disaffection in their classroom. In cases of multiple teachers, students were rated by the teacher who claimed to "know him/her the best." Students reported on their perceived control and their perceptions of teacher context. Children's school grades were obtained from school records. An overview of the constructs and reporters is provided in Figure 11.

All questionnaire assessments consisted of approximately equal numbers of positive and negative items. All items were answered on a scale of 1–4, which, for children's reports, ranged from "not at all true for me" to "very true for me" and, for teachers' reports of students, ranged from "not at all true for this student" to "very true for this student." For each scale or sub-

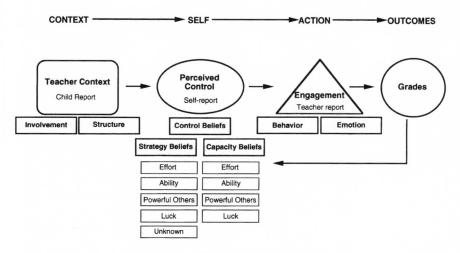

FIGURE 11.—An overview of the measures

scale, summary scores were calculated by creating average scores for positive and negative items separately, then reverse coding the negative scores and averaging the positive and negative scores within a scale. Therefore, all scores ranged from 1 to 4, with 4 indicating more of the corresponding construct, such as more engagement or more unknown strategy beliefs.

Engagement/Disaffection in School

Each student's teacher responded to 14 items assessing that child's behavioral and emotional motivation for learning during classroom activities (for sample items, see Table 2; as well as Skinner et al., 1990; and Wellborn, 1991). Behavioral engagement items (two positive and three negative) tapped teachers' perceptions of students' effort, attention, and persistence during the initiation and execution of learning activities. Emotional engagement items (three positive and six negative) tapped teachers' perceptions of children's emotional involvement in learning activities, including interest/boredom, happiness/sadness, anxiety, and anger. Cronbach's alpha by grade (averaged across times of measurement) was .92, .92, .89, .94, and .91 for teachers of students in grades 3, 4, 5, 6, and 7, respectively.

Perceived Control

Ten scales assessed children's beliefs about *strategies* for success and failure in school and their *capacities* to enact those strategies (for sample items, see Table 3). These items represent the short form of a longer scale (Skinner

TABLE 2

SAMPLE ITEMS FROM TEACHERS' REPORTS OF STUDENTS' ENGAGEMENT

Behavioral Engagement
In my class, this student . . .
  works as hard as he/she can. (+)
  does just enough to get by. (−)
  comes unprepared. (−)

When we start something new in class, this student . . .
  participates in discussions. (+)
  doesn't pay attention. (−)
  thinks about other things. (−)

Emotional Engagement
When we start something new in class, this student . . .
  is relaxed. (+)
  is bored. (−)

In my class, this student . . .
  is happy. (+)
  is enthusiastic. (+)
  is depressed. (−)
  is anxious. (−)
  is angry. (−)

When working on classwork in my class, this student appears . . .
  involved. (+)
  worried. (−)
  frustrated. (−)

NOTE.—From Wellborn (1991).

et al., 1983, 1988b; Skinner et al., 1990; Wellborn et al., 1989; all items and scoring procedures appear in Appendix A). The control beliefs subscale (six items) tapped children's generalized expectations about the extent to which they can produce success and avoid failure in school. Strategy beliefs tapped children's generalized expectancies about the extent to which certain potential causes are effective in producing desired and preventing undesired outcomes. Potential strategies in the academic domain included effort (five items, two positive and three negative), ability (four items), powerful others (four items), luck (four items), and unknown factors (four items). Capacity beliefs were assessed for all four known causes, namely, effort (six items), ability (four items), powerful others (four items), and luck (six items). Across age and time of measurement, the alphas ranged from .65 to .76. The breakdown of alphas by grade (averaged across times of measurement) appears in Table 4.[1]

[1] As can be seen, if .65 is considered the lower-bound satisfactory alpha (for a children's control scale of six or fewer items; Halpin & Ottinger, 1983), then a possible age difference in reliability can be detected. Of the ten scales, five fell below this level for third graders, and three were considerably lower (control, effort strategy, and luck capacity beliefs). However, there were no corresponding age differences in the patterns of test-retest reliability (cross-time stability) for any of these scales. Nevertheless, if patterns of age differences in

Unfortunately, the items assessing children's strategy and capacity beliefs for luck were omitted in the last year of data collection (measurement points 5 and 6). Since data on seventh graders were collected only in year 3, in general analyses of strategy and capacity luck beliefs do not include seventh-grade data, and any analyses including seventh-grade data do not include strategy or capacity for luck. The exceptions are the growth curve analyses, which include estimated seventh-grade values for luck.

To represent different profiles of control, two kinds of aggregate perceived control variables were formed for each child. First, aggregate capacity scores and strategy scores were calculated by combining capacity and strategy scales across causes. Because all capacity beliefs are considered positive, the four capacity scales (effort, ability, powerful others, and luck) were simply averaged. However, for strategy beliefs, some causes are positive and some negative. Hence, strategy beliefs indicating a reliance on uncontrollable or external factors, namely, ability, powerful others, luck, and unknown causes, were reverse coded before they were averaged with effort strategy beliefs. These aggregates are referred to as *Strategy beliefs* and *Capacity beliefs*. High scores on Capacity beliefs indicate that children perceive themselves as having access to a variety of means potentially important to school success. High Strategy beliefs indicate that children see school success and failure as caused more by internal and controllable means and less by external, uncontrollable, and unknown factors.

Second, aggregate scores were calculated to represent profiles of perceived control that were predicted to maximally promote or maximally undermine engagement. These scores, labeled *Promote* and *Undermine,* were based on the theoretical rationale described previously (see Figure 1 above), with the added methodological constraints that scores for beliefs about each cause would appear in each composite and that each item would appear in only one composite. The Promote composite reflected the following combination of beliefs: that effort is important *and* that one can oneself try hard (effort strategy times positive effort capacity); that ability is not essential to school success but that one does oneself possess high ability (additive inverse of ability strategy times positive ability capacity); that one is lucky and can influence powerful others (positive powerful others and luck capacity); and that generally one can influence school success and failure (control beliefs). The Undermine composite reflected the following combination of beliefs: that one lacks the capacity to exert effort (negative capacity beliefs); that one is low in ability (negative ability capacity beliefs); that teachers are running the show

---

correlations reveal that correlations involving these variables are lower for third graders, then one possible explanation is that low alphas are attenuating correlations. In each relation where this was the case, we examined age differences after disattenuating the correlations.

TABLE 3

Sample Items from the Assessment of Children's Perceived Control.

CONTROL BELIEFS

I can do well in school if I want to. (+)
I can't get good grades, no matter what I do. (−)

STRATEGY BELIEFS

Effort Strategy Beliefs

For me to do well in school, all I have to do is try hard. (+)
If I get bad grades, it's because I didn't try hard enough. (−)

Ability Strategy Beliefs

If I want to do well in school, I have to be smart. (+)
If I'm not smart, I won't get good grades. (−)

Powerful Others Strategy Beliefs

The best way for me to get good grades is to get my teacher to like me. (+)
I won't do well in school if my teacher doesn't like me. (−)

Luck Strategy Beliefs

For me, getting good grades is a matter of luck. (+)
If I get bad grades, it's because I'm unlucky. (−)

Unknown Strategy Beliefs

I don't know what it takes for me to get good grades in school. (+)
When I do badly in school, I usually can't figure out why. (−)

CAPACITY BELIEFS

Effort Capacity Beliefs

I can work really hard in school. (+)
When I'm in class, I can't seem to work very hard. (−)

Ability Capacity Beliefs

I would say I'm pretty smart in school. (+)
I don't have the brains to do well in school. (−)

Powerful Others Capacity Beliefs

I can get along with my teacher. (+)
I can't get my teacher to like me. (−)

Luck Capacity Beliefs

I am lucky in school. (+)
I am unlucky at my schoolwork. (−)

Note.—From Wellborn, Connell, and Skinner (1989).

TABLE 4

Reliability of Measurement of Children's Perceived Control by Grade Level Averaged across Times of Measurement

Student Grade Level	Control Beliefs	Strategy Beliefs					Capacity Beliefs			
		Effort	Ability	Powerful Others	Luck	Unknown	Effort	Ability	Powerful Others	Luck
3	.51	.58	.68	.72	.73	.62	.62	.65	.65	.56
4	.64	.67	.72	.69	.73	.65	.70	.76	.67	.67
5	.69	.67	.72	.72	.73	.70	.75	.79	.76	.69
6	.72	.66	.71	.72	.75	.72	.76	.77	.73	.66
7	.75	.69	.74	.76	..	.73	.75	.81	.78	..
All grades	.66	.65	.72	.72	.73	.68	.71	.75	.72	.64

Note.—Cronbach's alpha for each subscale was calculated for each grade level at each time of measurement. These values were averaged to obtain those presented in this table.

43

TABLE 5

SAMPLE ITEMS FROM THE ASSESSMENT OF TEACHER CONTEXT
(Students' Reports)

Involvement
My teacher knows me well. (+)
My teacher likes me. (+)
My teacher is always there for me. (+)
My teacher spends time with me. (+)
My teacher just doesn't understand me. (−)
My teacher doesn't seem to enjoy having me in his/her class. (−)
I can't count on my teacher when I need him/her. (−)
I can't depend on my teacher for important things. (−)

Structure
I know what my teacher expects of me in class. (+)
My teacher treats me fairly. (+)
My teacher shows me how to solve problems for myself. (+)
My teacher makes sure I understand before he/she goes on. (+)
My teacher keeps changing the rules on me. (−)
Every time I do something wrong, my teacher reacts differently. (−)
Even when I run into problems, my teacher doesn't help me. (−)
My teacher doesn't check to see if I'm keeping up. (−)

NOTE.—From Belmont, Skinner, Wellborn, and Connell (1992).

and that one cannot oneself influence them (powerful others strategy times negative powerful others capacity); that luck is a determining factor in school performance but that one is personally unlucky (luck strategy times negative luck capacity); and that generally the causes of school success and failure are unknown (unknown strategy beliefs).

The composite Promote and Undermine scores could be used to contrast the effects of those beliefs that were hypothesized to support children's engagement in the classroom with the effects of those that were hypothesized to lead to disaffection. Finally, these two scores could be combined to form a composite reflecting the optimal profile of perceived control. Referred to as *ConMax,* it was calculated by combining Promote with the additive inverse of Undermine. High scores on ConMax reflect the best possible combination of perceptions of control, whereas low scores reflect the most maladaptive combination of control beliefs possible. Procedures for calculating all scores are presented in Appendix A.

Teacher Context

All students reported on their experiences of involvement and structure in interactions with their teachers (for sample items, see Table 5; as well as Belmont, Skinner, Wellborn, & Connell, 1992). The involvement scale consisted of six items tapping students' perceptions of teachers' warmth, af-

TABLE 6

RELIABILITY OF MEASUREMENT OF TEACHER CONTEXT
BY STUDENT GRADE LEVEL AVERAGED ACROSS
TIMES OF MEASUREMENT

| | STUDENT REPORTS OF: | |
STUDENT GRADE LEVEL	Teacher Structure	Teacher Involvement
3	.84	.76
4	.88	.82
5	.91	.85
6	.89	.79
7	.90	.82
All grades	.88	.81

NOTE.—Teacher context was reported by students. Cronbach's alpha was calculated for each grade level at each time of measurement. These values were averaged to obtain those presented in this table.

fection, caring, and availability. The structure scale consisted of 19 items tapping students' views of teachers' consistency, contingency, and predictability. These scales overlapped moderately with teachers' ratings of the same dimensions of their interactions with students (Skinner & Belmont, 1993). Across grade and time of measurement, alphas ranged from .76 to .91. The breakdown of alphas by grade (averaged across times of measurement) appears in Table 6.

Academic Performance

At the end of the study, 414 children's grades were recorded for all years available in the students' records (for most students, these began in the first grade). Grades were converted from letters to numbers, from 1 (F or U−) to 12 (A or V). Aggregate grade scores were formed by averaging children's grades from classes tapping verbal ability (reading, language, and/or spelling) and math ability. The average for verbal grades was 8.93 (between a B and a B−; SD = 1.63), and the average for math grades was 8.96 (between a B and a B−; SD = 2.00).

As is typical, grades were highly reliable (the correlation between composite reading and composite math was .73) and stable across time. In addition, they be considered to be normed by teachers across grade. Hence, it did not make sense to examine age differences or growth curves in grades. However, we were interested in examining whether grades acted as a variable that "launched" subsequent trajectories of perceived control. As a result, for each child, we calculated two aggregate scores for school grades. Both averaged reading and math composites; however, the first set of scores included only grades that were earned prior to the study (i.e., from the beginning of kindergarten to the end of the second grade), and the second set of scores included all grade data collected for a given child.

SAMPLE AGGREGATION FOR DIFFERENT KINDS OF ANALYSES

A series of decisions were made about how to aggregate the sample for different analyses. On the one hand, several features of the study goals and design made it undesirable to conduct analyses using the entire sample, as would be done in typical interindividual differences analyses. First, the sample was not balanced by grade. This meant that any averages or correlations calculated on the whole sample would be overweighted by the values for fourth and fifth graders (who were most frequently assessed). In addition, any comparisons of correlation or regression coefficients between grades would favor the age group with the larger sample size.

On the other hand, several features made it undesirable to use the purely longitudinal subset of children, as would typically be done in developmental analyses. First, the number of children for whom we had complete longitudinal data was relatively small ($N = 222$); and, in general, as is typically the case, this group was slightly positively biased. For example, children who participated in the study at all six measurement points had significantly higher mean levels of teacher-rated engagement in the third grade (averaged over the fall and the spring) compared to children with fewer than six data points (3.32 and 3.17, respectively, $p < .05$). Second, in purely longitudinal designs, age is confounded with number of times previously tested, with the result that age is positively correlated with any bias introduced by repeated assessments. However, in our sequential design, we had seventh graders who had been tested in 2 previous years, but we also had fifth and sixth graders who had been tested in 2 previous years as well.

Hence, in this sample, sometimes cross-sectional age comparisons would provide the most representative picture of age changes. However, the cross-sectional data taken for the sample as a whole were "mixed," in that any comparison of grades included not only true cross-sectional comparisons (between groups) but also children who had been measured longitudinally (at both grades). If children followed longitudinally were included in analyses designed to compare independent samples (e.g., comparisons of correlation or regression coefficients between grades), then the dependent data would bias the results of the statistical tests.[2]

---

[2] We thank two anonymous reviewers for pointing this out.

Criteria for Aggregation

Because the analyses were designed to test both developmental and individual differences predictions, different subsamples were used for different analyses. Multiple criteria were used in creating subsamples, including consideration of bias in sampling, bias in statistical testing, and issues of power and developmental balance. In every case, overarching consideration was given to issues of bias. A subsample of children was never selected in a way that would introduce bias. Subsamples were always selected using a stratified random procedure. And conclusions were never based solely on the completely longitudinal subsample. In addition, subsamples were never created in a way that would compromise a statistical test. For example, in age comparisons of coefficients, no repeated-measures data were included.

When criteria for preventing the introduction of bias were met, we then attempted to maximize developmental representativeness by using samples that were balanced by age. Hence, in all substantive analyses, samples with equal or almost equal numbers of children of each age group were used. Finally, we were concerned with issues of power; therefore, within the constraints set by issues of bias and developmental representativeness, we tried to use the largest subsamples possible. Fortunately, the large size of the initial subject pool usually made it possible to identify subsamples in which different age groups had a minimum of 100 subjects each. The only exceptions were analyses involving academic performance because achievement data were available for only about 400 children; in these analyses, age groups sometimes contained only 70–80 subjects each. In most cases, however, it was not difficult to maintain sufficient power in the analyses. Descriptions of the specific samples and rationales for aggregation are provided in each results chapter.

DESCRIPTIVE ANALYSES

Initial analyses focused on the means, standard deviations, and correlations among the different indicators of context, self, action, and outcomes. In this first set of analyses, including the psychometric analyses reported previously, all subjects were included for whom we had complete data on the variable(s) of interest. However, for any given descriptive statistic, up to six different values, based on the six times of measurement, could be calculated. For example, the mean for control beliefs could be calculated for measurement time 1 (the fall of year 1) through measurement time 6 (the spring of year 3). If statistics were further broken down by grade, then even more values for each variable could be calculated (22 per variable).

Instead of including data for all measurement points or for only select measurement points, we reported statistics *averaged* across measurement points. For overall statistics, these were also averaged over age. So, for each alpha, mean, and correlation, that statistic was calculated 22 times, one for each measurement point and age, and then the values were averaged, first across measurement points for each age, then across age. So, for example, each alpha reported for fourth graders is actually the *mean* of six alphas calculated for fourth graders across the six measurement points. Even the standard deviation of each variable (e.g., the standard deviation of control beliefs) is the mean of up to six standard deviations. Hence, all statistics have their own standard deviations, each based on the variation of the statistic over measurement points. In general, these were small and indicated minor variations over measurement points. For example, the correlations between control and engagement for fourth graders did not differ much between fourth graders measured in the fall and those measured in the spring of year 1 or between fourth graders measured in spring of years 2 and 3.

Means and Standard Deviations

Table 7 presents the means and standard deviations of all the subscales of context, self, action, and outcomes averaged across age and time of measurement as well as broken down by grade level. Results of analyses of age differences in means and correlations are not presented in this section. This information is presented subsequently as part of more comprehensive analyses.

The general profile of control beliefs, presented in the first column of Table 7, was also consistent with published reports (e.g., Little & Lopez, 1997; Skinner et al., 1988a, 1988b; Skinner et al., 1990). In terms of strategy beliefs, children viewed effort as the most effective strategy, followed by ability; powerful others and luck were generally seen as not very central to school success and failure; unknown causes were also low. In terms of capacity beliefs, children perceived themselves as able and as possessing the capacities to exert effort and to influence powerful others (in this case, teachers); they viewed themselves as having less access to luck. Teachers' ratings of children's engagement were also consistent with previous work (Connell & Wellborn, 1991; Skinner & Belmont, 1993). Teachers rated students' engagement as higher than the midpoint of the scale (2.5) and as slightly higher on emotional than on behavioral engagement. In terms of context, students experienced teachers as both highly involved and as providing a great deal of structure; this is consistent with previous research (Skinner & Belmont, 1993).

For none of the variables was any evidence found for floor or ceiling effects or for a restricted range of variance. The highest ratings (control beliefs, $M = 3.42$) did not approach the highest point in the four-point scale, and the lowest scores (strategy luck, $M = 1.75$) did not approach the lowest

TABLE 7

Means and Standard Deviations of Context, Self, and Action Variables and Subscales by Student Grade Level Averaged across Times of Measurement

Variables	All Grades		3d Grade		4th Grade		5th Grade		6th Grade		7th Grade	
	Mean	SD	Mean	SD	Mean	SD	Mean	SD	Mean	SD	Mean	SD
Children's perceived control:												
ConMax	21.12	15.4	22.2	14.2	23.5	14.3	23.9	15.3	19.9	16.4	16.1	16.9
Promote	45.34	7.9	45.7	7.5	46.6	7.4	46.3	8.1	45.1	8.2	43.0	8.4
Undermine	24.32	9.0	23.6	9.0	23.0	8.3	22.5	8.7	25.4	9.6	27.1	9.5
Strategy beliefs	3.30	.51	2.29	.49	2.32	.48	2.26	.52	2.37	.53	2.40	.55
Capacity beliefs	2.34	.43	3.38	.49	3.42	.44	3.38	.40	3.23	.41	3.11	.39
Control beliefs	3.42	.53	3.40	.51	3.48	.50	3.50	.51	3.41	.55	3.29	.58
Strategy:												
Effort	3.16	.59	3.06	.63	3.19	.58	3.20	.58	3.20	.56	3.11	.59
Ability	2.56	.76	2.49	.80	2.56	.79	2.55	.76	2.52	.72	2.63	.72
Powerful others	1.76	.68	1.70	.76	1.61	.64	1.58	.64	1.85	.67	1.99	.70
Luck	1.75	.71	1.79	.80	1.75	.72	1.59	.62	1.78	.68	…	…
Unknown	1.86	.70	1.94	.76	1.90	.69	1.73	.67	1.90	.70	1.89	.67
Capacity:												
Effort	3.30	.57	3.37	.56	3.43	.53	3.38	.57	3.20	.59	3.06	.58
Ability	3.36	.63	3.44	.60	3.46	.59	3.41	.63	3.26	.65	3.17	.66
Powerful others	3.28	.68	3.35	.67	3.37	.64	3.31	.70	3.21	.67	3.07	.73
Luck	3.03	.58	3.06	.56	3.12	.60	3.03	.58	2.93	.58	…	…
Student engagement (teacher report):												
Behavior	3.04	.75	3.10	.71	3.11	.71	3.12	.78	2.96	.76	2.91	.74
Emotion	3.34	.52	3.42	.51	3.33	.51	3.54	.45	3.22	.58	3.33	.51
Average engagement	3.19	.60	3.26	.56	3.22	.61	3.33	.56	3.09	.62	3.12	.59
Teacher context (student report):												
Involvement	3.04	.68	3.18	.69	3.18	.69	3.12	.70	2.93	.64	2.77	.68
Structure	3.08	.54	3.11	.50	3.18	.50	3.20	.60	3.00	.53	2.90	.54
Average context	3.06	.57	3.14	.56	3.18	.57	3.18	.60	2.97	.55	2.85	.58

Note.—ConMax scores ranged from −66 to 66; promote and undermine scores ranged from 14 to 80; children's control beliefs, student engagement, and teacher context scores ranged from 1 (not at all true) to 4 (very true). Values were calculated for each grade level at each time of measurement. These values were averaged to obtain those presented in this table.

possible score, namely, 1.0. Most important, there was no indication of patterns of restricted variance by age. Hence, any age differences or changes in correlations or growth curves were not likely to be a function of these scale score properties.

Intraconstruct Correlations

Correlations between the subscales of perceived control (averaged across measurement and age) are contained in Table 8. Although factor analyses have confirmed that the 10 scales are distinct (Skinner et al., 1988b), the sets of beliefs are also related in a comprehensible fashion. As can be seen in Table 8, children who viewed themselves as being able to produce success and avoid failure in school (control beliefs) were also likely to endorse effort as a strategy and to report high capacities for all known causes, especially effort and ability; children with low control beliefs were more likely to endorse nonaction strategies, including ability, powerful others, and luck, and were especially likely to report that they simply did not know the causes of school success and failure (unknown strategy beliefs).

Capacity beliefs themselves showed, in general, a "positive manifold" (Little et al., 1995), suggesting that children who viewed themselves as having access to any of the causes also felt that they had access to the other causes. Especially closely related were capacity beliefs for effort and ability. Relative to capacity beliefs, strategy beliefs showed less coherence among the causal categories. In fact, effort strategy beliefs showed modest relations only with ability strategy beliefs; likewise, ability strategy beliefs showed only modest relations with strategy beliefs for the other causes (r ranging from .25 to .29); beliefs about the effectiveness of the three "external" causes—powerful others, luck, and unknown—were more highly intercorrelated (r ranging from .46 to .51). These correlational patterns are consistent with other published reports (e.g., Little & Lopez, 1997; Skinner et al., 1990).

The relations between capacity and strategy beliefs were not particularly high: for the same causes, correlations ranged from $-.38$ to $+.17$ and were in some cases positive (e.g., effort strategy and capacity) and in other cases negative (e.g., powerful others strategy and capacity). Most closely related to capacity beliefs seemed to be strategy beliefs about powerful others, luck, and unknown, with children who expressed low effort and ability capacity beliefs more likely to endorse the effectiveness of more "external," especially unknown, factors (average $r = -.47$).

The pattern of relations for ability strategy beliefs deserves brief note because it reveals something about their potentially positive and negative effects. On the one hand, children who endorsed ability as a strategy were also more likely to see effort as an effective means. On the other hand, students

TABLE 8

WITHIN-CONSTRUCT CORRELATIONS AVERAGED ACROSS STUDENT GRADE LEVELS AND TIMES OF MEASUREMENT

Children's Perceived Control	1	2	3	4	5	6	7	8	9
1. Control beliefs									
2. Strategy—effort	.21								
3. Strategy—ability	-.20	.25							
4. Strategy—powerful others	-.41	-.08	.29						
5. Strategy—luck	-.45	-.08*	.29	.51					
6. Strategy—unknown	-.58	-.11	.25	.46	.51				
7. Capacity—effort	.65	.17	-.22	-.43	-.42	-.58			
8. Capacity—ability	.65	.14	-.19	-.39	-.44	-.57	.67		
9. Capacity—powerful others	.47	.16	-.15	-.38	-.30	-.40	.49	.44	
10. Capacity—luck	.54	.10	-.16	-.29	-.33	-.44	.57	.61	.41

	Emotion
Student engagement (teacher report):	
Behavior	.71

	Structure
Teacher context (student report):	
Involvement	.79

NOTE.—Correlations were calculated for each grade level at each time of measurement. These values were averaged to obtain those presented in this table. All $p < .0001$ except where indicated.

* $p < .01$.

who believed that ability was a necessary condition for school success also gave higher endorsements to other nonaction strategies, including powerful others, luck, and unknown; furthermore, they saw themselves as having less control and as possessing consistently lower capacities. The pattern of age differences and age changes in the functions of ability strategy beliefs (described later) may illuminate the different components of conceptions of ability, for example, as an "internal" yet potentially uncontrollable cause.

In terms of children's perceptions of their teachers, the high correlation between teachers' involvement and their provision of structure ($r = .79$, $p <$ .001) suggested that children did not differentiate between their experiences of their teachers as warm and affectionate (as tapped by the involvement scale) and as consistent and contingent (as tapped by the structure scale). Although observational studies indicate that the two are objectively separable aspects of adult-child interaction (Baumrind, 1977; Skinner, 1986), we decided to combine child perceptions of involvement and provision of structure to form a summary indicator of the kinds of teacher-student interactions that should promote children's feelings of control.

IV. RESULTS OF ANALYSES EXAMINING AGE CHANGES IN THE FUNCTIONING OF INDIVIDUAL DIFFERENCES IN PERCEIVED CONTROL

The analyses described in this chapter were designed to test the model of individual differences in the functioning of perceived control and to determine whether any of its links operated differently for children of different ages. The general model, presented in Figure 11 above, holds that children's experiences of the structure and involvement provided by their teachers exerts an effect on their perceived control, which in turn influences their engagement in the classroom; the extent of children's engagement contributes to the level of their actual academic performance, which then feeds back on their perceived control.

We tested several aspects of this model. First, using structural equation modeling, we tested the fit between the overall model and the data. Of interest were the mediational effects of control and engagement: (1) Are the effects of teacher context on students' engagement mediated by children's perceived control? (2) Are the effects of perceived control on actual performance mediated by engagement? (3) Does actual performance exert a reciprocal effect on subsequent perceived control? In addition, we were interested in examining each individual link in the model: from teacher context to perceived control; from control to engagement; and from actual performance to control. Because the relations were predicted to be causal, we examined each link in the model across time, from the fall to the spring of the school year. The mediational and causal hypotheses are listed in Figure 8 above in the first two rows under *functional model.*

We also tested hypotheses that certain portions of the model would be invariant over this age range and that certain links would change with age. At each age from 8 to 13 years, we expected that the general model would hold: that teacher context would predict profiles of control, that aggregated control would predict engagement, that engagement would predict school performance, and that school performance would have a reciprocal effect on perceived control. We also predicted that, when the constructs of context and control were considered at a more differentiated level, developmental differences would emerge. These hypotheses are described in detail in later sections.

DEVELOPMENTAL DIFFERENCES IN THE MODEL OF CONTEXT, SELF, ACTION, AND OUTCOMES

The functional model was tested using structural equation modeling to evaluate the whole mediational model and using time-lagged and concurrent multiple regressions to examine the causal predictions about each link. Of primary interest were analyses that examined similarities and differences in these overall patterns across development.

Aggregation for Analyses of Age Differences in the Functioning of Perceived Control

Using criteria described in Chapter III above, we created subsamples for use in these analyses. For the overall analyses, each child was included in only one age group (i.e., no repeated-measures data were used), and a subsample was created that was closely balanced by age (total $N = 1,186$; $n = 213, 287, 203, 283,$ and 200 for grades 3, 4, 5, 6, and 7, respectively; when achievement data were included, total $N = 401$; $n = 82, 82, 80, 78,$ and 79 for grades 3, 4, 5, 6, and 7, respectively). Since the age comparisons involved developmental changes that took place in approximately the fourth and sixth grades, the explicit developmental comparisons were conducted using only children from grades 3, 5, and 7 (total $N = 616$). When achievement data were included, this sample was reduced to 241.

As a cross-check for these analyses of age differences, identical analyses of age changes were conducted using the longitudinal data. As mentioned previously, data from children for whom we had complete longitudinal data were slightly positively biased compared to the rest of the sample and so showed slightly higher levels of teacher context, perceived control, engagement, and school performance. However, the pattern of correlations and regressions, and especially the pattern of age *changes* in correlations and regressions, was virtually identical to that found in cross-sectional comparisons.

Interconstruct Correlations

Correlations among all the variables, averaged across times of measurement and then across age, are presented in Table 9. Table 10 includes selected interconstruct correlations by age, averaged across times of measure-

TABLE 9

Correlations between Constructs Averaged across Student Grade Levels and Times of Measurement

	Engagement (Teacher Report)			Teacher Context (Student Report)			Grades[a]		
	Behavior	Emotion	Total Engagement	Involvement	Structure	Total Context	Reading	Math	Average Achievement
Children's Perceived Control:									
ConMax	.38	.33	.39	.62	.68	.68	.35	.33	.36
Promote	.33	.28	.34	.59	.62	.64	.31	.28	.31
Undermine	−.35	−.31	−.36	−.55	−.62	−.61	−.33	−.32	−.35
Strategy	.24	.23	.26	.30	.42	.38	.33	.29	.33
Capacity	.36	.31	.37	.65	.68	.71	.33	.30	.34
Control beliefs	.33	.29	.34	.44	.50	.49	.40	.36	.40
Strategy:									
Effort	.10	.08	.09	.10	.20	.17	.16	.11*	.15**
Ability	−.06**	−.04*	−.05**	−.21	−.22	−.14	.07[b]	.04[b]	.06[b]
Powerful others	−.21	−.19	−.22	−.42	−.51	−.49	−.22	−.21	−.23
Luck	−.26	−.25	−.27	−.30	−.43	−.37	−.22	−.22	−.24
Unknown	−.30	−.27	−.31	−.38	−.46	−.44	−.26	−.26	−.27
Capacity:									
Effort	.34	.27	.34	.49	.55	.54	.34	.32	.35
Ability	.32	.28	.33	.44	.48	.48	.29	.28	.31
Powerful others	.25	.22	.26	.69	.66	.71	.23	.18	.22
Luck	.33	.28	.33	.45	.46	.48	.22	.24	.25

NOTE.—Correlations between constructs were calculated at each grade level and time of measurement. These correlations were averaged to obtain those presented in this table. Except where indicated, $p < .001$.

[a] Student grades were the average of each student's grade history. Correlations with grades are based on a random selection of unique students balanced by grade level. Third grade $N = 82$, fourth grade $N = 82$, fifth grade $N = 80$, sixth grade $N = 78$, seventh grade $N = 79$.

[b] Not significant.

* $p < .05$.

** $p < .01$.

TABLE 10

CORRELATIONS BETWEEN CONSTRUCTS BY GRADE LEVEL AVERAGED ACROSS TIMES OF MEASUREMENT

	STUDENT GRADE LEVEL									
	STUDENT ENGAGEMENT (Teacher Report)					TEACHER CONTEXT (Student Report)				
	3	4	5	6	7	3	4	5	6	7
Children's perceived control:										
ConMax	.40	.35	.42	.42	.34	.70	.64	.69	.68	.70
Promote	.36	.28	.38	.34	.32	.61	.59	.65	.67	.68
Undermine	−.34	−.34	−.39	−.41	−.32	−.60	−.58	−.62	−.61	−.64
Strategy	.27	.26	.28	.31	.16**	.36	.30	.34	.42	.49
Capacity	.33	.32	.43	.40	.36	.73	.66	.74	.70	.71
Control beliefs	.31	.31	.41	.38	.28	.51	.44	.47	.51	.52
Strategy:										
Effort	.10*	.08*	.16**	.12*	.01[a]	.07[a]	.10**	.13**	.23	.31
Ability	−.13**	.05[a]	.01[a]	.02[a]	.05[a]	−.17**	−.24	−.21	−.26	−.24
Powerful others	−.27	−.23	−.22	−.26	−.14**	−.42	−.50	−.50	−.50	−.53
Luck	−.28	−.20	−.31	−.29	…	−.26	−.33	−.40	−.47	…
Unknown	−.31	−.29	−.30	−.34	−.30	−.41	−.36	−.42	−.49	−.54
Capacity:										
Effort	.38	.30	.40	.36	.26	.61	.48	.54	.56	.53
Ability	.24	.33	.37	.41	.30	.51	.45	.49	.49	.46
Powerful others	.21	.16	.31	.26	.35	.66	.69	.78	.69	.75
Luck	.31	.28	.35	.39	…	.47	.45	.46	.53	…
Student engagement (teacher report)	…	…	…	…	…	…	…	…	…	…
Teacher context (student report)	.33	.23	.32	.24	.33	…	…	…	…	…

	AVERAGE ACHIEVEMENT[b]				
Children's perceived control:					
ConMax	.35**	.22[a]	.39	.43	.48
Promote	.23*	.16[a]	.43	.36**	.46
Undermine	−.37	−.23*	−.31**	−.46	−.46
Strategy	.23*	.26[a]	.31**	.47	.32**
Capacity	.42	.15[a]	.39	.40	.54
Control beliefs	.32**	.24*	.56	.46	.46
Strategy:					
Effort	−.03[a]	.15[a]	.25*	.25[a]	.06[a]
Ability	.04[a]	.07[a]	.08[a]	.04[a]	.03[a]
Powerful others	−.29**	−.08[a]	−.16[a]	−.36**	−.28*
Luck	−.21[a]	−.07[a]	−.40*	−.39**	…
Unknown	−.15[a]	−.24*	−.20[a]	−.44	−.36
Capacity:					
Effort	.47	.18[a]	.39	.41	.44
Ability	.16[a]	.23*	.40	.40	.50
Powerful others	.35**	−.01[a]	.22[a]	.24*	.36**
Luck	.38	.15[a]	.43**	.07[a]	…
Student engagement (teacher report)	.37	.57	.68	.68	.49
Teacher context (student report)	.32**	.09[a]	.33**	.21[a]	.28*

NOTE.—Correlations between constructs were calculated at each time of measurement. These correlations were averaged to obtain those presented in this table. All $p < .001$ except where indicated.

[a] Not significant.

[b] Student grades were the average of each student's grade history. Correlations with grades are based on a random selection of unique students balanced by grade level. Third grade $N = 82$, fourth grade $N = 82$, fifth grade $N = 80$, sixth grade $N = 78$, seventh grade $N = 79$.

* $p < .05$.

** $p < .01$.

ment. As can be seen, all the bivariate links predicted by the model—namely, between context and self (perceived control), between self and action (engagement), and between action and outcomes (school performance)—were significant.

As expected, children's experiences with teacher context were related to their perceived control. Considering the different aspects of perceived control, it seemed that teacher context was especially important to children's views of their capacities and to their reports of "external" strategies. The correlates of teachers' involvement compared to their provision of structure revealed (as expected from the high intercorrelations between these two aspects of teacher context) few differential relations to perceived control. The two possible exceptions were strategy beliefs for powerful others and luck. Children's perceptions that other people and luck were forces in their own school performance were associated less with teachers' involvement (average $r = -.36$) and more with the structure that teachers provided (average $r = -.47$).

Also as expected, children's perceived control was related to their engagement in the classroom. The strongest bivariate predictors of engagement were control and capacity beliefs; the strongest negative relations were found for the "external" strategies, especially unknown strategy beliefs. The aggregate control scales showed the expected relations to teachers' ratings of students' engagement (r ranging from $-.36$ to $.39$). Although total capacity beliefs seemed more closely related to engagement than were total strategy beliefs, the profile of beliefs expected to promote and the profile expected to undermine engagement seemed to show correlations that, although opposite in direction, were of about the same magnitude.

Also consistent with hypotheses, robust correlations between engagement and grades indicated that children who were more engaged in school also earned higher grades in both math and verbal subjects. Finally, variables that were not adjacent in the model nevertheless showed significant relations to each other. Teacher context was related to students' engagement; teachers' provision of structure (r ranging from $.24$ to $.31$) had slightly higher correlations with engagement than did teachers' involvement (r ranging from $.20$ to $.26$). In addition, children's grades were related to their perceived control. Grades were most strongly related to children's control beliefs and capacity effort beliefs. Grades were also modestly related to students' perceptions of teacher context, both structure and involvement (r ranging from $.14$ to $.25$).

Structural Equation Modeling

Structural equation analyses were used to test the mediational predictions of the model across time, specifically, (1) whether the effects of teacher

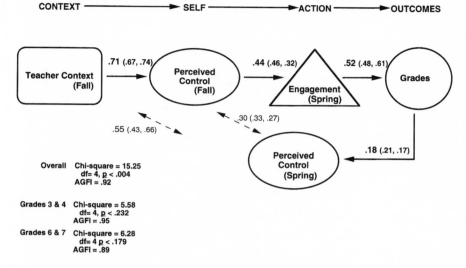

CONTEXT ─────────▶ SELF ─────────▶ACTION ────────▶OUTCOMES

FIGURE 12.—Structural equation models of the mediational model of context, self, action, and outcomes. Total $N = 280$; grades 3 and 4 $N = 162$; grade 6 and 7 $N = 84$.

context in the fall on students' engagement in the spring were mediated by children's perceived control in the fall, (2) whether the effects of perceived control in the fall on children's school performance were mediated by their engagement in the classroom in the spring, and (3) whether school performance exerted a reciprocal direct effect on perceived control in the spring. We also allowed perceived control, which was measured in both the fall and the spring, to correlate across time.

The results of the structural equation modeling using children from all grades ($N = 280$) are presented in Figure 12. As can be seen, the data showed a good fit with the model ($\chi^2 = 15.25$, $df = 4$, $p < .004$; AGFI $= .92$). The chi-square value was significant because of the large sample size; however, the adjusted goodness-of-fit index indicated a reasonable fit. In addition, an indicator of fit that is less sensitive to sample size, namely, the ratio of chi square to degrees of freedom, at 3.8, was well within the range of acceptable values of 1–5 proposed for this index (Byrne, 1989).

The results of the structural equation modeling separately for children in grades 3 and 4 ($N = 162$) and for children in grades 6 and 7 ($N = 84$) are also presented in Figure 12. The model was a good fit for the data from both groups, as indicated by the chi-square ratios, the adjusted goodness-of-fit indices, and the chi-square/degrees-of-freedom ratios (1.4 and 1.6, for the younger and older groups, respectively). Analyses of age differences in the model parameters indicated that the coefficients for two paths differed between children in grades 3 and 4 and those in grades 6 and 7: (1) between children's engagement and

TABLE 11

<small>Multiple Regressions Examining the Effects of Teacher Context and Student Achievement in the Fall on Children's Perceived Control in the Spring and the Effect of Perceived Control in the Fall on Student Engagement in the Spring</small>

Independent variables	Unique β
Dependent variable: Children's perceived control (ConMax, spring):	
$R^2 = .59$, $N = 627$:	
Teacher context (fall)	.179**
Children's perceived control (ConMax, fall)	.635**
$R^2 = .56$, $N = 282$:	
Average student achievement	.168*
Children's perceived control (ConMax, fall)	.680**
Dependent variable: Student engagement (spring):	
$R^2 = .58$, $N = 624$:	
Children's perceived control (ConMax, fall)	.154**
Student engagement (fall)	.689**

<small>NOTE.—Student engagement was reported by teachers. Teacher context was reported by students.</small>
<small>* $p < .001$.</small>
<small>** $p < .0001$.</small>

their grades and (2) between students' reports of teacher context in the fall and their perceived control in the spring. In both cases, the older children's parameter estimates were significantly higher than younger children's. However, overall, the models did not differ appreciably by age.

Time-Lagged Regressions

In order to test the causal predictions from the model, we used time-lagged regressions to examine whether each link would hold when the dependent variable was *change* in the target outcome from fall to spring. Table 11 contains the results of the time-lagged regressions, which are consistent with the causal hypotheses of the functional model. As can be seen, the regressions indicated that students' ratings of teacher context in the fall predicted children's perceived control in the spring, even controlling for the strong effect of perceived control in the fall. Likewise, average performance (grades) also predicted changes in perceived control from fall to spring. In addition, the time-lagged regressions indicated that students' perceived control in the fall predicted changes in engagement from fall to spring, despite the high stability of teachers' ratings of students' engagement.

Summary of the Results on the Mediational Model

Data were consistent with a cyclic model of beliefs and performance. Data were consistent with hypotheses that the effects of teacher context on students' engagement would be mediated by children's perceived control and that the effects of students' perceived control on their academic achievement would be mediated by their engagement in the classroom. In addition, actual performance showed the predicted feedback effect on perceived control. The mediational model held at a general level for children across this age range.

AGE DIFFERENCES IN THE ANTECEDENTS OF CONTROL

Previous findings were consistent with the causal and mediational hypotheses of the model. However, we wished to examine more closely two specific links: (1) antecedents of control, that is, the effects of prior performance and teacher context on students' perceived control; and (2) consequences of control, that is, the influence of perceived control on students' engagement. These analyses are described in the next two sections.

According to the functional model, individual differences in perceived control should be shaped, not only by the amount of structure and involvement provided by teachers to a particular child, but also by the level of the child's own academic performance. The previous analyses showed that, at a general level, these links hold for children across middle childhood. In these next analyses, we examined the links from context and performance to different aspects of children's perceived control.

We hypothesized that, although both teacher context and individual performance would predict students' perceived control, they would change in their centrality or salience as predictors as children developed. Younger children's perceived control should be more influenced by teacher context than that of older children. We reasoned that, in general, younger children are more dependent on social cues than older children. In addition, children in the third grade should still be in the process of constructing their domain-specific perceived control and so should be more open to social information (Carton & Nowicki, 1994). We also expected that older children's perceived control would be influenced more by their individual performances than would younger children's (Stipek, 1984b). These hypotheses are listed in Figure 8 above in the row on age differences under the heading *functional model*.

We did not formulate specific hypotheses about the aspects of perceived control that would be likely to be differentially affected by teacher context compared to academic performance. It might make sense that teacher context would have a greater effect on beliefs about the role of powerful others, whereas academic performance might have a stronger effect on beliefs about ability. However, as discussed in Chapter I above, social cues can also influence whether attributions are made to effort or to ability (e.g., Graham, 1984), so we considered these analyses exploratory.

In terms of age differences, we also expected, in a general way, that, if younger children's perceived control is focused more on effort and older children's more on ability, then the effects of the antecedents might also be differentially focused for children of these two ages. Specifically, it seemed possible that, for younger children, experiences with teachers and information about academic performance might have a stronger effect on beliefs about *effort* and that, for older children, social context and individual performance might have a greater effect on beliefs about *ability*. However, again, these analyses were considered exploratory.

Performance Predicts Control: Multiple Regressions and Age Interactions

The previous analyses indicated that children's perceived control was predicted by their own prior performance. In the next analyses, we examined the "feedback" effect of grades on different aspects of perceived control. The zero-order correlations between different aspects of control and grades were ambiguous in this regard because they contained both feedback effects of grades on control *and* "feedforward" effects of control on grades through their effects on engagement. Hence, to isolate "feedback" effects, we examined the relations between different aspects of control and grades while controlling for the feedforward mechanism, namely, engagement. We also examined age differences in these feedback effects. We expected that the effects of grades on control would be greater for older than for younger children, especially the feedback effects on capacity ability beliefs.

In each case, the independent variables were average achievement (grades) and teachers' ratings of students' engagement, and the dependent variable was an aspect of perceived control. In general, two regression equations were calculated for each aspect of control beliefs considered (see Table 12). The first, using the concurrent balanced sample of students ($n = 401$), entered both independent variables simultaneously (see the first three columns of Table 12). The second included the effects of grade level (grades 3–7) and a linear interaction term created by multiplying average achievement by grade level. A significant interaction term for a given aspect of perceived control indicated that the relation between achievement and that aspect of perceived control differed for children as a function of grade (see the last three columns of Table 12).

As can be seen, achievement exerted an effect on all aspects of perceived control except strategy and capacity luck, even when controlling for engagement. Strongest "feedback" effects were found, as predicted, for control and capacity beliefs for effort and ability. An age interaction was found for ability capacity beliefs. This was followed up using the subsample of third, fifth, and seventh graders ($n = 241$). In this analysis, independent variables included average achievement, dummy-coded grade variables to contrast third to fifth

TABLE 12

RESULTS OF MULTIPLE REGRESSIONS EXAMINING THE EFFECTS OF CHILDREN'S ACHIEVEMENT ON THEIR PERCEIVED CONTROL, CONTROLLING FOR THEIR ENGAGEMENT

DEPENDENT VARIABLES	MAIN EFFECT MODEL, R^2	INDEPENDENT VARIABLES, β		MODEL WITH INTERACTION, R^2	GRADE LEVEL AND INTERACTION, β	
		Average Achievement	Student Engagement (Teacher Report)		Grade Level	Grade Level × Average Achievement
ConMax	.18	.207***	.275***	.21	.599**	.555†
Promote	.13	.186***	.228***	.16	-.618*	.607*
Undermine	.18	-.197***	-.279***	.21	.499*	-.431
Strategy beliefs	.12	.254***	.140*	.13	-.186	.323
Capacity beliefs	.16	.197***	.260***	.24	-.685**	.546†
Control beliefs	.20	.286***	.217***	.21	-.425†	.466
Strategy:						
Effort	.02	.126*	.039	.04	-.046	.239
Ability	.02	.135*	-.183*	.02	.065	.019
Powerful others	.08	-.130*	-.182**	.09	.124	.004
Luck	.10	-.092	-.263***	.10	.074	-.102
Unknown	.11	-.151**	-.225***	.12	.303	-.465
Capacity:						
Effort	.17	.207***	.263***	.23	-.418†	.212
Ability	.13	.177**	.234***	.22	-.957***	.889**
Powerful others	.07	.123*	.169**	.09	-.361	.273
Luck	.09	.134†	.207**	.17	.095	-.476

NOTE.—Data from one time of measurement for each student with achievement data were selected maintaining the criteria that data were balanced by grade level. $N = 401$.

* $p < .05$.
** $p < .01$.
*** $p < .001$.
† $p < .10$.

graders and fifth to seventh graders, and the interaction scores for achievement, formed by multiplying achievement scores by the two dummy-coded grade variables. This analysis revealed a linear increase in the effects of achievement on ability capacity beliefs. In fact, achievement showed no feedback effect on ability capacity beliefs for third graders ($\beta = .12$, N.S.), compared to moderate effects for fifth graders ($\beta = .26$, $p < .05$) and strong effects for seventh graders ($\beta = .38$, $p < .001$).

Teacher Context and Performance Uniquely Predict Control: Multiple Regressions and Age Interactions

The previous analyses showed that children's perceived control was predicted by their own prior performance (in this case, grades). In addition, the zero-order correlations between perceived control and students' reports of social context (in this case, teachers) also suggested that context may play a role in children's sense of control. In the next analyses, we examined whether context and performance have differential unique effects on different aspects of control; for example, context may be more central to strategy beliefs, whereas performance may be more important to capacity beliefs. We also determined whether the unique contributions of context and performance to control differed as a function of age. We expected that context factors would become less important and performance more important as determinants of perceived control as children progress from the third to the seventh grade.

In each case, the independent variables were students' ratings of teacher context and achievement (average grades) and students' engagement (because we wanted to examine the unique feedback effects of achievement), and the dependent variable was an aspect of perceived control. In general, two regression equations were calculated for each aspect of control beliefs considered (see Table 13). The first, using the concurrent balanced sample of students with achievement data ($n = 401$), entered all independent variables simultaneously (see the first four columns of Table 13). The second included the effects of grade level (grades 3–7) and two linear interaction terms created by multiplying average achievement by grade level and teacher context by grade level. A significant interaction term for a given aspect of perceived control indicated that the relation between that independent variable (achievement or teacher context) and that aspect of perceived control differed for children as a function of grade (see the last four columns of Table 13).

In general, the unique coefficients suggested that the effects of teacher context and achievement were additive and relatively homogeneous across these ages. Compared to the zero-order correlations, the multiple regressions

TABLE 13

RESULTS OF MULTIPLE REGRESSIONS EXAMINING THE EFFECTS OF TEACHER CONTEXT AND CHILDREN'S ACHIEVEMENT ON CHILDREN'S PERCEIVED CONTROL, CONTROLLING FOR STUDENT ENGAGEMENT

DEPENDENT VARIABLES	MAIN EFFECT MODEL, R^2	INDEPENDENT VARIABLES, β			MODEL WITH INTERACTIONS, R^2	GRADE LEVEL AND INTERACTIONS, β		
		Teacher Context (Student Report)	Average Achievement	Student Engagement (Teacher Report)		Grade Level	Grade Level × Teacher Context	Grade Level × Average Achievement
ConMax	.54	.637***	.173***	.099*	.56	−.543*	.197	.439†
Promote	.47	.609***	.154***	.060	.48	−.591*	.227	.487*
Undermine	.47	−.573***	−.166***	−.121**	.48	.424	−.143	−.334
Strategy beliefs	.19	.279***	.239***	.063	.22	−.435	.479	.180
Capacity beliefs	.55	.654***	.162***	.080†	.57	−.585*	.135	.445*
Control beliefs	.36	.422***	.264***	.101*	.36	−.214	−.103	.440
Strategy:								
Effort	.03	.092†	.121*	.014	.08	−.664†	.908**	.020
Ability	.10	−.313***	.152**	−.047	.11	−.121	.119	.028
Powerful others	.29	−.482***	−.104*	−.050	.29	.031	−.082	.077
Luck	.15	−.232***	−.060	−.216**	.16	.001	−.072	−.006
Unknown	.24	−.370***	−.132*	−.123*	.26	.191	−.024	−.414
Capacity:								
Effort	.42	.525***	.179***	.119*	.44	−.241	−.029	.163
Ability	.31	.444***	.154**	.112*	.35	−.889**	.081	.825**
Powerful others	.49	.682***	.087*	−.019	.49	−.340	.270	.135
Luck	.30	.478***	.081	.107	.33	.139	.249	−.667†

NOTE.—Data from one time of measurement for each student with achievement data were selected maintaining the criteria that data were balanced by grade level. $N = 401$.

* $p < .05$.

** $p < .01$.

*** $p < .001$.

† $p < .10$.

showed that students' ratings of teacher context continued to predict all aspects of perceived control, even when controlling for achievement (and engagement). In addition, teacher context continued to predict powerful others strategy and capacity most strongly, but it also continued to predict other external strategies, other capacity beliefs, and control beliefs as well.

However, no support was found for the general prediction that teacher context would become *less* important to children's perceived control as they got older. Children's experiences of teacher context showed a unique and significant effect on almost all aspects of their control, at each age level. In fact, the single age interaction involving teacher context (followed up as described previously) indicated that teacher context became *more* important to older children, at least in terms of their strategy beliefs for effort. The relation between students' ratings of teacher context and their effort strategy beliefs was not significant in grade 3 or grade 5 (βs = $-.03$ and $.01$, respectively), but it was significantly higher in grade 7 ($\beta = .49$, $p < .001$). As can also be seen, achievement continued to exert effects on all aspects of control except strategy and capacity beliefs for luck, even after controlling for the strong effects of teacher context (and engagement).

Summary of Results on Age Differences in the Antecedents of Perceived Control

Children's perceived control was predicted both by their experiences with teachers and by their own academic performance. In general, both were unique predictors of most aspects of control all across this age range. Children's experiences with teachers were especially important to their strategy and capacity beliefs about powerful others but also showed effects on beliefs about other external strategies and capacity beliefs. As expected, children's academic performance was especially important as a predictor of their beliefs about their own ability and control, but it also shaped all children's beliefs except their strategy and capacity beliefs about luck.

Considering the effects of teacher context and achievement together revealed several interesting patterns involving beliefs about ability and effort. The first was for strategy beliefs for ability: although strategy ability was *negatively* predicted by teacher context, it showed a *positive* feedback effect from achievement. This was the only set of beliefs that was predicted in different directions by the two antecedent variables. For example, control and capacity beliefs, which were predicted positively by achievement, were also predicted positively by teacher context. And, although unknown strategy beliefs were predicted negatively by teacher context, they were also predicted negatively by students' achievement.

Second, the two findings in which the effects of antecedents differed as a function of age both operated in the same way: the antecedents were *stronger* predictors of control for older children. As expected, individual performance was a stronger predictor of capacity ability beliefs for older children; this increase was linear. In addition, and counter to general expectations that teacher context would become *less* important as children aged, the oldest children's beliefs about the effectiveness of effort as a strategy were more closely related to their experiences of their teachers than were those of younger children. This pattern, in which older children's beliefs about effort and ability seemed to be shaped more strongly by contextual *and* individual factors, may reflect older children's increased sensitivity to all sources of information about their control, perhaps also combined with increased differentiation as to which sources will shape which aspect of control beliefs. It may be that experiences of teachers as structured and warm were considered better sources of information about the potential effectiveness of effort, whereas an individual's own previous performance would be considered better information about his or her own ability.

AGE DIFFERENCES IN THE EFFECTS OF CONTROL ON ENGAGEMENT

A differentiated assessment of perceived control allowed the examination of multiple predictors of children's engagement as well as the exploration of age differences in the aspects of perceived control that promote and undermine engagement at different ages. We first discuss the basis for general predictions about the aspects of control that influence engagement and then detail hypotheses about age differences in these relations. Hypotheses are summarized in Table 14.

Consequences of Perceived Control for Engagement

Several theories contributed to hypotheses about the individual effects of different kinds of beliefs. As predicted by expectancy-value models and by theories of perceived competence and self-efficacy, control beliefs were expected to promote engagement, as were beliefs in one's own capacities. Extending these theories, we also predicted that engagement would be promoted by all capacity beliefs, and not just by convictions about the capacity to exert effort and possess ability. Having access to any potential means should bolster control. Even perceptions that one has the capacity to influence powerful others or to be lucky have been found to exert unique positive effects on engagement (Skinner et al., 1990). Consistent with locus of control, learned helplessness, and attribution theories, we predicted that engagement would be undermined by beliefs that powerful others and luck are major

TABLE 14

HYPOTHESES ABOUT DEVELOPMENTAL DIFFERENCES IN CONSEQUENCES OF PERCEIVED CONTROL

Effects of Different Aspects of Perceived Control on Engagement
1. Children's engagement is promoted by beliefs in control and capacities (including effort, ability, powerful others, and luck).
2. Children's engagement is undermined by beliefs in "external" strategies (including powerful others, luck, and unknown factors).
3. Beliefs in *effort* as a strategy will promote engagement for children who also have high effort capacity beliefs but will undermine engagement for children with low effort capacity beliefs.
4. Beliefs in *ability* as a strategy will operate similarly to beliefs about effort as a strategy for younger children but will come to undermine engagement for older children.

Age Differences in Effects of Control on Engagement
5. Capacity and control beliefs will promote engagement for children all across the age range.
6. Strategy beliefs will show different effects depending on the age of the child:
    a) For the youngest children (ages 8 and 9), beliefs about effort and unknown strategies will be stronger predictors of engagement.
    b) For the middle age group (ages 10 and 11), children's beliefs about "external" strategies (powerful others and luck) will be stronger predictors of engagement.
    c) For the oldest children (ages 12 and 13), beliefs about ability as a strategy will be a stronger predictor of engagement.

determinants of school performance or that the determinants of academic success and failure are unknown.

A lack of clarity exists about the effects of strategy beliefs about ability and effort. At first glance, it may seem that the belief that ability is an important strategy for school success has advantages because ability is an internal cause. However, it can also be viewed as a stable and uncontrollable cause, in which case reliance on ability could interfere with reengagement in the face of failures or setbacks. A possible developmental interpretation holds that strategy beliefs centered on ability will have a positive effect for young children because a young child's conception of ability is undifferentiated from that of effort and so is seen as unstable and controllable. Only when children form mature conceptions of ability as stable and immutable would ability strategy beliefs undermine engagement.

In terms of effort strategy beliefs, most control theories hold that attributing school performance (both success and failure) to effort is positive (e.g., Weiner, 1985a). However, when attributions are separated into strategy and capacity beliefs, it is also possible to argue that the conviction that effort is an important cause of school success and failure has positive effects on engagement *if and only if* one also believes that one has the capacity to exert effective effort (Skinner et al., 1990). Otherwise, a strong belief in the effectiveness of effort simply increases guilt and self-blame, by making more salient one's own incapacity to exert effort or one's lack of ability (Covington & Omelich, 1979).

Developmental Differences in the Aspects of Perceived Control That Predict Engagement

Hypotheses about age differences were based on normative changes in children's conceptions of causes (for a summary of hypotheses, see Table 14). As described in Chapter II above, in early elementary school, children have an undifferentiated conception of effort as a relatively all-encompassing cause and also often report that the causes of school success and failure are simply unknown. Therefore, we hypothesized that younger children's (grades 3 and 4) engagement was more likely to be regulated by their beliefs about effort and unknown factors, with children who endorsed higher effort and lower unknown strategy beliefs showing higher subsequent engagement.

At about age 9 (grade 4), children normatively develop a conception of chance, luck, and noncontingent causes as distinct from effort. After this shift, we predicted that noncontingent causes, such as powerful others and luck, would become more salient in their effects on students' engagement in the classroom. Finally, at about age 12 (grade 6), children normatively make sufficient cognitive progress that they are able to distinguish conceptions of ability from those of effort. Hence, when mature conceptions of ability first emerge, we predicted that individual differences in beliefs about the importance of ability as a strategy would come to play a more central role in children's engagement in school activities.

In terms of control and capacity beliefs, we predicted that their effects would remain invariant and positive across the entire age range. At all ages, we expected that children with higher beliefs in their own control and capacities would show higher engagement in school activities. If any age differences were found, we thought that they would be likely to correspond to the pattern of changing salience predicted for strategy beliefs, that is, from effort to powerful others to ability. In response to the question of how individual differences in perceived control can continue to predict performance despite developmental changes, the answer may be that control in general continues to be an important contributor to children's engagement but that the aspects of control, and especially the causal categories used to interpret performance, may nevertheless change with age (Skinner, 1995).

Control Predicts Engagement: Multiple Regressions and Age Interactions

Multiple regression analyses were also used to determine the unique contribution of different aspects of control to students' engagement and to examine whether these relations differed as a function of developmental level (grade 3 vs. grade 5 vs. grade 7). For these analyses, the dependent variable in each case was teachers' ratings of students' engagement. In general, three regression equations were calculated for each set of beliefs considered (see Tables 15 and 16). The first set of regression equations was used to get an estimate of the unique (main) effects of different beliefs; in these equations, using the concurrent balanced sample, all beliefs in a set were entered simultaneously (see first two columns of Tables 15 and 16). The second set, designed to detect linear interactions with age, also used the balanced sample and entered all belief scores, a dummy-coded grade variable (grades 3–7), and the interaction scores for each belief, formed by multiplying each belief score by the dummy-coded grade variable. Significant interaction terms indicated that the relation between students' engagement and that aspect of perceived control differed for children as a function of grade (see columns 3 and 4 of Tables 15 and 16).

The third set of regression equations, designed as follow-ups to locate age differences in relations, used the subsample of third, fifth, and seventh graders and entered all belief scores, two dummy-coded grade variables to contrast third to fifth graders and fifth to seventh graders, and the interaction scores for each belief, formed by multiplying each belief score by the two dummy-coded grade variables. Significant interaction terms indicated that the relation between students' engagement and that aspect of perceived control differed between children in grade 3 and grade 5 or between children in grade 5 and grade 7. These follow-ups were performed only when significant linear interactions were found, and the results are reported in the text. Finally, models were run for grades 3, 5, and 7 separately. These models are summarized in the last three columns of Tables 15 and 16. In addition, comparisons of the zero-order correlations between the variables at different ages were also helpful in interpreting interactions. These correlations were presented in Table 6 above.

The effects of composite perceived control scores on students' engagement were examined first (Table 15). In general, they showed few developmental differences. ConMax, which reflected the optimal profile of perceived control, was significantly and positively related to engagement, and this relation was consistent across all ages (r ranging from .34 to .42). When composite scores for Promote and Undermine were entered simultaneously, it was found that *both* beliefs made significant unique contributions to students' engagement; however, these relations did not differ as a function of age.

In the last of the regressions assessing the effects of aggregate scores, both total Strategy and total Capacity beliefs made unique contributions to children's engagement in the classroom. In addition, although the age interaction was not significant for total Strategy beliefs, it was significant for total Capacity beliefs. Follow-up regressions comparing regression coefficients by

TABLE 15

RESULTS OF MULTIPLE REGRESSIONS EXAMINING THE RELATION BETWEEN BOTH CHILDREN'S PERCEIVED CONTROL AND STUDENT ENGAGEMENT AND GRADE LEVEL DIFFERENCES (Dependent Variable: Student Engagement [Teacher Report])

Independent Variables, Children's Perceived Control	Main Effect Model, R^2	Independent Variable, β	Model with Interaction, R^2	Interaction, IV × Grade Level, β	3d-Grade Model,[a] β	5th-Grade Model,[a] β	7th-Grade Model,[a] β
ConMax	.15	.393***	.16	−.109	.40**	.44**	.37***
Promote	.16	.136***	.16	.078	−.18*	.30**	.25*
Undermine	...	−.292***	...	−.079	−.28**	.18†	−.15
Strategy beliefs	.15	.091**	.15	−.054	−.01	.03	−.12
Capacity beliefs	...	.339***	...	.334**	.36**	.43***	.48***

NOTE.—IV = independent variables. N = 1,186.

[a] The model included only students in the grade indicated. Third grade N = 213. Fifth grade N = 208. Seventh grade N = 200.

* p < .05.
** p < .01.
*** p < .001.
† p < .10.

TABLE 16

RESULTS OF MULTIPLE REGRESSIONS EXAMINING THE RELATION BETWEEN BOTH CHILDREN'S PERCEIVED CONTROL AND STUDENT ENGAGEMENT AND GRADE LEVEL DIFFERENCES (Dependent Variable: Student Engagement [Teacher Report])

Independent Variables, Children's Perceived Control	Main Effect Model, R^2	Independent Variable, β	Model with Interactions, R^2	Interaction, IV × Grade Level, β	3d-Grade Model,[a] β	5th-Grade Model,[a] β	7th-Grade Model,[a] β
Control beliefs	.12	.343***	.12	-.016	.320***	.416***	.310***
Strategy	.10		.11				
Effort		.061*		-.175	.084	.160*	-.007
Ability		-.003		.225	-.138†	-.081	-.048
Powerful others		-.113***		.185	-.127†	-.194*	.048
Unknown		-.243***		-.255†	-.166*	-.095	-.304***
Capacity	.15		.16				
Effort		.226***		-.755**	.395***	.355***	-.097
Ability		.151***		.504*	.017	.051	.393***
Powerful others		.074*		.361*	.024	.099	.291***

NOTE.—IV = independent variables. $N = 1,186$

[a] The model included only students in the grade indicated. Third grade $N = 213$. Fifth grade $N = 203$. Seventh grade $N = 200$.

* $p < .05$.
** $p < .01$.
*** $p < .001$.
† $p < .10$.

grade (grade 3 vs. grade 5 vs. grade 7) revealed that total Capacity beliefs made a stronger unique contribution to children's engagement as children moved from grade 3 ($\beta = .36$, $p < .001$) to grade 5 ($\beta = .43$, $p < .001$), which did not differ from grade 7 ($\beta = .48$, $p < .001$).

In general, the regression analyses with the aggregate scores, representing profiles of perceived control, did not show marked age differences in their relations to students' engagement. However, the analyses of the five different strategy and four different capacity beliefs allowed us to test predictions that specific sets of beliefs—those referring to the causal effects of effort, ability, powerful others, luck, and unknown—would change in their relations to engagement with age.

Because of the overlap among beliefs, we conducted these analyses in several steps (see Table 16). First, we entered all strategy beliefs simultaneously. Second, we entered all capacity beliefs simultaneously. Because seventh graders had not reported on strategy or capacity beliefs for luck, these analyses do not include data on luck. As can be seen from the first two columns of Table 16, when all remaining strategy beliefs were considered simultaneously, each made a unique contribution to students' engagement, with the exception of strategy ability beliefs. When considering all remaining capacity beliefs simultaneously, we found that, despite the positive manifold of beliefs, capacity beliefs for each of the three causes made a unique contribution to children's engagement.

We then examined age differences, as described above, first examining the linear interaction with age, then performing follow-ups to compare grade 3 with grade 5 and grade 5 with grade 7. Because seventh graders had not reported on strategy or capacity beliefs for luck, regression models examining age interactions do not include those beliefs. The regressions testing the linear interaction terms, summarized in columns 3 and 4 of Table 16, revealed significant interaction terms for powerful others and unknown strategy and all three capacity beliefs, indicating age differences in their relations to engagement.

The regressions using dummy codes to compare grades indicated the bases for these differences. Beliefs about powerful others as a strategy decreased in their centrality to engagement from grade 5 to grade 7. In grades 3 and 5, children's powerful others strategy beliefs made a unique contribution to their engagement, but, by grade 7, they no longer did. In addition, unknown strategies were more predictive of engagement for seventh than for fifth graders; the unique contribution of unknown strategies was significant (and negative) for third and seventh graders.

Unexpectedly, age interactions were also found for capacity beliefs. Beliefs about effort capacity were replaced by beliefs about ability capacity as unique predictors of engagement from the third to the fifth grade. As indicated by the separate age regressions, in the third and fifth grades, children's

73

engagement was uniquely predicted by effort, not by ability capacity; however, by the seventh grade, effort capacity no longer uniquely predicted engagement, whereas ability capacity was significant. An interesting unpredicted age interaction was also found for powerful others capacity beliefs. It seems that their unique importance to engagement may increase with age. Although they made no unique contribution to engagement in grades 3 and 5, they were related by grade 7. Perhaps, as children become increasingly aware of the importance of teachers to the evaluation of their school performance, they come to appreciate their own role in influencing teachers.

Age Differences in Correlations among Strategy Beliefs

To examine whether these age differences in the relative salience of effort and ability causes might be due to the differentiation of ability from effort, we determined whether the correlations between ability and effort strategy or between ability and effort capacity beliefs decreased from grade 3 to grade 7. Although correlations between capacity beliefs for effort and ability were high and did not differ by grade (r ranging from .50 to .71), correlations between *strategy* beliefs for effort and ability did decrease as a function of grade level (grade 3 $r = .38$, grade 5 $r = .27$, p's $< .01$; grade 7 $r = .12$, N.S.).

In addition, an examination of the correlations between effort and the external causes by age suggested that beliefs about the effectiveness of effort may also become more differentiated from beliefs about such strategies as powerful others, luck, and unknown over this age range. At the youngest ages, effort strategy beliefs were *not* correlated with external strategy beliefs. However, effort strategy beliefs became progressively more negatively correlated with the external strategy beliefs from the third to the seventh grade. This pattern of increasingly negative correlations was found for the relations between strategy effort and all three external causes: powerful others (r's with effort $= .07$, $.01$, $-.08$, $-.16$, and $-.20$ for grades 3, 4, 5, 6, and 7, respectively), luck (r's with effort $= .11$, $-.01$, $-.08$, and $-.19$ for grades 3, 4, 5, and 6, respectively), and unknown (r's with effort $= .10$, $-.01$, $-.13$, $-.18$, and $-.28$ for grades 3, 4, 5, 6, and 7, respectively).

Finally, an examination of the correlations between ability and external strategy beliefs showed that, although ability strategy beliefs became progressively more differentiated from effort, they maintained their positive relations to external causes. The connection between ability as a strategy and all three external causes was high and stable over the entire age range, r ranging from .17 to .37 for strategy ability and powerful others, from .20 to .41 for strategy ability and luck, and from .19 to .34 for strategy ability and unknown. This pattern of progressive correlational differentiation is consistent with the findings of other large-scale studies (Little & Lopez, 1997).

Summary of Results on Age Differences in the Consequences of Perceived
Control for Engagement

Children's engagement in the classroom was predicted uniquely by many different aspects of their perceived control. Especially strong negative predictors were uncontrollable and external strategy beliefs. Especially strong positive predictors were control and capacity beliefs.

Although no overall pattern of age differences was found for aggregate control beliefs, several specific aspects of perceived control did show age-related changes in their connections to children' engagement. As hypothesized, unknown strategy beliefs were a significant predictor for third- but not fifth-grade children. However, unknown was again a significant predictor of engagement in the seventh grade, perhaps as a consequence of the transition to middle school (Connell & Furman, 1984). Follow-up analyses of the unique relations between unknown strategy beliefs and engagement were consistent with this explanation. The unique effect of unknown strategy beliefs was also significant for the sixth graders ($\beta = -.33$, $p < .001$), who were in the first year of the transition.

The most interesting developmental trends involved beliefs about effort and ability, although they were found, not as predicted in strategy beliefs, but instead in capacity beliefs. Capacity effort was the only unique capacity beliefs predictor of engagement in grades 3 and 5. However, capacity effort was no longer a unique predictor of engagement after children entered the seventh grade; effort was replaced by capacity ability and capacity powerful others. Follow-up analyses supplemented the interpretation of this developmental trend, in that by the sixth grade *both* capacity effort ($\beta = .22$, $p < .01$) and capacity ability ($\beta = .24$, $p < .01$), but not capacity powerful others ($\beta = .01$, N.S.), made unique contributions to engagement. It seems that, from a "baseline" in grade 3, when the only unique predictor of engagement is capacity beliefs for effort, an additional unique predictor, capacity ability, is added to capacity effort in grade 6. Following this, capacity powerful others replaced capacity effort as a unique predictor of engagement in grade 7.

Examination of age differences in the correlations among strategy beliefs suggested one basis for these developmental changes in the aspects of perceived control that predict engagement across the elementary school years. Strategy beliefs about effort became successively more differentiated from beliefs about ability (progressing from a positive relation to independence) as well as from strategy beliefs about external causes, including powerful others, luck, and unknown causes (progressing from independence to negative relations).

V. RESULTS OF ANALYSES EXAMINING INDIVIDUAL DIFFERENCES IN THE DEVELOPMENT OF PERCEIVED CONTROL AND ACTION

The previous set of analyses focused on individual differences in children's perceived control, how these could be predicted by the social context provided by teachers and by children's own prior performance, and how, in turn, they could have an impact on children's engagement and subsequent performance on school tasks. In addition, we examined developmental changes in the functioning of these individual differences.

This second set of analyses focused, not on the development of individual differences, but instead on individual differences in development. The primary goal of this set of analyses was to describe normative developmental trajectories of teacher context, perceived control, and children's engagement from age 8 to age 13 years and to examine predictors of individual differences in these trajectories across the same 5-year period. We also conducted some exploratory analyses. Hypotheses about normative development and about predictors of individual differences in trajectories are detailed below. They are also summarized in Table 17. The exploratory analyses are described in the last sections of this chapter.

HYPOTHESES ABOUT DEVELOPMENTAL CHANGE

The first set of hypotheses involved predictions about patterns of normative change during the elementary school years. We expected regular age-graded changes in children's engagement and their perceptions of control. Hypotheses about age-graded changes in children's experiences of their teachers were more tentative. The predictions and rationales are presented in this section.

TABLE 17

HYPOTHESES ABOUT INDIVIDUAL DIFFERENCES IN DEVELOPMENT

NORMATIVE CHANGES IN CONTEXT, SELF, ACTION, AND OUTCOMES

1. Engagement will decline steadily over this age range, perhaps more sharply during the transition to middle school starting in the sixth grade.
2. Context will not decline, unless decreases in involvement are seen beginning in the sixth grade.
3. Different aspects of perceived control will show different developmental trajectories:
   a) Control and capacity beliefs will remain relatively stable, perhaps declining slightly in the third grade.
   b) Strategy beliefs will become more differentiated from each other over time:
      i) Strategy effort beliefs will remain high and stable.
      ii) Strategy ability beliefs will decline slightly starting in the fifth grade.
      iii) Strategy powerful others and luck beliefs will decline more rapidly and starting earlier.
      iv) Strategy unknown will decline but may increase again during the transition to middle school.

PREDICTORS OF INDIVIDUAL DIFFERENCES IN DEVELOPMENT

Overall, Significant Individual Differences in Trajectories Will Be Found for Each of the Variables

4. The development of perceived control over 5 years (from grade 3 to grade 7) will be promoted by a more supportive teacher context and higher individual academic performances.
5. The development of engagement over 5 years will be promoted by control and capacity beliefs and undermined by strategy beliefs about "external" causes (powerful others, luck, and unknown factors).

Comparison of Models

6. Grades are more likely to *launch* individual trajectories of perceived control.
7. *Ambient level* of context is more likely to support individual trajectories of perceived control.
8. The relation between trajectories of perceived control and engagement is more likely to be consistent with a *change-to-change* model.

Hypotheses about Normative Change in Context, Self, and Action

Engagement

We expected that students' engagement would show a gentle decline across this age range, perhaps accelerating as children made the transition to middle school in sixth grade. This trend is part of the steady deterioration that has been found in children's intrinsic motivation for school, beginning in kindergarten and continuing until the end of high school (Anderman & Maeher, 1994; Eccles & Midgley, 1989; Eccles, Midgley, et al., 1993; Eccles et al., 1998; Harter, 1978, 1981a, 1981b). The bases of this trend are not completely clear (Stipek & Daniels, 1988). One view is that it is based in the organization of schools, which in general do not provide children opportunities for competence (and other fundamental human needs, such as autonomy and relatedness). The cumulative effects of this deprivation are manifest in increasing disaffection from school (Connell & Wellborn, 1991; Eccles et al., in press; Eccles & Midgley, 1989; Eccles et al., 1998; Skinner, 1995).

Perceived Control

Different aspects of control were expected to show different patterns of normative change. Children's estimates of control and of their capacities were expected to remain relatively stable across this age range, although it was possible that gentle declines might characterize the earliest ages. Children's estimates of their competence, in general, decline across early childhood, as children distinguish their actual capacities from their wishes and desires (Stipek, 1984b). This is also the beginning of the age at which children's estimates of ability first correlate with their school grades (Stipek, 1984a). Although this task was expected to be completed by the third grade, it seemed possible that the end of this trend would be seen in gentle decreases in perceptions of control and capacities and perhaps especially in capacity beliefs about luck.

Children's strategy beliefs were expected to show more robust patterns of normative change from age 8 to age 13. Following cross-sectional studies, we expected that strategy beliefs would show increasing differentiation from each other according to causal categories (Little & Lopez, 1997; Skinner et al., 1988a). We expected that beliefs about effort as a strategy would be high and relatively stable. Ability strategy was expected to decline slightly, as it was differentiated from effort. Beliefs about powerful others and luck were expected to decline even more, as they were distinguished from effort and their limited controllability was recognized. Strategy beliefs for unknown causes were likely to decline. However, we expected that they might show an increase as children entered middle school (in the sixth grade) because unknown strategy beliefs often increase during transitions (Connell & Furman, 1984).

Teacher Context and Academic Performance

We did not expect to see normative patterns of change in either children's school performance or their perceptions of teacher context, although the reasons differed. School performance was expected to be relatively stable since grades are themselves developmentally normed. Neither did we expect "developmental" change in children's views of their teachers because we expected their perceptions to be based (at least in part) on their actual interactions with their teachers. Since teachers changed every year, we did not expect linear trends in children's reports of teachers' behavior. Moreover, we did not expect any developmental changes in the cognitive processes that children used to interpret their interactions with teachers.

We did consider the possibility that normative changes in the school system might produce regular changes in children's interactions with teachers as they progress through the elementary school years (Eccles et al., in press). If this were the case, then we would expect to see decreases in students' reports of teachers' involvement, starting when the multipleteacher format took effect, in about sixth grade (Roeser et al., 1996).

Hypotheses about Predictors of Individual Differences in Developmental Change

As described previously, we expected that different models would best characterize different predictors of change. We predicted that the *launch* model, in which children's trajectories are a function of their initial differential starting levels, would provide a good account of the relations between actual performance and perceived control. We expected that children who are academically successful in their early school years would be initiating a positive cycle of control beliefs and experiences, whereas children who instead experience failure in their early years would initiate a downward spiral.

In contrast, we expected the *ambient-level model*, in which trajectories are shaped by the average level of support provided while the trajectory is unfolding, would be more consistent with social predictors of the development of perceived control. That is, children whose teachers maintained involvement and continued to provide structure over time would show positive trajectories of control. However, teachers would not need to show ever increasing levels of support to contribute to the positive development of students' control.

Third, we expected the *change-to-change* model, which looks at changes in one trajectory as a function of changes in another, to provide a good description of the relation between perceived control and engagement. That is, children whose control was increasing over time would show corresponding increases in their engagement in the classroom, whereas children whose control decreased would show increasingly greater disaffection in school.

OVERVIEW

Overview of the Analyses

The analyses of developmental trajectories were conducted in three steps. In step 1, normative trajectories across the ages from 8 to 13 years were determined for constructs of interest, namely, teacher context, engagement, and aspects of control. These were determined using the hierarchical linear model approach to estimate group growth curves (HLM [also called the random effects or general linear mixed model]; Bailey, Burchinal, & McWilliam, 1993; Bryk & Raudenbush, 1992; Burchinal & Appelbaum, 1991; Francis, Fletcher, Steubing, Davidson, & Thompson, 1991; Willett, Ayoub, & Robinson, 1991).

In step 2, we examined whether systematic differences in individual trajectories could be found for context, self, and action. By using a general linear mixed model of HLM, we were able to estimate individual growth curves for each child across the ages from 8 to 13 years. From the HLM analyses, we output individual growth curve parameter estimates for intercepts and linear slopes.

In step 3, we used these scores as interindividual differences variables that allowed us to test different models of the predictors of individual differences in developmental trajectories of control and engagement. For each link, we attempted to test all three developmental models. The launch model examined whether initial levels of the predictor variable related to patterns of change in the outcome variable. The ambient-level model examined whether the average level of the predictor variable while the target trajectory was unfolding was related to the trajectory of the outcome variable. And the change-to-change model examined whether the trajectory of the predictor was related to the trajectory of the outcome.

Each step is presented in turn. Because the use of growth curves to estimate individual trajectories is relatively new, we first present a more detailed description of the framework that we used, namely, the HLM approach. Examples of how the data were organized for these analyses and the SAS code used to perform them are included in Appendix B.

Overview of the Individual Growth Curve Modeling Procedure

We were interested in the HLM procedure because, when it is applied to longitudinal data, it can be used to estimate the parameters of group and individual change simultaneously. It does so, essentially, by regressing repeated measures of a variable against time, estimating both fixed and random model effects simultaneously. The fixed effects estimate population curves. Random effects estimate the variation between the population trajectory and individual trajectories. Individual growth curves are estimated with respect to the population curve; as a result, the estimates for an individual are based on the variation of his or her observed value from the expected value for that individual based on the population curve. This procedure allows for the estimation of missing data points for an individual; estimates are based on available data points for that individual and population estimates.

Determining the Shape of the Population Growth Curve

In order to calculate group and individual growth curves, however, several preliminary steps are necessary. First, decisions need to be made about the general shape of the curve for each variable of interest for the population and for individuals. Growth curves can be estimated for many trends, such as linear or curvilinear, and it is important to identify the appropriate population shape of the curve for a target variable. This can be accomplished theoretically or empirically, but it is important to determine whether the data are consistent with the shape of the curve used. It has been suggested that the shape can be determined by examining a plot of raw individual growth curves. This may be effective when subjects are few, but it was not a feasible method with our sample size. Nevertheless, we did examine a random sample of individual curves to obtain a sense of the homogeneity of the trajectory shapes.

Estimating Group and Individual Growth Curves

Once the appropriate shape for the general growth curve has been determined for each variable, the corresponding population growth curves can be estimated. These describe the pattern of normative change in a variable over the age range or time points used. In this same step, it is possible to estimate parameters of individual growth curves and to determine empirically whether there is significant variation among these parameters. If so, then it is possible to use the estimated parameters as interindividual difference variables, representing individual change in the target variable over time. Using HLM models, it is possible at this same step to answer substantive questions, such as group differences in growth curves (by entering a fixed-effects independent variable for groups) or the effects of repeated measures of an independent variable (by entering a time-varying covariate). However, we used HLM analyses only to estimate parameters of group and individual growth curves for our target variables. In all subsequent analyses examining predictors of individual differences in the slopes of growth curves, we output the individual parameters (intercepts and linear slopes) estimated in the HLM analyses and then used these individual difference variables in regular multivariate regression analyses.

One advantage of remaining within the HLM framework to test substantive hypotheses is that the HLM procedure weights subjects' data based on the number of measurement points for which each child has actual data. Thus, cases with more observations are weighted more heavily. However, once the HLM procedure is used to output individual parameter estimates, these are unweighted. As a result, if these parameter estimates are used in regressions, equal importance is placed on all individual estimates regardless of the number of observations on which each is based. Since estimates based on fewer observations rely more on population slopes, one net effect might be reduced individual variability.[3]

Hence, we decided to use weighted regressions for all analyses that included individual estimates output by HLM. Specifically, each child's score was weighted by the number of observations (1–6) for the dependent variable used in the analysis. Because the current data set was relatively complete (e.g., over 750 children had four or more observations), the weighting procedure did not alter the pattern of substantive findings. However, in less complete data sets, weighting may be essential to maximize individual variability. The results of all the unweighted regressions are available on request.

Estimating Individual Parameters from Incomplete Longitudinal Data

One feature of the HLM procedures is that they allow estimation of individual growth curve parameters for children who do not have complete data. Hence, for these analyses, every child in the sample could be included who was assessed at at least one measurement point on the variable of interest, and the HLM procedure, using the child's actual data and information about group parameters, could estimate individual growth curve parameter scores for that child.

Because the entire age range in this sample was from the fall of grade 3 to the spring of grade 7, it was possible to estimate parameters for all children based on trajectories covering 10 points (point 1 corresponding to the fall of grade 3 and point 10 corresponding to the spring of grade 7). However, because the maximum number of *actual* assessment points in which a child could have participated was six (twice a year over the 3 years of the study), all individual growth curve scores were estimated using from one to six actual assessment points (average number of points = 3). The procedure for estimating individual parameters for children with incomplete data (e.g., for engagement growth curves), is essentially the same as asking, "Given that you were this engaged at this point in time and this engaged at this point in time [two actual measurement points], and given that the group growth curve slope for engagement looked like this [population parameter], what is your individual growth curve likely to be [individual estimate]?" For a child with only one measurement point, the HLM procedures relied heavily on the group growth curve estimates. Since individual growth curves are estimated from a child's actual data and group estimates, individual estimates do not bias the group data.

It is important to note that the current data set provided an excellent

---

[3] We thank Margaret Burchinal for pointing this out.

basis for determining accurate estimates of individual parameters. As noted above, for each child, there were many actual time points (up to six, with an average of three). In addition, there were a large number of subjects at each time point, which contributed to stable estimates of mean level at each time. Finally, as can be seen from Figure 9 above, a large percentage of the data was longitudinal, resulting in robust estimates of individual change from each point to the next.

Nevertheless, because we wanted to understand the effects of estimating data in these analyses, we performed cross-checks of two kinds. First, we successively deleted children with the fewest number of actual data points (e.g., deleting all children who had only one data point on a given variable, then also deleting those with only two points, etc.) and repeatedly calculated both group and individual estimates on the successively more complete longitudinal sample. By the time estimates were based only on children with at least four consecutive data points, a significant increase in the intercepts had been detected (indicating, as expected, a positive selection bias in the more longitudinal sample), but there was no change in the shape of the slope for any variable.

As a second cross-check, we completed individual regressions for each child on the key variables of interest, using only actual data for each child (children with only one measurement point on a variable were excluded). We then correlated the individual beta weights (slopes) based on these regressions with the individual slopes estimated using HLM. For all the variables that we examined, correlations between slopes calculated using these two methods were well above .9. These cross-checks indicated that the variation in individual growth curves (the target of our hypotheses) was a function of the variation in the actual data.

Hence, we were satisfied that, as argued by statistical experts (Bailey et al., 1993; Burchinal & Appelbaum, 1991; Francis et al., 1991; Willett et al., 1991), the estimated growth curves and their parameters corresponded closely to the original data on which they were based. As a final point of reference, every figure that depicts estimates of the group growth curve for a variable has the observed mean values for each time of measurement in that growth curve superimposed over it. In this way, the extent of the discrepancy between estimated and observed data can be discerned graphically.

Interpreting Covariation between Growth Curves

Just like typical correlations, the pattern of covariation between estimates of linear slopes of growth curves should be interpreted relative to the mean and variation of the estimates. For example, a significant positive correlation between the estimated slopes of two growth curves means that children who have higher scores on one slope estimate also have higher scores on the other slope estimate and, correspondingly, that children who have lower scores on one slope estimate also have lower scores on the other.

However, depending on the range and average population curves, a "high" score on a slope estimate of a growth curve may reflect different patterns of change. For example, if the population curve increases (as is typically the case with many developmental variables studied, such as vocabulary), then a "high" estimate of the slope of a growth curve may reflect actual increases in a variable over time, whereas a low score may reflect, not a decrease, but a *slower rate of increase* over time. In contrast, if the population curve is generally decreasing (as do many motivational variables), then a low estimate of the slope of a growth curve may indicate a pattern of decline, but a high estimate may indicate either a slower rate of decline or more relative stability. Hence, we describe the normative growth curves in our target variables before we examine the three developmental models of interest.

NORMATIVE CHANGE

Estimating Population and Individual Parameters

We used an empirical procedure to identify the shape of the population growth curve for each target variable. The HLM approach with unbalanced data allowed us to include all study participants ($N = 1,608$) and up to 10 times of measurement for each participant. For each model, the dependent variable was the repeated measures of the target variable of interest. Linear, quadratic, and cubic relations between time of measurement (independent variables) and the target variable were tested by including time, time squared, and time cubed as fixed effects in the HLM. Additional fixed effects in the model included the sex of the student, the wave (1 or 2) in which the first measurement was completed, and the interactions between these two variables and the three time variables. Interactions between independent variables tested whether the shape of the curve differed for different groups, such as between boys and girls or between waves.

Both the intercept and time of measurement were specified as random effects. This was done to obtain estimates of the intercept and the linear growth curve coefficient for each individual's growth curve of the target variable. Independent variables were excluded (using criteria of a parameter estimate less than .005 or a p value greater than .05) until a model remained that included time, significant higher-order time effects, and all other significant fixed effects or interactions. If a higher-order time effect or interaction was significant, then all lower-order terms remained in the model. The goal was to find the simplest accurate equation needed to represent the nor-

TABLE 18

RESULTS OF THE FULL HIERARCHICAL LINEAR MODEL PREDICTING CHILDREN'S PERCEIVED CONTROL
FROM THE THIRD TO THE SEVENTH GRADE (Dependent Variable: Repeated Measures of
Children's Perceived Control [ConMax])

Independent Variables	Unique Estimate	SE (Unique Estimate)	F	p Value
Intercept	22.67	2.57	. . .	. . .
Time of measurement (linear trajectory)	1.33	1.64	3.06	.081
Time^2 (quadratic trajectory)	−.17	.33	1.30	.254
Time^3 (cubic trajectory)	.00	.02	.01	.937
Student sex (male)	−3.33	2.55	1.70	.192
Wave (1)	−1.59	2.77	.30	.587
Interactions:				
Time × sex	.76	1.70	.20	.655
Time^2 × sex	−.17	.35	.23	.630
Time^3 × sex	.00	.02	.01	.920
Time × wave	−.27	1.80	.02	.881
Time^2 × wave	.08	.37	.05	.817
Time^3 × wave	.00	.02	.00	.952

NOTE.—Time of measurement was coded from 1 to 10, where 1 = the fall of the third grade and 10 = the spring of the seventh grade.

mative shape of the growth curve of the target variable for the population group(s) considered.

Illustration of How the Shape of a Population Growth Curve Was Determined

This procedure is illustrated with the variable indexing children's profiles of perceived control, ConMax. The dependent variable was the repeated measures of ConMax over the 10 times of measurement. Time was coded 1–10, from the fall of grade 3 to the spring of grade 7. The full model, including tests for linear, quadratic, and cubic curves and for differences as a function of sex and wave, is presented in Table 18. As can be seen, only the main effect of time was marginally significant.

Excluding terms using the criteria described above resulted in the final equation for ConMax depicted in Table 19. This equation describes the population growth curve for ConMax. The linear term for time was significant, as was time squared, indicating that the population growth curve for ConMax could be described as containing linear and curvilinear components. A time by sex interaction was found, indicating that the linear component of the curves differed for boys and girls. In addition, the main effect for wave and the wave × time interaction were significant, indicating that the two waves differed in mean level of ConMax (with the second wave starting higher) and that the linear component of the curves differed by wave (with the second

TABLE 19

Hierarchical Linear Model Results Depicting the Final Group Model (Final Model) and the Model Used to Estimate Individual Growth Curves (Reduced Model) for Perceived Control, Engagement, and Teacher Context from 3rd to 7th Grade

Independent Variables	Final Model				Reduced Model			
	Unique Estimate	SE (Unique Estimate)	F	p Value	Unique Estimate	SE (Unique Estimate)	F	p Value
Dependent Variable: Repeated Measures of Children's Perceived Control (ConMax)								
Intercept	22.570	1.39	...	...	27.850	1.16	...	...
Time of measurement	1.513	.40	18.22	.000	−.811	.20	39.07	.000
Time²	−.211	.03	44.86	.000	...	...	...	...
Student sex (male)	−.161	1.24	.02	.897	−.192	1.26	.02	.878
Wave (1)	−3.874	1.28	9.10	.003	−4.894	1.29	14.50	.000
Interactions:								
Time × sex	−.810	.22	13.46	.000	−.804	.23	12.82	.000
Time × wave	.764	.23	11.12	.001	.989	.23	18.48	.000

	DEPENDENT VARIABLE: REPEATED MEASURES OF STUDENT ENGAGEMENT (Teacher Report)							
Intercept	3.471	.05	...	...	3.431	.04	...	...
Time of measurement	−.056	.02	.06	.805	−.036	.01	46.35	.000
Time²	.002	.00	6.39	.012	...	...	...	...
Student sex (male)	−.204	.03	56.24	.000	−.205	.03	56.62	.000
Wave (1)	−.210	.07	8.47	.004	−.002	.05	.00	.967
Interactions:								
Time × wave	.118	.03	18.92	.000	.015	.01	3.47	.063
Time² × wave	−.010	.00	16.24	.000	...	...	...	...

	DEPENDENT VARIABLE: REPEATED MEASURES OF TEACHER CONTEXT (Student Report)							
Intercept	3.333	.05	...	...	3.479	.04	...	...
Time of measurement	.006	.02	1.54	.215	−.058	.01	91.49	.000
Time²	−.006	.00	18.54	.000	...	...	...	...
Student sex (male)	−.131	.03	23.33	.000	−.131	.03	23.23	.000
Wave (1)	−.161	.05	9.65	.002	−.192	.05	13.69	.000
Interactions:								
Time × wave	.025	.01	8.24	.004	.031	.01	12.82	.000

NOTE.—Time of measurement was coded from 1 to 10, where 1 = the fall of the third grade and 10 = the spring of the seventh grade. The "final model" depicts the equation describing the population growth curve. The "reduced model" is the model used to estimate growth curve parameters for individuals.

87

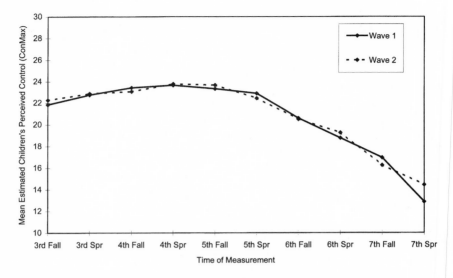

FIGURE 13.—Observed and estimated normative trajectories of children's profiles of perceived control (ConMax) from grade 3 to grade 7 for two waves of students. ConMax scores could range from −66 to 66.

wave declining faster). Figure 13 depicts the estimated growth curves for the two waves.

The reduced model for perceived control (ConMax) is also presented in Table 19. It depicts the equation that we used to estimate growth curve parameters for individuals. We used the estimate of the slope (the linear term) to describe ConMax growth curves. However, because the curvilinear term was also significant, we controlled for this when estimating individual slopes. Because of the significant interaction with sex, we decided to examine sex differences in all subsequent equations; in order to do so, we excluded sex from the final model from which individual growth curves were obtained.

Finally, we considered the main effects and the interaction involving wave. Because the difference between waves was only 1 year, and because waves varied as additional teachers were recruited, we decided that wave effects were not substantively significant (Baltes, Cornelius, & Nesselroade, 1980), and we therefore did not try to examine their exact pattern. However, in acknowledgment of their statistical significance, we did control for wave in estimating individual trajectories. As in all subsequent analyses in which wave effects were found, those effects were small (see Figure 13). Individual estimates of the slope of the growth curve for ConMax were calculated controlling for and not controlling for wave; they were almost identical ($r = .996$). Likewise, the effects of controlling for curvilinearity in this and subsequent variables were small. Just as with wave, individual estimates of the slope of the growth curve for target variables calculated controlling for curvilinearity were almost identical to those calculated when not controlling for curvilinearity (r ranging from .97 to .99).

Table 19 also contains the final and reduced models for engagement and teacher context. As with ConMax, the final models are the complete HLM models that resulted from eliminating terms that did not meet criteria for significance. These final models describe the population growth curves for engagement and teacher context. The reduced models are the equations used to estimate individual intercepts and linear slopes for each child.

As can be seen from the final models, not just the linear components but also the quadratic components were significant. This indicated that both engagement and teacher context contained some curvilinearity. As with ConMax, we used the estimate of the slopes to describe individual curves for engagement and teacher context. However, as can be seen from the reduced models, we controlled for curvilinearity and wave main effects and their interactions in calculating these individual estimates. In addition, we did not control for sex so that it would be possible to examine interactions with sex in subsequent analyses.

Analyses of Normative Development of Context, Self, and Action

These analyses focused on describing the age-graded pattern of normative change in key variables across 5 years, from the beginning of grade 3 to the end of grade 7. The population estimates for the growth curves for perceived control (ConMax), engagement, and teacher context are presented in Figures 14–16. For comparison purposes, the actual average mean levels of each variable at each time of measurement are superimposed over the estimates. Table 20 includes the observed and estimated means and standard deviations for each time of measurement for the three main variables.

Perceived Control

As can be seen in Figure 14 above, the normative trajectory of ConMax was curvilinear. Pairwise comparison of adjacent means using dependent t tests showed that ConMax started high ($M = 22.32$) and was stable in third grade, increased slightly between the spring of grade 3 and the fall of grade 4, and then was stable again until the fall of grade 5 ($M = 24.61$). From then on, ConMax began to decline rapidly, showing significant decreases from fall to spring during grades 5, 6, and 7 ($M = 12.62$ by the spring of seventh grade).

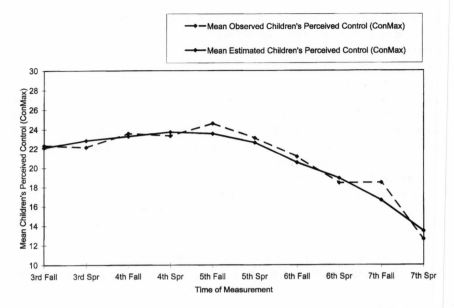

FIGURE 14.—Observed and estimated normative trajectories of children's profiles of perceived control (ConMax) from grade 3 to grade 7. ConMax scores could range from −66 to 66.

Engagement

In Figure 15, the population growth curve, which was also curvilinear, shows that children's engagement started off relatively high ($M = 3.25$ in the fall of grade 3) and remained stable, with a slight decline beginning when children entered middle school ($M = 3.10$ in the fall of grade 6) and again from the fall to the spring of grade 7 ($M = 2.95$ in the spring of grade 7).

Teacher Context

In Figure 16, the population growth curve (which again was curvilinear) showed that children's perceptions of their interactions with teachers began high ($M = 3.21$ in the fall of grade 3) and were also relatively stable until the end of grade 5, at which point they began a gradual decline ($M = 2.77$ in the spring of grade 7). Of course, children were rating different teachers each year, so strong patterns of normative change were not expected. Teacher context did, however, show a consistent pattern of change from fall to spring *within* several school years. Children's ratings of their teachers declined slightly from the fall to the spring of the school year at each grade, but they recovered again *between* years for grades 3, 4, and 5. After grade 5,

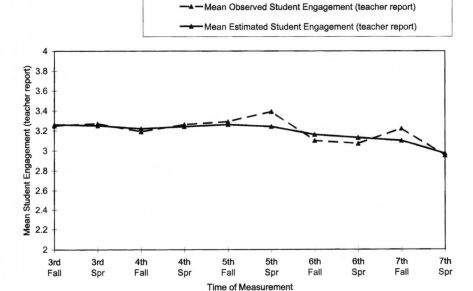

FIGURE 15.—Observed and estimated normative trajectories of children's engagement from grade 3 to grade 7. Scores for teachers' reports of students' engagement could range from 1 to 4.

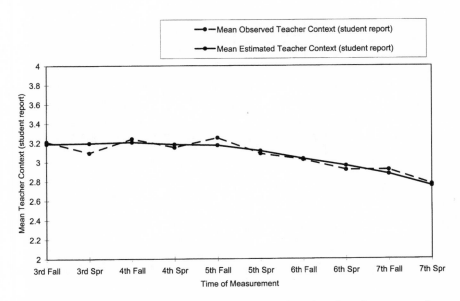

FIGURE 16.—Observed and estimated normative trajectories of teacher context from grade 3 to grade 7. Scores for students' reports of teacher context could range from 1 to 4.

TABLE 20

MEANS AND STANDARD DEVIATIONS OF OBSERVED AND ESTIMATED CONSTRUCTS BY TIME OF MEASUREMENT

TIME OF MEASUREMENT	CHILDREN'S PERCEIVED CONTROL		STUDENT ENGAGEMENT (TEACHER REPORT)		TEACHER CONTEXT (STUDENT REPORT)	
	Observed	Estimated	Observed	Estimated	Observed	Estimated
3d grade, fall	22.3	22.1	3.25	3.26	3.21	3.19
	(14.3)	(9.9)	(.55)	(.42)	(.52)	(.37)
3d grade, spring	22.1	22.8	3.27	3.25	3.09	3.19
	(14.2)	(9.9)	(.58)	(.42)	(.57)	(.37)
4th grade, fall	23.6	23.3	3.19	3.22	3.24	3.21
	(13.3)	(9.6)	(.60)	(.40)	(.53)	(.35)
4th grade, spring	23.3	23.7	3.26	3.24	3.15	3.18
	(15.4)	(9.9)	(.62)	(.42)	(.62)	(.37)
5th grade, fall	24.6	23.6	3.28	3.26	3.25	3.17
	(14.3)	(10.4)	(.54)	(.38)	(.58)	(.36)
5th grade, spring	23.1	22.6	3.39	3.24	3.09	3.11
	(16.4)	(11.4)	(.58)	(.39)	(.67)	(.38)
6th grade, fall	21.1	20.5	3.10	3.16	3.02	3.03
	(16.2)	(11.8)	(.61)	(.41)	(.55)	(.36)
6th grade, spring	18.4	18.9	3.07	3.13	2.92	2.95
	(16.5)	(13.0)	(.64)	(.43)	(.54)	(.38)
7th grade, fall	18.5	16.6	3.22	3.10	2.92	2.87
	(16.7)	(13.9)	(.58)	(.42)	(.58)	(.41)
7th grade, spring	12.6	13.4	2.95	2.97	2.77	2.75
	(16.7)	(14.7)	(.56)	(.43)	(.57)	(.43)

NOTE.—Standard deviations are given in parentheses.

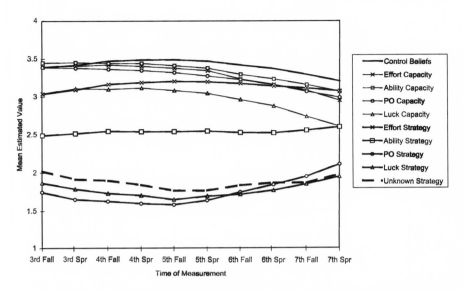

FIGURE 17.—Normative trajectories of different aspects of children's perceived control from grade 3 to grade 7. Beliefs scores could range from 1 to 4.

however, no between-year recoveries occurred, and children's experiences of their teachers declined steadily.

Different Aspects of Perceived Control

We used the same procedure to calculate group and individual estimates for all other variables used in subsequent analyses. The population estimates for the 10 aspects of perceived control appear in Figure 17. As can be seen, control and capacity beliefs were generally higher than strategy beliefs. All capacity beliefs were generally stable, with the exception of luck capacity beliefs, which showed the most marked decline over time. However, capacity for effort and powerful others also showed significant decreases across each school year.

As expected, effort was the strategy that received the highest endorsement, followed by ability, and both these beliefs were relatively stable, with effort strategy increasing slightly over time. The nonaction strategy beliefs (powerful others, unknown, and luck) were the lowest and showed decreases until grade 5, when they began to increase slightly. The patterns of change for strategy beliefs are consistent with the general developmental trends described for these kinds of beliefs in many cultural contexts (Little & Lopez, 1997).

To understand the trends for powerful others and unknown strategy be-

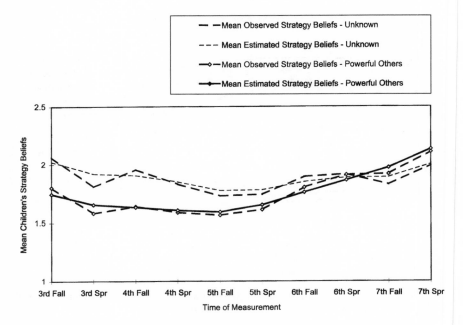

Figure 18.—Observed and estimated normative trajectories of children's powerful others and unknown strategy beliefs from grade 3 to grade 7. Strategy beliefs scores could range from 1 to 4.

liefs a bit better, we compared the estimates with actual averages from each measurement point (see Figure 18). As can be seen, both these beliefs showed regular changes *within* several school years. Beliefs that the causes of school success and failure were unknown improved (i.e., declined) from fall to spring of each year for grades 3 and 4, presumably as children became more accustomed to the structure of their particular classrooms. Then, unknown beliefs relapsed again at the beginning of each subsequent new year, although not to the same levels as the beginning of the previous year. However, starting between the spring of grade 5 and the fall of grade 6, as children entered middle school, unknown strategy beliefs showed no more within-year improvements (declines) but instead worsened (increased) steadily. This pattern is consistent with the notion that unknown strategy beliefs are sensitive to the effects of transitions (Connell & Furman, 1984).

Precision

The precision of the individual slope parameter estimates was reflected in the standard errors. In general, the linear growth curve trajectories were precisely estimated. For example, the standard errors of the estimated growth

TABLE 21

MEANS AND STANDARD DEVIATIONS OF ESTIMATED GROWTH
CURVE SLOPES

	GROWTH CURVE SLOPE ESTIMATES	
CONSTRUCTS	Mean	SD
Children's perceived control:		
ConMax	−.636	.899
Promote	−.240	.374
Undermine	.422	.658
Strategy	−.007	.024
Capacity	−.032	.028
Control beliefs	−.012	.026
Strategy beliefs:		
Effort	−.003	.021
Ability	.000	.039
Powerful others	.036	.056
Luck	.001	.064
Unknown	−.011	.039
Capacity beliefs:		
Effort	−.036	.021
Ability	−.032	.033
Powerful others	−.035	.055
Luck	−.008	.019
Student engagement (teacher report)	−.030	.022
Teacher context (student report)	−.040	.020

curve slopes of engagement ranged between .042 and .059 ($M = .06$) and of ConMax ranged between 1.17 and 1.80 ($M = 1.55$). There was significant variation in the linear growth curve estimates of all the variables (see entries under the heading *final models* in Table 19 above). Hence, all variables were used in subsequent interindividual analyses. To do so, we output individual estimates for intercepts and linear slopes for the target variables. They were used as individual difference variables in subsequent regression analyses (see Zimmer-Gembeck, 1997; and Appendix B).

INDIVIDUAL DIFFERENCES IN THE DEVELOPMENT OF CONTEXT, SELF, AND ACTION

Descriptive Analyses

Table 21 depicts the means and standard deviations of the estimates of the slopes of the individual growth curves. These represent the average and variation of individual curves from grade 3 to grade 7 for each variable. To

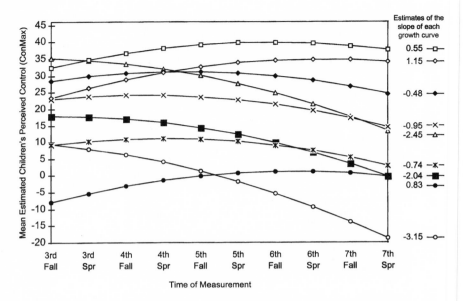

Figure 19.—Individual trajectories of children's profiles of perceived control (ConMax) from grade 3 to grade 7 and slope estimates for nine children. ConMax scores could range from −66 to 66. The estimate of the slope of the population growth curve for ConMax was −0.636.

aid in the interpretation of these estimates, we include Figure 19, which depicts several individual growth curve coefficients and their corresponding curves. These students' curves were selected to highlight the range of scores for each variable as well as to show a student with an individual trajectory resembling the normative trajectory of −.636 (estimate = −.74).

To test the developmental models, we used the estimates of the slopes of individual growth curves as the dependent variables in multiple regression analyses. In addition, for each construct, and for each child, we obtained a launch or initial level variable from the HLM analysis (in this case, the estimate of the intercept of the growth curve) as well as an ambient-level variable, or the average of the variable across all points of measurement (in this case, the actual average across all available measurement points from the third to the seventh grade). The means and standard deviations for these two estimates appear in Table 22.

Because we intended to regress the estimates of the slopes of the growth curves for each outcome variable on all three aspects of the antecedent variables (launch, ambient level, and slope of the growth curve), it was important to examine the intercorrelations among these variables. The correlations appear in Table 23. The significant correlations among the intercept estimates reflect the time 1 (fall of third grade) intercorrelations among the variables.

TABLE 22

MEANS AND STANDARD DEVIATIONS OF ESTIMATED GROWTH CURVE INTERCEPTS AND
AMBIENT LEVELS

CONSTRUCTS	GROWTH CURVE INTERCEPT		AMBIENT LEVEL	
	Mean	SD	Mean	SD
Children's perceived control:				
ConMax	24.75	8.12	20.97	14.25
Promote	46.89	3.73	45.48	7.14
Undermine	21.98	5.38	24.55	8.27
Strategy	3.06	.19	3.01	.31
Capacity	3.48	.28	3.31	.47
Control beliefs	3.50	.24	3.42	.46
Strategy beliefs:				
Effort	3.18	.27	3.16	.49
Ability	2.54	.46	2.54	.65
Powerful others	1.53	.41	1.76	.59
Luck	1.73	.49	1.76	.65
Unknown	1.95	.42	1.92	.61
Capacity beliefs:				
Effort	3.50	.27	3.30	.51
Ability	3.53	.31	3.35	.55
Powerful others	3.46	.29	3.27	.57
Luck	3.08	.27	3.03	.52
Student engagement (teacher report)	3.33	.40	3.17	.54
Teacher context (student report)	3.30	.32	3.09	.52

NOTE.—Ambient level is the average of that variable across all observed values for each child.

As can be seen, for a few variables (e.g., engagement, total strategy), there were modest but significant *negative* correlations between intercepts and slopes of the trajectories. These indicated that children who started higher declined *more* from grade 3 to grade 7 than children who started lower. The dependence between intercepts and slopes is usually considered a methodological issue (Willett et al., 1991), in that children who begin higher have more room to decline in their slopes. Consistent with this interpretation, we entered the intercept of the variable as an independent variable when examining predictors of that variable's growth curves.

As can also be seen, for each variable, high correlations were found between its estimated intercept and its ambient level (r ranging from .78 to .94). This was due to the relatively high stability of the variables over time. Hence, this high relation was especially pronounced for variables that were characterized by less change over time and so had flatter growth curves (e.g., engagement and context). Pragmatically, this high correlation meant that intercept and average levels could not be entered as independent variables in the same regression equations; hence, unfortunately, we could not test hypotheses about the unique contribution of launch versus ambient-level developmental

TABLE 23

CORRELATIONS AMONG BOTH INDIVIDUAL ESTIMATED GROWTH CURVE SLOPES AND INTERCEPTS AND AMBIENT LEVELS

	1	2	3	4	5	6	7	8	9	10	11
1. Engagement GC intercept											
2. Engagement ambient level	.94										
3. Engagement GC slope	−.35	−.09									
4. ConMax GC intercept	.42	.40	−.11								
5. ConMax ambient level	.41	.45	−.01a	.88							
6. ConMax GC slope	.23	.28	.13	.28	.66						
7. Promote GC intercept	.38	.36	−.11	.89	.81	.33					
8. Promote ambient level	.36	.39	−.02a	.79	.91	.60	.90				
9. Promote GC slope	.20	.25	.13	.31	.64	.88	.36	.67			
10. Undermine GC intercept	−.37	−.36	.12	−.90	−.73	−.14	−.62	−.54	−.21		
11. Undermine ambient level	−.41	−.44	.01a	−.81	−.93	−.61	−.62	−.71	−.53	.80	
12. Undermine GC slope	−.13	−.18	−.14	−.03a	−.39	−.85	−.13	−.32	−.56	−.16	.41
13. Strategy GC intercept	.24	.22	−.07*	.47	.37	.06*	.32	.27	.10	−.52	−.40
14. Strategy ambient level	.31	.32	.01a	.48	.56	.39	.37	.44	.34	−.45	−.59
15. Strategy GC slope	.15	.17	.10	.05*	.27	.52	.12	.24	.36	.06*	−.27
16. Capacity GC intercept	.40	.38	−.10	.94	.82	.27	.86	.76	.30	−.83	−.75
17. Capacity ambient level	.39	.44	.00a	.83	.95	.61	.78	.87	.60	−.69	−.87
18. Capacity GC slope	.18	.24	.17	.15	.52	.91	.20	.47	.81	−.04a	−.50
19. Teacher context GC intercept	.32	.31	−.08	.68	.64	.29	.65	.61	.31	−.60	−.59
20. Teacher context ambient level ...	.29	.33	−.02a	.61	.70	.44	.60	.67	.46	−.51	−.65
21. Teacher context GC slope	.03a	.08	.18	−.01a	.27	.58	.04a	.26	.55	.09	−.25
22. Grade 2 achievement	.48	.50	−.06a	.30	.34	.15	.28	.30	.15	−.26	−.32
23. Average achievement	.62	.63	−.06a	.37	.43	.24	.33	.38	.23	−.32	−.43

	12	13	14	15	16	17	18	19	20	21	22
1. Engagement GC intercept											
2. Engagement ambient level											
3. Engagement GC slope											
4. ConMax GC intercept											
5. ConMax ambient level											
6. ConMax GC slope											
7. Promote GC intercept											
8. Promote ambient level											
9. Promote GC slope											
10. Undermine GC intercept											
11. Undermine ambient level											
12. Undermine GC slope	.09										
13. Strategy ambient level	-.27	.78									
14. Strategy ambient level	-.58	-.27	.33								
15. Strategy GC slope	-.03a	.42	.43	.06*							
16. Capacity GC intercept	-.37	.33	.51	.25	.87						
17. Capacity ambient level	-.81	.01a	.31	.45	.13	.54					
18. Capacity GC slope	-.10	.33	.37	.09	.72	.66	.20				
19. Teacher context GC intercept	-.25	.26	.41	.20	.64	.74	.39	.91			
20. Teacher context ambient level	-.54	-.12	.15	.38	-.02a	.27	.65	.05*	.36		
21. Teacher context GC slope	-.09a	.23	.31	-.09a	.28	.29	.10a	.21	.21	.01a	
22. Grade 2 achievement	-.14	.28	.42	.16	.35	.41	.21	.25	.27	.05a	.82
23. Average achievement											

NOTE.—N ranged from 993 to 1,474. N ranged from 334 to 410 for correlations with grade 2 achievement and average achievement. GC = growth curve. Student engagement was reported by teachers. Teacher context was reported by students. $p < .01$ unless noted.

[a] Not significant.

* $p < .05$.

TABLE 24

RESULTS OF MULTIPLE REGRESSIONS EXAMINING LAUNCH AND CHANGE-TO-CHANGE RELATIONS
BETWEEN CHILDREN'S PERCEIVED CONTROL AND SLOPES OF THE GROWTH CURVES OF STUDENT
ENGAGEMENT (Dependent Variable: Slope of the Growth Curve
of Student Engagement [Teacher Reports])

Independent Variables	R^2	Children's Perceived Control Intercept; Launch, β	Children's Perceived Control Slope; Change to Change, β	Student Engagement Intercept, β
ConMax	.02	. . .	.13***	. . .
ConMax	.16	.03	.22***	(−.40)
Promote	.02	. . .	.09*	. . .
Undermine	. . .	. . .	.08**	. . .
Promote	.16	−.05	.14***	(−.39)
Undermine	. . .	−.09*	−.13***	. . .
Strategy beliefs	.03	. . .	.01	. . .
Capacity beliefs	. . .	. . .	.16***	. . .
Strategy beliefs	.17	.06*	.08*	(−.41)
Capacity beliefs	. . .	.03	.21***	. . .

NOTE.—Analyses were weighted by the number of times of measurement of teacher-reported student engagement.
N ranged from 1,258 to 1,271.
 * $p < .05$.
 ** $p < .01$.
 *** $p < .001$.

models. However, although the correlations between intercept and ambient level, on the one hand, and the slope of the growth curve for the same variable, on the other, were significant, they were low enough to allow us to investigate the independent effects of change-to-change versus launch models and of change-to-change versus ambient-level models.

Individual Differences in the Development of Engagement

The first set of regressions used estimates of individual slopes of engagement as the dependent variable, examining them as a function of different aspects of perceived control. For each set of proposed perceived control antecedents, we included both the launch variables (intercepts of the growth curves) and the change-to-change variables (slopes of the growth curve). As described above, to correct for the negative correlation between slope and intercept for engagement, we also included the engagement intercept as an independent variable. Finally, to examine whether these effects differed between boys and girls, we included main effects and interaction terms for sex.

The results of these regressions for the aggregate perceived control scores, representing profiles of control beliefs, appear in Table 24 (except for the interactions with sex, which are described below). As can be seen, after controlling for the intercept of engagement, only the *slope* of ConMax made a significant unique positive contribution to children's engagement growth curves. The intercept of ConMax did not "launch" children's engagement. When Promote and Undermine aggregate scores were considered together, a similar pattern was found, although the intercept of the growth curve of Undermine also made a marginally significant contribution.

Regressions comparing total strategy and capacity beliefs showed a slightly different pattern, with total *capacity* beliefs showing the expected strong unique change-to-change effect, but with total *strategy* beliefs showing only a small change-to-change effect as well as a small launch effect. We concluded that, as predicted from the change-to-change model, individual differences in the development of children's engagement from the third to the seventh grade closely corresponded to individual differences in the development of children's optimal control profiles. Nevertheless, a contribution from the launch model was also apparent: a modest effect was found in which children who started out "rich" in strategy beliefs become "richer" in engagement over time and children who started out "poor" in strategy beliefs become "poorer" over time.

Subgroup Analyses

In order to graphically depict the extent to which children's trajectories of perceived control shaped their trajectories of engagement, we estimated growth curves for children with very high perceived control (the top 10% of the ConMax trajectories) and very low perceived control (the lowest 10% of the ConMax trajectories). These are plotted in Figure 20. As can be seen, the average trajectory of engagement for children with high estimated slopes of the growth curve of control is completely different from that for children with the lowest control slopes, and the two trajectories even appear to become more divergent over time.

We plotted one additional subgroup analysis, to test an alternative to the notion that trajectories of control help shape trajectories of engagement. We reasoned that children who are very good in school (i.e., who received good grades) have higher perceived control and also show positive trajectories of engagement. Hence, it seemed possible that, once grades were controlled for, there would be no relation between trajectories of control and engagement. As can be seen in Figure 21, this was not the case. Although there were marked differences in engagement trajectories as a function of grades (between children who had A and B averages and children who had C averages or below), within each of these groups, levels of the slope of the perceived control growth curves (the top 10% vs. the lowest 10%) continued to distinguish children's trajectories of engagement.

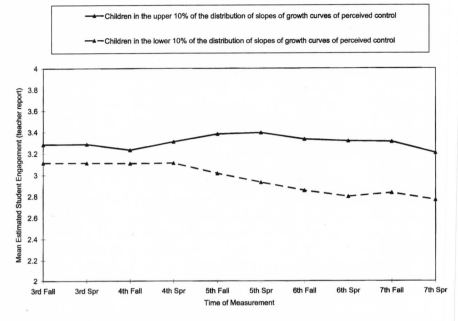

FIGURE 20.—Normative trajectories of children's engagement from grade 3 to grade 7 for children in the top and bottom deciles of the distribution of slopes of perceived control (ConMax). Scores for teachers' reports of students' engagement could range from 1 to 4.

Effects of Different Aspects of Perceived Control

Analyses of individual beliefs separately allowed us to pinpoint the unique change-to-change and launch effects of different aspects of perceived control on engagement trajectories. Results of the regression models examining each strategy and capacity belief separately appear in Table 25. A clear pattern emerged. For control and capacity beliefs, every belief showed a significant change-to-change effect: *changes* in beliefs significantly predicted the slope of the trajectories of engagement; however, no strong unique launch effects were found. In contrast, for strategy beliefs, only three strategies showed significant relations to the slope of the engagement trajectories: powerful others, luck, and unknown strategy beliefs. And, for each of these beliefs, significant unique effects were found for *both* launch and change-to-change variables.

An examination of sex differences in all the models looking at the effects of perceived control on the slope of the growth curves for engagement, revealed only two significant interactions: for strategy beliefs for effort and for strategy beliefs for unknown causes. The slope of the growth curve for strategy unknown was a significant (negative) predictor of the slope of the engage-

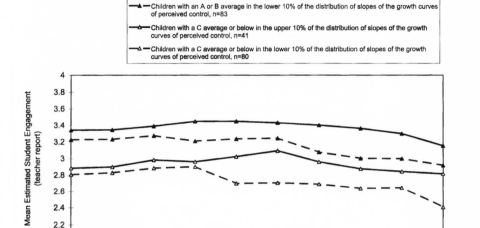

FIGURE 21.—Normative trajectories of engagement from grade 3 to grade 7 for children in the top and bottom deciles of the distribution of slopes of perceived control (ConMax) and with high or low average achievement. Scores for teachers' reports of students' engagement could range from 1 to 4.

ment trajectories for boys only. The growth curve for strategy effort was an additional unique (and positive) predictor of the slope of the engagement trajectories for girls. No other aspects of beliefs or aggregate beliefs, either estimated as intercepts or slopes of the growth curves, showed an interaction with sex in predicting the slope of engagement trajectories.

Individual Differences in the Development of Perceived Control

Teacher Context as a Predictor of the Development of Perceived Control

The next set of regressions contrasted change-to-change and ambient-level indicators of teacher context as predictors of children's trajectories of control beliefs. Specifically, in each model, the dependent variable was the slope of the growth curve of a different aspect of perceived control; independent variables included the average across all time points of students' reports of teacher context (the ambient-level variable), the slope of the growth curve for teacher context (the change-to-change variable), and the estimated intercept of the growth curve for the corresponding dependent variable.

These models are summarized in Table 26. In general, for each aggre-

TABLE 25

Unique Effects of Different Aspects of Children's Perceived Control on Slopes
of the Growth Curves of Student Engagement (Dependent Variable: Slope
of the Growth Curve of Student Engagement [Teacher Reports])

Independent Variables	R^2	Children's Perceived Control Intercept; Launch, β	Children's Perceived Control Slope; Change to Change, β	Student Engagement Intercept, β
Control beliefs	.16	.01	.22***	(−.40)
Strategy:				
Effort	12	.04	.07*	(−.34)
Ability	.11	.04	.03	(−.33)
Powerful others	.12	−.10**	−.14***	(−.36)
Luck	.15	−.12*	−.16***	(−.39)
Unknown	.15	−.13***	−.21***	(−.40)
Capacity:				
Effort	.16	.01	.21***	(−.38)
Ability	.15	.06*	.18***	(−.40)
Powerful others	.17	.05	.24***	(−.37)
Luck	.19	.01	.22***	(−.42)
Unique effects of strategies[a]	.15			(−.41)
Effort		N.S.	N.S.	
Ability		.09**	.08**	
Powerful others		N.S.	N.S.	
Luck		N.S.	N.S.	
Unknown		−.16***	−.22***	
Unique effects of capacities[a]	.23			(−.43)
Effort		N.S.	.09**	
Ability		N.S.	N.S.	
Powerful others		N.S.	.15***	
Luck		N.S.	.14***	

Note.—Analyses were weighted by the number of times of measurement of student engagement. Student engagement was reported by teachers. N ranged from 967 to 1,337.

[a] Intercepts and slopes of the growth curves of children's perceived control constructs were simultaneously entered, and backward elimination of nonsignificant effects was used to achieve final models.

* $p < .05$.
** $p < .01$.
*** $p < .001$.

gate and separate aspect of perceived control, a strong unique change-to-change effect of teacher context was found (M of coefficients = .33). Although relatively weaker, consistent unique ambient-level effects of teacher context were also found for almost all aspects of perceived control (M of coefficients = .18). However, although the coefficients for strategy and capacity beliefs for effort and for strategy ability were statistically significant, they were less than .10.

The extent to which the slope of the growth curve of teacher context shaped the development of children's perceived control is depicted graphi-

TABLE 26

UNIQUE EFFECTS OF TEACHER CONTEXT ON THE SLOPE OF THE GROWTH CURVES OF
ASPECTS OF CHILDREN'S PERCEIVED CONTROL

| | | INDEPENDENT VARIABLES | | |
DEPENDENT VARIABLES	R^2	Teacher Context Ambient Level, β	Teacher Context Slope (Change to Change), β	Dependent Variable Intercept, β
ConMax	.40	.18***	.53***	(.08)
Promote	.39	.19***	.49***	(.15)
Undermine	.36	−.29***	−.39***	(−.35)
Strategy	.24	.17***	.28***	(−.31)
Capacity	.44	.19***	.58***	(−.04)
Control beliefs	.21	.18***	.36***	(.05)
Strategy:				
Effort	.16	.09***	.18***	(−.33)
Ability	.26	−.09***	−.10***	(−.52)
Powerful others	.55	−.25***	−.24***	(−.67)
Luck	.64	−.14***	−.09***	(−.80)
Unknown	.32	−.25***	−.23***	(−.52)
Capacity:				
Effort	.32	.09**	.43***	(.25)
Ability	.19	.14***	.35***	(.06)
Powerful others	.50	.36***	.50***	(−.35)
Luck	.13	.13***	.24***	(.13)

NOTE.—Analyses were weighted by the number of times of measurement of children's perceived control. Teacher context was reported by students. N ranged from 980 to 1,368.

** $p < .01$.

*** $p < .001$.

cally in Figure 22. Children were selected who started high versus low on perceived control; then their trajectories of control were shown for two groups: children who reported high versus low subsequent slopes of teacher context. As can be seen, for children who initially were either high or low in perceived control, declining slopes of the trajectories of teacher context led to declining slopes of the trajectories of perceived control, whereas stable or slightly increasing slopes of teacher context led to the maintenance of a positive sense of control.

One interpretation of these models, which were contrary to predictions that ambient level of teacher context (and not change in teacher context) would be the better predictor of individual differences in the development of control, takes the normative shape of the trajectories into consideration. The normative trend for children's experiences of interactions with teachers was one of decline. Hence, the stronger than expected effects of change-to-change models suggested that, although teacher support did not need to be increasing over time for perceived control to develop optimally, it could not be deteriorating over time. Declines in children's experiences of teacher sup-

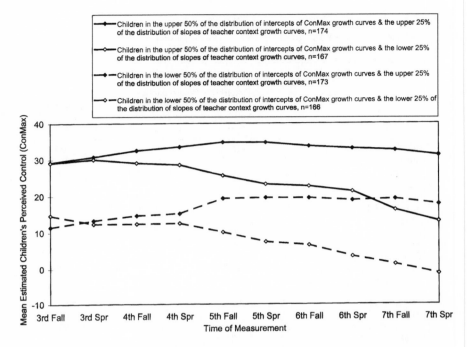

FIGURE 22.—Normative trajectories of children's profiles of perceived control (ConMax) from grade 3 to grade 7 for children grouped by the slopes of their growth curves of teacher context and also grouped by the intercepts of their growth curves of perceived control. ConMax scores could range from −66 to 66. Teacher context was reported by students.

port were more predictive of declines in control than were lower overall average levels of support.

Sex Differences in the Effects of Teacher Context

An examination of sex differences in these models revealed an interesting pattern. For the growth curves of three aggregate control scores, the relation with ambient level of teacher context differed as a function of sex. In each case, the connection between teacher context ambient-level scores and the slope of the growth curves for control was greater for boys than for girls (p's $< .01$). Students' reports of teacher context showed sex interactions for (1) the slope of the Undermine growth curves ($\beta = -.15$, $p < .01$, for boys, but $\beta = -.03$, N.S., for girls), (2) the slope of the Strategy growth curves ($\beta = .14$, $p < .01$, for boys, but $\beta = .02$, N.S., for girls), and (3) the slope of the Capacity growth curves ($\beta = .26$, $p < .001$, for boys, but $\beta = .11$, $p <$

TABLE 27

CORRELATION BETWEEN SLOPES OF THE GROWTH CURVES OF CHILDREN'S PERCEIVED
CONTROL AND THE LAUNCH VARIABLE, AVERAGE ACHIEVEMENT PRIOR TO THE THIRD GRADE

Slopes of Growth Curves of Children's Perceived Control	Average Achievement prior to Third Grade	Slopes of Growth Curves of Children's Perceived Control	Average Achievement prior to Third Grade
ConMax	.15**	Strategy:	
Promote	.15**	Powerful others	.06
Undermine	−.09	Luck	.04
Strategy	.09	Unknown	−.09
Capacity	.10	Capacity:	
Control beliefs	.22***	Effort	.12*
Strategy:		Ability	.20***
Effort	.03	Powerful others	.02
Ability	.03	Luck	.13*

NOTE.—N ranged from 331 to 339.
* $p < .05$.
** $p < .01$.
*** $p < .001$.

.01, for girls). Given that fifteen interactions with sex were examined, this pattern does not constitute major sex differences in the teacher context predictors of the development of children's perceived control. However, the consistency of the pattern does suggest that, when it comes to supporting control trajectories, the ambient level of teacher context of involvement and structure may be especially important to boys.

Academic Performance as a Predictor of the Development of Perceived Control

To examine the launch effects of grades on children's trajectories of perceived control, we used the aggregate grade scores that included children's grades *prior* to the beginning of the study (up to the end of second grade) and correlated them with the estimates of the slopes of the growth curves for different aspects of control. These appear in Table 27. As can be seen, children's prior grades predicted patterns of change from the third to the seventh grade for four control variables: control beliefs, capacity for effort, capacity for luck, and, especially, capacity for ability. Interpretations of these findings should reflect the fact that, since school grades tend to be highly stable, launch effects may not be empirically distinguishable from ambient-level effects. The extent of the effect of grades on control is depicted in Figure 23, which pictures the trajectories of ConMax for children with high (A or B average grades) versus low (grades C average or below) performance

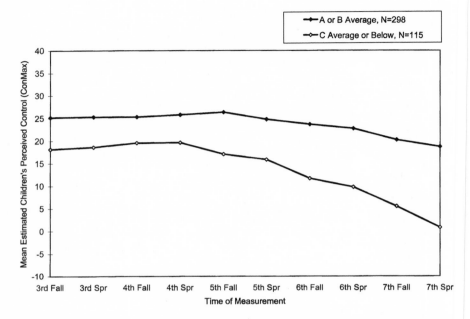

FIGURE 23.—Normative trajectories of children's profiles of perceived control (ConMax) from grade 3 to grade 7 for children grouped by their average achievement prior to grade 3. ConMax scores could range from −66 to 66.

in the second grade. The trajectories do not touch and appear to become increasingly divergent over time.

Unique Effects of Teacher Context and Academic Performance

Since the development of perceived control was related to both early school performance (i.e., second-grade grades) and children's changing perceptions of their interactions with teachers, we decided to examine the unique effects of these antecedents, in regressions containing both as independent variables (along with the intercept of the control dependent variable). The results of these regressions appear in Table 28.

For all aspects of control, teacher context continued to exert its effects. In addition, children's initial grades also uniquely predicted the slope of their trajectories of beliefs about their capacity ability as well as the slope of their trajectories for control beliefs and external (powerful others, luck, and unknown) strategy beliefs. The effects of achievement on the development of other aspects of capacity beliefs (effort and luck) were no longer significant once the effects of teacher context were controlled. It is also interesting to note that the only strong unique predictors of the development of strategy

TABLE 28

SLOPES OF THE GROWTH CURVES OF TEACHER CONTEXT AND AVERAGE ACHIEVEMENT
PRIOR TO THIRD GRADE AS PREDICTORS OF THE SLOPE OF THE GROWTH CURVES OF
CHILDREN'S PERCEIVED CONTROL

| | | INDEPENDENT VARIABLES | | |
DEPENDENT VARIABLES	R^2	Slope of Teacher Context, β	Average Achievement prior to 3d Grade, β	Intercept of the Dependent Variable, β
ConMax	.39	.61***	.15**	(.05)
Promote	.32	.54***	.09	(.14)
Undermine	.39	−.47***	−.20***	(−.32)
Strategy	.25	.25***	.21***	(−.37)
Capacity	.45	.66***	.12**	(−.01)
Control beliefs	.20	.36***	.26***	(−.11)
Strategy:				
Effort	.18	.10	.09	(−.41)
Ability	.26	−.13**	.05	(−.51)
Powerful others	.55	−.37***	−.07	(−.58)
Luck	.61	−.12**	−.11**	(−.77)
Unknown	.36	−.22***	−.24***	(−.55)
Capacity:				
Effort	.28	.48***	.07	(.20)
Ability	.20	.40***	.22***	(.01)
Powerful others	.42	.59***	.06	(−.19)
Luck	.06	.17***	.08	(.14)

NOTE.—Analyses were weighted by the number of times of measurement of children's perceived control. Teacher context was reported by students. N ranged from 329 to 334.

  ** $p < .01$.
  *** $p < .001$.

and capacity beliefs for powerful others were children's changing perceptions of teacher context.

Summary of Results on Individual Differences in the Development of Control and Engagement

The normative growth curves replicated the finding that children's engagement in school declines during the elementary school years and verified that the "elbow" for disaffection begins during the transition to middle school, between the fifth and the sixth grades (Eccles & Midgley, 1989; Eccles et al., 1998). At the same time, children also reported declines in their experiences of their teachers as involved and structured (Roeser et al., 1996). In addition, children's perceived control, which began at a relatively high level in grade 3, showed decreases in beliefs about the capacity to exert effort and influence powerful others and increases in beliefs about the role of powerful others and unknown strategies in school success and failure.

An interesting *within*-year pattern was also detected, in that engagement and teacher context, as well as some aspects of perceived control (e.g., powerful others and unknown strategy beliefs), showed slight declines within a school year (from fall to spring) that, in the early elementary school years, were offset by "recoveries" during the summer (from spring of one year to fall of the next). Starting in the summer between the fifth and the sixth grades, however, no more "recoveries" were seen, with the result that the subsequent sharper declines within the school year cumulatively led to normative decreases in both teacher context (as reported by students) and students' engagement (as reported by teachers).

As hypothesized, the relations between individual differences in the development of perceived control and engagement were consistent with a change-to-change developmental model. Individual differences in the trajectories of children's engagement were predicted most strongly by their trajectories of perceived control. As children's perceived control improved, remained stable, or decreased over time, so too did their engagement. Unique predictors of the development of engagement were children's capacity beliefs for effort, powerful others, and luck. Both change-to-change and launch effects were found for children's beliefs about external strategies. Children who, at the beginning of the third grade, reported higher beliefs in the effectiveness of external strategies also showed more deterioration in their trajectories of engagement over the elementary school years.

Individual differences in children's trajectories of perceived control over the 5 years from grade 3 to grade 7 were predicted uniquely both by their level of achievement prior to the third grade and by changes in their experiences of teachers over the course of the study. Early achievement launched positive trajectories of beliefs about both control and ability as a capacity. In contrast, poor early academic performance launched maladaptive trajectories of beliefs about luck and unknown strategies. Trajectories of teacher context predicted trajectories of all aspects of perceived control; teacher context was the only strong unique predictor of strategy and capacity beliefs about powerful others. Ambient level of teacher context was especially important to boys' trajectories of perceived control.

Counter to predictions, change-to-change (and not ambient-level) models were better accounts of the relations between students' experiences of teacher context and the development of children's perceived control. One explanation for this pattern is that in general children's experiences of their teachers' involvement and the structure that they provided were declining over this age range. If the optimal development of children's sense of control requires at least a threshold amount of teacher support, then changes in children's experiences with teachers may be a better indicator (than average level) of whether teacher support crosses below that threshold.

Individual Differences and Development of Perceived Control and Action: Exploratory Analyses

In the last phase of the analyses, we explored whether the predictors of individual differences in development would differ as a function of the age of the child. It could be possible, for example, that increases in engagement when children were in the early grades might be better predicted by corresponding declines in unknown control, whereas, at later ages, increases in engagement might be better predicted by increases in perceptions of ability capacity. In other words, the goal of these analyses was to explore whether the aspects of perceived control that predict changes in engagement across time differ as a function of the portion of the normative trajectory that serves as the target outcome. For example, children's engagement in school remains relatively stable until the end of fifth grade and then declines sharply. The question then becomes, Do the factors that predict individual differences in development when that development is relatively flat remain the same as the predictors of individual development when that path, in general, is declining?

As with predictions from the functional model, we expected teacher context to predict trajectories of control at all ages, but we also expected involvement to be especially important for the development of control at younger ages. We expected that the same age changes that occurred in the predictors of individual differences in engagement would also hold for age changes in the predictors of individual differences in the development of engagement. That is, we expected that trajectories of perceived control would relate to trajectories of engagement at all ages but that specific aspects of control (effort and unknown as opposed to ability) would become progressively more important as children proceeded from the third to the seventh grade. These hypotheses are summarized in Table 29.

Patterns of Engagement

To explore these possibilities, we used data on 2–year (four-point) developmental trajectories that began during two different developmental periods: (1) 2-year trajectories starting when children were in the fall of third grade and spanning the third and fourth grades; (2) 2-year trajectories starting when children were in the fall of sixth grade and spanning the sixth and seventh grades. Regression analyses similar to those described in the last section were completed in order to compare developmental models, such as launch and change to change. However, in each regression, interaction terms for initial grade were added to see whether relations between predictors and outcomes differed for children at different developmental levels.

TABLE 29

Hypotheses about Age Differences in Predictors of Individual Differences
in Development

Effects of Context on the Development of Perceived Control
1. Both involvement and structure will predict individual differences in 2-year trajectories of control across the age range.
2. Relative to 2-year trajectories of the oldest children (whose trajectories began in the fall of grade 6), 2-year trajectories of the youngest children (whose trajectories began in the fall of grade 3) will be influenced more strongly by teacher involvement.

Effects of Control on the Development of Engagement
3. Both control and capacity beliefs will predict individual differences in the development of engagement all across this age range.
4. Relative to the oldest children, the youngest children's 2-year trajectories of engagement will be influenced more strongly by trajectories of their beliefs in effort and unknown strategies.
5. Relative to the youngest children, the oldest children's 2-year trajectories of engagement will be influenced more strongly by trajectories of their beliefs in ability as a strategy.

Estimation of Two-Year Growth Curve Scores

As a first step, group and individual intercept and slope estimates for the 2-year trajectories were calculated for all the variables. We used the same procedures as described previously to determine the shape of the 2-year population growth curve for each variable. First, the full model was calculated, this time also including a main effect for initial grade (grade 3 vs. grade 6) and interactions between the time variables (time, time squared, and time cubed) and initial grade. The full model for ConMax is presented in Table 30. As can be seen, not only were the linear (time) and curvilinear (time squared) components significant, but the cubic component (time cubed) was also significant.

In a second set of steps, the final model was determined by eliminating variables according to the criteria described in the previous section. The final model for ConMax is presented in Table 31 and was the simplest accurate depiction of the population curve for that variable. As can be seen, the effects of all three time variables were still significant, indicating that the population growth curve for ConMax contained linear, quadratic, and cubic trends; in addition, the interaction between initial grade and time was significant, indicating that the linear component of ConMax differed between the two initial grade groups. The positive sign on the coefficient indicates that the older children's ConMax growth curves contained significantly more linear change than the younger children's.

The reduced model (also shown in Table 31 for ConMax) depicts the model used to estimate individual children's intercepts and slopes for ConMax. As with the other variables, we used the linear component of the slopes

TABLE 30

Results of the Full Hierarchical Linear Model Predicting 2-Year Trajectories of Children's Perceived Control (Grades 3–4 and Grades 6–7)

Independent Variables	Unique Estimate	SE(Unique Estimate)	F	p Value
Intercept	26.769	5.21	. . .	. . .
Time (the fall of the 3d or 6th grade to the spring of the next year; linear trajectory)	−4.860	8.10	9.31	.002
Time^2 (quadratic trajectory)	1.720	3.66	9.26	.002
Time^3 (cubic trajectory)	−.304	.49	10.10	.002
Initial grade (3d)	−5.268	6.05	.76	.384
Student sex (male)	1.480	5.50	.07	.788
Wave (1)	9.643	5.82	2.74	.098
Interactions:				
Time × initial grade	6.725	9.30	.52	.470
Time^2 × initial grade	−1.912	4.12	.22	.643
Time^3 × initial grade	.282	.55	.27	.650
Time × sex	−11.540	8.40	1.89	.169
Time^2 × sex	5.860	3.71	2.50	.114
Time^3 × sex	−.852	.49	3.01	.083
Time × wave	−12.616	8.89	2.02	.156
Time^2 × wave	4.666	3.91	1.43	.232
Time^3 × wave	−.500	.51	.94	.331

Note.—Time was coded from 1 to 4, where 1 indicates each student's measurement in the fall of the first year and 4 indicates measurement in the spring of the second year.

of the growth curves. If sex, curvilinear, or wave terms or their interactions were significant, we controlled for them when estimating individual slopes. The final and reduced models for engagement and teacher context are also presented in Table 31.

Descriptive Statistics for Two-Year Trajectories

The means and standard deviations of the slopes of the 2-year growth curves of all the variables used in these analyses are presented in Table 32, separately for the two initial grade groups. Table 33 contains the means and standard deviations of the launch (intercept) and ambient-level scores (average of actual scores across 2 years) for the two initial grade groups. The actual and estimated values for all variables at each time of measurement are presented in Table 34. The estimated 2-year trajectories for ConMax, engagement, and teacher context are presented in Figures 24–26. The observed values at each time of measurement for these variables are superimposed over the estimates.

As can be seen in these tables and figures, and as discussed in the previous sections on normative development, some variables showed different

TABLE 31

Results of Final and Reduced Hierarchical Linear Models Predicting 2-Year Trajectories (Grades 3–4 and Grades 6–7)

Independent Variable	Final Model				Reduced Model			
	Unique Estimate	SE (Unique Estimate)	F	p Value	Unique Estimate	SE (Unique Estimate)	F	p Value
	Dependent Variable: Children's Perceived Control (ConMax)							
Intercept	30.93	3.07	…	…	25.74	.92	…	…
Time (the fall of the first year to the spring of the second year)	−12.22	4.41	8.95	.003	−2.31	.33	17.27	.000
Time²	5.19	1.92	8.77	.003	…	…	…	…
Time³	−.78	.25	9.50	.002	…	…	…	…
Initial grade (3d)	−3.39	1.35	6.31	.120	−2.25	1.27	3.15	.077
Student sex (male)	−4.59	.78	34.99	.000	−4.60	.78	35.21	.000
Wave (1)	4.57	2.11	4.69	.030	…	…	…	…
Interactions:								
Time × initial grade	3.02	.47	40.54	.000	2.77	.44	39.19	.000
Time × wave	−4.28	1.69	6.42	.011	…	…	…	…
Time² × wave	.91	.33	7.52	.006	…	…	…	…

DEPENDENT VARIABLE: STUDENT ENGAGEMENT (Teacher Report)

Intercept	3.92	.14	⋯	⋯	3.23	.04	⋯	⋯
Time (the fall of the first year to the spring of the second year)	−1.21	.21	3.69	.055	−.03	.01	.32	.571
Time²	.58	.10	4.91	.027	⋯	⋯	⋯	⋯
Time³	−.08	.01	6.20	.013	⋯	⋯	⋯	⋯
Initial grade (3d)	−.90	.20	20.40	.000	.14	.03	29.33	.000
Student sex (male)	−.21	.03	58.56	.000	−.21	.03	57.81	.000
Wave (1)	−.06	.05	1.63	.201	−.05	.05	1.14	.285
Interactions:								
Time × initial grade	1.78	.31	33.15	.000	⋯	⋯	⋯	⋯
Time² × initial grade	−.84	.14	36.60	.000	⋯	⋯	⋯	⋯
Time³ × initial grade	.12	.02	38.45	.000	⋯	⋯	⋯	⋯
Time × wave	.04	.02	6.99	.008	.04	.02	7.07	.008

DEPENDENT VARIABLE: TEACHER CONTEXT (Student Report)

Intercept	3.75	.12	⋯	⋯	3.17	.03	⋯	⋯
Time (the fall of the first year to the spring of the second year)	−1.03	.18	39.12	.000	−.07	.01	23.67	.000
Time²	.45	.08	37.48	.000	⋯	⋯	⋯	⋯
Time³	−.06	.01	37.94	.000	⋯	⋯	⋯	⋯
Initial grade (3d)	.08	.05	2.53	.113	.12	.05	6.55	.011
Student sex (male)	−.15	.03	30.65	.000	−.16	.03	31.10	.000
Wave (1)	.18	.08	4.66	.031	⋯	⋯	⋯	⋯
Interactions:								
Time × initial grade	.06	.02	11.56	.001	.06	.02	10.83	.001
Time × wave	−.19	.07	7.85	.005	⋯	⋯	⋯	⋯
Time² × wave	.04	.01	7.46	.007	⋯	⋯	⋯	⋯

NOTE.—Time was coded from 1 to 4, where 1 indicates each student's measurement in the fall of the first year and 4 indicates measurement in the spring of the second year in the study. The "reduced model" is the model used to estimate growth curve parameters for individuals. The "final model" depicts the equation describing the population growth curve.

TABLE 32

MEANS AND STANDARD DEVIATIONS OF ESTIMATED GROWTH CURVE SLOPES
FROM GRADE 3 TO GRADE 4 AND GRADE 6 TO GRADE 7

| | GROWTH CURVE SLOPE ESTIMATES | | | |
| | Grades 3–4 | | Grades 6–7 | |
CONSTRUCTS	Mean	SD	Mean	SD
Children's perceived control:				
ConMax	.497	2.27	−2.162	1.57
Promote	.149	.99	−.998	.66
Undermine	−.489	1.26	1.120	.91
Strategy	.038	.04	−.037	.02
Capacity	−.003	.07	−.063	.06
Control levels	.024	.03	−.065	.04
Strategy:				
Effort	.031	.07	−.072	.04
Ability	−.004	.06	.020	.03
Powerful others	−.058	.10	.081	.04
Luck	−.020	.11	. . .	. . .
Unknown	−.081	07	.016	.03
Capacity:				
Effort	.010	.05	−.067	.05
Ability	.009	.06	−.047	.05
Powerful others	−.022	.09	−.075	.08
Luck	.038	.08	. . .	. . .
Student engagement (teacher				
report)	−.005	.07	.001	.08
Teacher context (student report)	−.009	.06	−.068	.07

starting points (intercepts) and some different patterns of change (growth curves) for children whose 2-year trajectories began in the third as opposed to the sixth grade. For ConMax, initial starting levels were not so different for third and sixth graders (M's = 22.32 and 21.13, respectively). However, third graders' ConMax improved slightly over the next 2 years, whereas sixth graders' ConMax declined sharply. This resulted in very different 2-year linear population slopes (.497 and −2.162 for third and sixth graders, respectively) and ambient levels (22.84 and 18.65 for third and sixth graders, respectively).

In Figure 24, the amount of curvilinearity in the ConMax variables removed in the estimates by controlling for quadratic and cubic trends was also apparent. Not captured in the descriptive statistics, but apparent in the plots of actual scores, was that the "location" of change in ConMax was different for the two grade groups. As can also be seen in Figure 24, for children in grades 3–4, ConMax was relatively stable during the school year (from fall to spring) but improved between school years; in contrast, for the sixth to seventh graders, ConMax was stable between school years but showed marked declines during school years. To highlight the similarity between the two

TABLE 33

MEANS AND STANDARD DEVIATIONS OF ESTIMATED GRADES 3–4 AND GRADES 6–7 GROWTH CURVE INTERCEPTS AND AMBIENT LEVELS

| | Grades 3–4 | | | | Grades 6–7 | | | |
| | GC Intercept | | Ambient Level | | GC Intercept | | Ambient Level | |
Constructs	Mean	SD	Mean	SD	Mean	SD	Mean	SD
Children's perceived control:								
ConMax	21.57	8.72	22.84	12.98	22.89	13.93	18.65	16.04
Promote	45.88	3.88	46.28	6.63	46.49	6.08	44.56	7.91
Undermine	24.74	6.14	23.41	7.73	23.90	8.28	26.11	9.17
Strategy	2.93	.17	3.03	.32	3.05	.21	2.98	.33
Capacity	3.41	.29	3.40	.43	3.31	.43	3.19	.51
Control beliefs	3.39	.22	3.46	.43	3.50	.36	3.37	.51
Strategy:								
Effort	3.06	.25	3.16	.51	3.30	.30	3.16	.50
Ability	2.57	.46	2.56	.69	2.50	.46	2.53	.66
Powerful others	1.81	.46	1.65	.59	1.73	.41	1.89	.62
Luck	1.83	.53	1.79	.69	...	...	...	.64
Unknown	2.16	.44	1.93	.62	1.88	.50	1.92	.64
Capacity:								
Effort	3.37	.27	3.40	.47	3.29	.43	3.16	.54
Ability	3.42	.30	3.45	.51	3.33	.50	3.24	.60
Powerful others	3.43	.33	3.36	.55	3.31	.40	3.16	.61
Luck	2.99	.26	3.07	.52	...	...	...	...
Student engagement (teacher report)	3.24	.36	3.23	.56	3.08	.51	3.08	.55
Teacher context (student report)	3.22	.27	3.19	.50	3.08	.44	2.94	.53

NOTE.—Ambient level is the average of that variable across all observed values for each child. GC = growth curve.

TABLE 34

Means and Standard Deviations of Observed and Estimated Values by Initial Grade Level and Time of Measurement

	Grade 3 at First Measurement							
	3d Grade, Fall		3d Grade, Spring		4th Grade, Fall		4th Grade, Spring	
	Observed	Estimated	Observed	Estimated	Observed	Estimated	Observed	Estimated
Children's perceived control:								
ConMax	22.32	22.10	22.12	22.98	23.57	23.13	23.32	23.62
Promote	46.39	46.15	44.93	46.17	46.62	46.47	46.56	46.51
Undermine	24.17	24.02	22.88	23.28	22.99	23.24	23.10	22.76
Control beliefs	3.42	3.41	3.37	3.42	3.48	3.47	3.48	3.48
Strategy:								
Effort	3.07	3.08	3.06	3.10	3.18	3.16	3.19	3.19
Ability	2.50	2.54	2.49	2.52	2.57	2.56	2.54	2.54
Powerful others	1.80	1.78	1.58	1.67	1.64	1.66	1.59	1.57
Luck	1.86	1.89	1.71	1.82	1.81	1.81	1.69	1.75
Unknown	2.06	2.05	1.81	1.93	1.95	1.92	1.83	1.84
Capacity:								
Effort	3.41	3.39	3.32	3.40	3.45	3.41	3.40	3.42
Ability	3.44	3.43	3.43	3.44	3.46	3.44	3.46	3.46
Powerful others	3.42	3.42	3.28	3.38	3.41	3.37	3.32	3.33
Luck	3.04	3.05	3.09	3.10	3.15	3.13	3.10	3.16
Student engagement (teacher report)	3.25	3.27	3.27	3.24	3.19	3.21	3.26	3.19
Teacher context (student report)	3.21	3.21	3.09	3.19	3.24	3.20	3.15	3.18

	6th Grade, Fall		6th Grade, Spring		7th Grade, Fall		7th Grade, Spring	
GRADE 6 AT FIRST MEASUREMENT	Observed	Estimated	Observed	Estimated	Observed	Estimated	Observed	Estimated
Children's perceived control:								
ConMax	21.13	20.84	18.42	18.59	18.46	16.87	12.62	13.96
Promote	45.79	45.54	44.29	44.50	43.94	43.30	41.65	42.14
Undermine	24.73	24.92	26.16	26.05	26.00	26.72	28.76	28.43
Control beliefs	3.44	3.43	3.36	3.37	3.35	3.30	3.21	3.24
Strategy:								
Effort	3.23	3.23	3.15	3.15	3.12	3.11	3.10	3.08
Ability	2.53	2.52	2.51	2.54	2.60	2.58	2.65	2.65
Powerful others	1.80	1.81	1.91	1.89	1.91	1.96	2.11	2.07
Luck	...	...	...	...	...	...	...	...
Unknown	1.89	1.89	1.91	1.91	1.82	1.89	1.99	1.94
Capacity:								
Effort	3.24	3.23	3.15	3.16	3.12	3.10	2.99	3.00
Ability	3.31	3.28	3.20	3.24	3.20	3.18	3.12	3.12
Powerful others	3.26	3.24	3.15	3.16	3.13	3.09	2.98	2.99
Luck	...	...	...	...	...	...	...	...
Student engagement (teacher report)	3.10	3.09	3.07	3.09	3.22	3.11	2.94	3.04
Teacher context (student report)	3.02	3.01	2.92	2.94	2.92	2.87	2.77	2.77

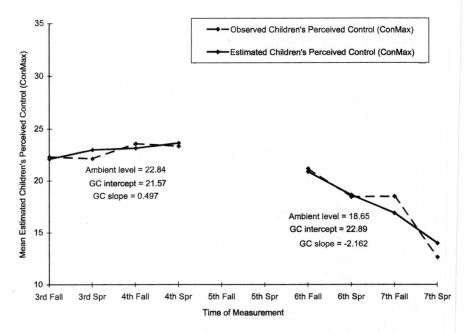

FIGURE 24.—Observed and estimated normative 2-year trajectories of children's profiles of perceived control (ConMax). GC = growth curve. ConMax scores could range from −66 to 66.

grade groups, it could be argued that the "bad news" for profiles of control occurred during school years, whereas the "good news" occurred *between* school years. However, the good news for third to fourth graders was improvements in profiles of control, whereas for sixth to seventh graders it was maintenance of control. The bad news for third to fourth graders was stability of control, whereas for sixth to seventh graders it was marked decreases in profiles of control.

Two-year trajectories of teachers' ratings of students' engagement are presented in Figure 25. This figure shows that engagement was relatively stable (growth curves = −.005 and .0001) but higher in grades 3–4 than in grades 6–7, as reflected in the higher intercepts (3.24 and 3.08, respectively) and ambient levels (3.23 and 3.08, respectively). However, the relative stability of the linear slope was a better representation of the actual pattern of change for children initially in third grade than for older children. The small linear component for the children initially in sixth grade included actual stability from fall to spring of sixth grade, combined with increases between the spring of sixth and the fall of seventh grade and marked declines from the fall to the spring of seventh grade.

For students' ratings of teacher context, depicted in Figure 26, third to

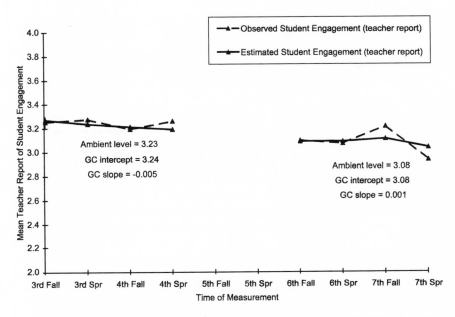

FIGURE 25.—Observed and estimated normative 2-year trajectories of children's engage-ment. GC = growth curve. Scores for teachers' reports of students' engagement could range from 1 to 4.

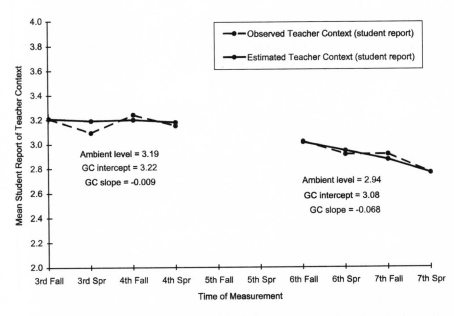

FIGURE 26.—Observed and estimated normative 2-year trajectories of teacher context. GC = growth curve. Scores for students' reports of teacher context could range from 1 to 4.

fourth graders reported more supportive interactions with teachers than did sixth to seventh graders—both initially (intercepts = 3.22 and 3.08, respectively) and in ambient level (intercepts = 3.19 and 2.94, respectively). For both grade groups, the relatively small linear slopes (−.0009 and −.068, respectively) did not capture patterns of within-year change that seemed somewhat greater.

Finally, we examined the correlations among the intercepts, ambient levels, and slopes of the target variables. As with the 5-year trajectories, the correlations between launch scores (intercepts) and ambient levels were too high to allow them to be tested in the same regressions. Hence, as with the previous analyses, change-to-change models were compared only with launch models when examining the effects of control on the development of engagement, and change-to-change models were compared only with ambient-level models when examining the effects of teacher context and achievement on the development of control.

One additional complication was apparent when the correlations between intercepts and linear slopes for the same variables were examined. For children initially in grade 3, these within-variable correlations were either low or nonsignificant. However, for the older children (initially in grade 6), the correlations were significant and sometimes high. For example, the correlation between the intercept and the slope for teachers' ratings of students' engagement was −.72 ($p < .001$). There are several possible interpretations for age differences in these relations (see Chapter VI below). Nevertheless, in order to control for them statistically, in addition to entering the intercept of the dependent variable (as in previous analyses) we also entered an interaction score, namely, the cross-product of grade and the intercept of the dependent variable. Interaction effects are listed in the regression models in which age differences were examined.

Age Differences in Predictors of Two-Year Engagement Trajectories

Table 35 contains the unique main effects of launch and change-to-change indicators for each belief individually. When the results of these analyses are compared to those of the analyses of 5-year engagement trajectories (see Tables 24 and 25 above), it can be seen that the aspects of control that uniquely predicted the slopes of the 2-year engagement trajectories were similar. Most of the strategy beliefs had significant effects, especially those for external causes (powerful others, luck, and unknown); capacity beliefs were also strong predictors, especially effort and ability.

One difference between the patterns of predictors for the slopes of the 2- and the 5-year engagement trajectories was clear, however. In the analyses of the predictors of 5-year engagement slopes, the change-to-change control

TABLE 35

UNIQUE RELATIONS BETWEEN DIFFERENT ASPECTS OF CHILDREN'S PERCEIVED CONTROL AND 2-YEAR SLOPES OF THE GROWTH CURVES OF ENGAGEMENT (Grades 3–4 and Grades 6–7) (Dependent Variable: Slope of the Growth Curve of Student Engagement [Teacher Report])

INDEPENDENT VARIABLES	R^2	INTERCEPT (Launch), β	SLOPE (Change to Change), β	STUDENT ENGAGEMENT INTERCEPT, β	3D-GRADE MODEL		6TH-GRADE MODEL	
					Launch, β	Change to Change, β	Launch, β	Change to Change, β
ConMax	.20	.13***	.15***	(−.47)	.21***	.19***	.10**	.11***
Promote	.20	.01	.10**	(−.47)	.08	.11*	−.03	.11**
Undermine		−.13**	−.05		−.17**	−.07	−.11*	−.03
Strategy	.20	−.02	−.02	(−.47)	.09*	.06	−.07*	−.05
Capacity		.16***	.15***		.18***	.13**	.17***	.16***

NOTE.—Analyses were weighted by the number of times of measurement of teacher-reported student engagement. N ranged from 1,293 to 1,309. Third-grade model N ranged from 1,293 to 1,309. Third-grade model N ranged from 677 to 682. Sixth-grade model N ranged from 616 to 627.

* $p < .05$.
** $p < .01$.
*** $p < .001$.

variables were more likely to be significant and usually were more strongly related to the slope of engagement than the launch variables. For the 2-year slopes, however, more launch effects were significant, and, in almost every case, launch effects were larger in magnitude than change-to-change effects (although we did not test this for significance).

The difference in pattern probably reflects the difference between launching a 2-year and launching a 5-year trajectory. When the trajectory is shorter, a launch variable must exert an effect only over the near future, whereas, when the trajectory is more extended (such as over 5 years), variables that may have initially launched a pattern of change over time may be overshadowed by subsequent developments. And, if these developments are captured in change-to-change variables, these will show stronger relations to individual differences in change over time.

Of primary interest, however, was the pattern of age changes in the predictors of individual differences in the development of engagement. Tables 36–39 present the regressions separately for launch (intercept) and change-to-change (slope) indicators for control variables, testing for interactions with initial grade. Using the dummy-coding procedure described previously, comparisons were conducted between children whose 2-year trajectories began in the third grade and those whose 2-year trajectories began in the sixth grade.

The aggregate control measures are presented in Table 36 (launch) and Table 37 (change to change), and each of the eight control variables separately are given in Table 38 (launch) and Table 39 (change to change). In these analyses, a significant interaction between a given aspect of perceived control and initial grade indicated that the predictors of children's 2-year engagement trajectories differed between children whose trajectories spanned the third and fourth grades (when children were ages 8–10 and engagement was normatively stable) and children whose trajectories spanned the sixth and seventh grades (when children were ages 11–13 and engagement was normatively declining).

An examination of the aggregate control scores (Tables 36 and 37) revealed few age differences in the relations between profiles of perceived control and the slopes of the engagement trajectories. Two sets of control profiles launched 2-year trajectories for children of both age groups: children who were initially high in aggregate Capacity beliefs showed more positive subsequent 2-year trajectories of engagement, whereas children who started off initially high on the profile of maladaptive beliefs (Undermine) had subsequently more negative engagement trajectories. In addition, two profiles of beliefs showed positive change-to-change relations with slopes of engagement: ConMax and Promote.

The only two interactions with age that were significant involved aggregate Strategy and Capacity beliefs. Strategy beliefs were more important in launching trajectories of engagement for children initially in the third grade

TABLE 36

The Launch Effect of Children's Perceived Control on 2-Year Slopes of the Growth Curves of Student Engagement (Grades 3–4 and Grades 6–7) and Interactions with Student Grade Level (Dependent Variable: Slope of the Growth Curve of Student Engagement [Teacher Report])

Independent Variables	R^2	Intercept (Launch), β	Student Engagement Intercept, β	Grade Level and Interactions, β			3d-Grade Model, Launch, β	6th-Grade Model, Launch, β
				Initial Grade 3 vs. 6	Launch × Grade Level 3 vs. 6	Student Engagement Intercept × Grade Level 3 vs. 6		
ConMax	.28	.20*	(.59)	−.01	−.12	(−1.08)	.11**	.06†
	.29		(.57)	−.01		(−1.08)		
Promote		.11			−.14		.02	−.06
Undermine		−.16			−.16		−.14**	−.12**
	.30		(.56)	.00		(−1.07)		
Strategy		.21*			−.23**		.07†	−.07*
Capacity		.14			−.03		.11*	.10**

Note.—Analyses were weighted by the number of times of measurement of teacher-reported student engagement. N ranged from 1,293 to 1,309. Third-grade model N ranged from 677 to 682. Sixth-grade model N ranged from 616 to 627.

* $p < .05$.
** $p < .01$.
† $p < .10$.

TABLE 37

The Change-to-Change Effect of Children's Perceived Control on 2-Year Slopes of the Growth Curves of Student Engagement (Grades 3–4 and Grades 6–7) and Interactions with Student Grade Level (Dependent Variable: Slope of the Growth Curve of Student Engagement [Teacher Report])

				Grade Level and Interactions, β				
Independent Variables	R^2	Slope (Change to change), β	Student Engagement Intercept, β	Initial Grade 3 vs. 6	Change to Change × Grade Level 3 vs. 6	Student Engagement Intercept × Grade Level 3 vs. 6	3d-Grade Model, Change to Change, β	6th-Grade Model, Change to Change, β
ConMax	.28	.05			.03		.09*	.07**
			(.64)	−.01		(−1.10)		
Promote	.30	.02			.11		.12**	.13***
Undermine		.05			−.01		.05	.02
			(.65)	−.01		(−1.13)		
Strategy	.29	.10			−.10		.03	−.03
Capacity		−.07			.15*		.04	.11***
			(.64)	−.01		(−1.10)		

NOTE.—Analyses were weighted by the number of times of measurement of teacher-reported student engagement. N ranged from 1,292 to 1,309. Third-grade model N ranged from 677 to 682. Sixth-grade model N ranged from 616 to 627.

* $p < .05$.
** $p < .01$.
*** $p < .001$.

TABLE 38

THE LAUNCH EFFECT OF CHILDREN'S PERCEIVED CONTROL ON 2-YEAR SLOPES OF THE GROWTH CURVES OF STUDENT ENGAGEMENT (Grades 3–4 and Grades 6–7) AND INTERACTIONS WITH STUDENT GRADE LEVEL (Dependent Variable: Slope of the Growth Curve of Student Engagement [Teacher Report])

INDEPENDENT VARIABLES	R^2	INTERCEPT (Launch), β	STUDENT ENGAGEMENT INTERCEPT, β	GRADE LEVEL AND INTERACTIONS, β			3D-GRADE MODEL, LAUNCH, β	6TH-GRADE MODEL, LAUNCH, β
				Initial Grade 3 vs. 6	Launch × Grade Level 3 vs. 6	Student Engagement Intercept × Grade Level 3 vs. 6		
Control beliefs	.31	.39***	(.56)	−.01	−.30**	(−1.07)	.18***	.05†
Strategy:								
Effort	.29	.09	(.67)	−.01	−.12	(−1.14)	.02	−.05
Ability	.29	.05	(.68)	−.01	−.07	(−1.15)	.00	−.04
Powerful others	.31	−.35***	(.56)	.00	.26***	(−1.06)	−.21***	.00
Unknown	.29	.01	(.71)	−.01	−.07	(−1.20)	−.04	−.08*
Capacity:								
Effort	.30	.19*	(.62)	−.01	−.10	(−1.13)	.12**	.08***
Ability	.30	.30***	(.62)	.00	−.20*	(−1.13)	.16***	.08***
Powerful others	.30	.12	(.66)	−.01	−.08	(−1.15)	.08*	.02

NOTE.—Analyses were weighted by the number of times of measurement of teacher-reported student engagement. N ranged from 1,379 to 1,398. Third-grade model N ranged from 710 to 720. Sixth-grade model N ranged from 669 to 678.

* $p < .05$.
** $p < .01$.
*** $p < .001$.
† $p < .10$.

TABLE 39

THE CHANGE-TO-CHANGE EFFECT OF CHILDREN'S PERCEIVED CONTROL ON 2-YEAR SLOPES OF THE GROWTH CURVES OF STUDENT ENGAGEMENT (Grades 3–4 and Grades 6–7) AND INTERACTIONS WITH STUDENT GRADE LEVEL (Dependent Variable: Slope of the Growth Curve of Student Engagement [Teacher Report])

INDEPENDENT VARIABLES	R^2	SLOPE (Change to Change), β	STUDENT ENGAGEMENT INTERCEPT, β	GRADE LEVEL AND INTERACTIONS, β			3D-GRADE MODEL, CHANGE TO CHANGE, β	6TH-GRADE MODEL, CHANGE TO CHANGE, β
				Initial Grade 3 vs. 6	Change to Change × Grade Level 3 vs. 6	Student Engagement Intercept × Grade Level 3 vs. 6		
Control beliefs	.31	.27***	(.62)	−.01	−.15†	(−1.12)	.16***	.10***
Strategy:								
Effort	.29	.06	(.67)	−.01	−.06	(−1.15)	.02	−.02
Ability	.29	.05	(.67)	−.01	−.03	(−1.15)	.04	.00
Powerful others	.30	.18*	(.66)	.00	−.09	(−1.14)	.15***	.01
Unknown	.30	−.15†	(.70)	−.01	.08	(−1.17)	−.11**	.00
Capacity:								
Effort	.29	.13†	(.69)	−.01	−.11	(−1.17)	.07*	.00
Ability	.30	.08	(.65)	−.01	.00	(−1.12)	.09*	.07*
Powerful others	.31	−.13†	(.70)	−.01	.24***	(−1.19)	.03	.16***

NOTE.—Analyses were weighted by the number of times of measurement of teacher-reported student engagement. N ranged from 1,379 to 1,398. Third-grade model N ranged from 710 to 720. Sixth-grade model N ranged from 669 to 678.

* $p < .05$.
** $p < .01$.
*** $p < .001$.
† $p < .10$.

(relative to children initially in the sixth grade). In contrast, changes in Capacity beliefs were more important predictors of changes in engagement for older children (compared to younger children).

An examination of age interactions in the effects of individual beliefs (Tables 38 and 39) revealed the basis of these trends. Significant age changes were found in several of the predictors of individual differences in children's linear slopes of engagement. First, control beliefs exerted a stronger effect on children's engagement trajectories for younger (compared to older) children. Although significant at both ages, the launch and change-to-change effects were significantly greater for children whose trajectories began in the third than for those whose trajectories began in the sixth grade.

Second, younger children's engagement trajectories were shaped more by their strategy beliefs (relative to older children). For children initially in grade 3, trajectories of engagement across 2 school years were launched by initial beliefs about powerful others as a strategy and by changes in strategy beliefs about both powerful others and unknown causes. For older children, the only significant effect of strategy beliefs was a launch effect for unknown strategy beliefs.

Finally, capacity beliefs were important in launching and shaping children's 2-year trajectories of engagement. Capacity ability showed both launch and change-to-change effects; launch effects were significantly greater for younger compared to older children. Children's capacity beliefs for effort launched their 2-year engagement trajectories at both ages but showed significant change-to-change effects only for younger children. In contrast, children's capacity beliefs about powerful others exerted a significantly greater change-to-change effect for older (than for younger) children.

It was interesting to note that, in addition to the age differences in causal categories, there were also age differences in the kinds of beliefs that predicted patterns of engagement across time. Overall, third graders had more variables that launched the development of engagement than did sixth graders. Perhaps because third graders were nearer to the absolute beginning of their engagement trajectories (which presumably began in the first grade), early factors could exert a greater launch effect. It is possible that, once trajectories are well under way (as they are with, e.g., sixth graders), fewer variables can exert effects in shaping them.

Age Differences in Predictors of Two-Year Trajectories of Perceived Control

Analyses parallel to those described previously were completed with indicators of teacher context (ambient-level and change-to-change variables) as the independent variables and the 2-year slopes of different aspects of perceived control as the dependent variables (see Table 40). These analyses

TABLE 40

Unique Effects of Teacher Context Ambient Level and 2-Year Slopes on 2-Year Slopes of the Growth Curves of Aspects of Children's Perceived Control (Grades 3–4 and Grades 6–7)

Dependent Variables	R^2	Teacher Context Ambient Level, β	Teacher Context Slope; Change to Change, β	Dependent Variable Intercept, β	3d-Grade Model Ambient Level, β	3d-Grade Model Change to Change, β	6th-Grade Model Ambient Level, β	6th-Grade Model Change to Change, β
ConMax	.38	.30***	.34***	(−.47)	.32***	.29***	.35***	.41***
Promote	.27	.29***	.30***	(−.38)	.28***	.27***	.31***	.36***
Undermine	.41	−.23***	−.30***	(−.57)	−.20**	−.30***	−.27***	−.36***
Strategy	.10	.15***	.23***	(.08)	.13**	.21***	.13***	.31***
Capacity	.39	.30***	.36***	(−.49)	.24***	.37***	.40***	.40***
Control beliefs	.09	.08**	.22***	(.13)	.08†	.29***	.17***	.19***
Strategy:								
Effort	.08	.13***	.08**	(−.23)	.13**	.01	.16***	.17***
Ability	.09	−.08**	−.05†	(−.30)	−.12**	−.04	.02	−.08†
Powerful others	.39	−.23***	−.20***	(−.61)	−.17***	−.22***	−.12**	−.32***
Unknown	.31	−.16***	−.15***	(−.57)	−.17***	−.14***	−.09**	−.21***
Capacity:								
Effort	.24	.18***	.25***	(−.43)	.10†	.33***	.23***	.22***
Ability	.14	.12***	.27***	(−.24)	.04	.39***	.16***	.26***
Powerful others	.46	.41***	.31***	(−.58)	.31***	.32***	.53***	.39***

Note.—Analyses were weighted by the number of times of measurement of children's perceived control. Teacher context was reported by students. N ranged from 1,333 to 1,382. Third-grade model N ranged from 727 to 746. Sixth-grade model N ranged from 606 to 637.

** $p < .01$.

*** $p < .001$.

† $p < .10$.

showed a pattern similar to that for 5-year trajectories. Although significant main effects were found for almost all aspects of perceived control, teacher context had the strongest effects on individual differences in the development of children's strategy and capacity beliefs about powerful others.

At the same time, the patterns also showed one striking difference. In the 5-year trajectories of beliefs, change-to-change aspects of teacher context were (unexpectedly) found to be stronger predictors than ambient-level variables. However, in the 2-year trajectories of beliefs, ambient-level teacher context variables were consistently significant and occasionally more strongly related to control than change-to-change effects.

Of primary interest were differences in the relations between teacher context and trajectories of control as a function of grade level. These regressions were conducted separately for ambient level of teacher context (Table 41) and for change-to-change models (Table 42). In these analyses, significant age interaction terms for given aspects of perceived control indicated that predictors of the development of an aspect of perceived control differed as a function of children's grade (grades 3–4 as opposed to grades 6–7).

As can be seen in the fifth columns of Tables 41 and 42, several age interactions were found. They all took the same form: effects were more strongly pronounced for children who were initially in the third grade (compared to older children). However, follow-ups in which the effects of teacher context on trajectories of control were examined for each grade group separately (the last two columns of Tables 41 and 42) revealed that most of these age interactions were not of great substantive interest. For all change-to-change models, and for all the ambient-level models for capacity beliefs, the basis for the age differences was the same. Children from the two different grade groups grades 3–4 and grades 5–6) both showed significant effects; however, the coefficient for the younger age group was significantly greater than that for the older group. For example, the change-to-change effect of teacher context on children's trajectories of capacity effort beliefs was significant for both groups of children (βs = .38 and .23, p's < .001, for grades 3–4 and grades 5–6, respectively); however, the coefficient for the younger children was significantly greater (compared to that for older children). Likewise, the ambient-level effect of teacher context on trajectories of powerful others strategy beliefs was significant for both groups of children (βs = −.31 and −.12, p's < .01, for grades 3–4 and grades 5–6, respectively); however, the coefficient for the younger children was significantly lower (compared to that for older children).

However, in three cases, the significant differences between the coefficients for younger and older children seemed to carry substantive weight. All three cases were for ambient-level effects of teacher context, and, in all three cases, the trajectories were kinds of uncontrollable strategy beliefs. Significant differences were found between the betas for younger and older children,

TABLE 41

EFFECTS OF THE AMBIENT LEVEL OF TEACHER CONTEXT ON 2-YEAR SLOPES OF THE GROWTH CURVES OF CHILDREN'S PERCEIVED CONTROL (GRADES 3–4 AND GRADES 6–7) AND GRADE LEVEL INTERACTIONS

DEPENDENT VARIABLES	R^2	TEACHER CONTEXT AMBIENT LEVEL, β	DEPENDENT VARIABLE INTERCEPT, β	GRADE LEVEL AND INTERACTIONS, β			3D-GRADE MODEL, AMBIENT LEVEL, β	6TH-GRADE MODEL, AMBIENT LEVEL, β
				Initial Student Grade Level 3 vs. 6	Teacher Context Ambient Level × Grade Level 3 vs. 6	Dependent Variable Intercept × Grade Level 3 vs. 6		
ConMax	.34	.98***	(−1.45)	1.06***	−.97***	(.88)	.55***	.41***
Promote	.25	.88***	(−1.34)	.96***	−.88***	(.90)	.49***	.36***
Undermine	.37	−.76***	(−1.38)	−.86***	.79***	(.75)	−.42***	−.29***
Strategy	.17	.57***	(−1.21)	.77***	−.73***	(1.15)	.26***	.13**
Capacity	.33	.79***	(−1.37)	.64***	−.53***	(.74)	.56***	.47***
Control beliefs	.08	.01	(.74)	−.23	.28	(−.68)	.12*	.18***
Strategy:								
Effort	.14	.20*	(−1.01)	.17	−.12	(.81)	.13**	.15***
Ability	.15	−.38***	(−1.07)	−.59***	.59***	(.81)	−.14***	.02
Powerful others	.51	−.77***	(−1.85)	−1.09***	1.07***	(1.29)	−.31***	−.12**
Unknown	.33	−.65***	(−1.18)	−.94***	.90***	(.63)	−.26***	−.09**
Capacity:								
Effort	.21	.57***	(−1.07)	.57***	−.52***	(.58)	.35***	.25***
Ability	.08	.46***	(−.34)	.52***	−.47*	(.05)	.26***	.16***
Powerful others	.43	.64***	(−1.19)	.24	−.09	(.49)	.56***	.61***

NOTE.—Analyses were weighted by the number of times of measurement of children's perceived control. Teacher context was reported by students. N ranged from 1,333 to 1,382. Third-grade model N ranged from 727 to 746. Sixth-grade model N ranged from 606 to 637.

* $p < .05$.
** $p < .01$.
*** $p < .001$.

TABLE 42

EFFECTS OF THE 2-YEAR SLOPES OF TEACHER CONTEXT ON THE GROWTH CURVES OF CHILDREN'S PERCEIVED CONTROL (Grades 3–4 and Grades 6–7) AND GRADE LEVEL INTERACTIONS

| DEPENDENT VARIABLES | R^2 | TEACHER CONTEXT SLOPE (Change to Change), β | DEPENDENT VARIABLE INTERCEPT, β | GRADE LEVEL AND INTERACTIONS, β | | | 3D-GRADE MODEL, CHANGE TO CHANGE, β | 6TH-GRADE MODEL, CHANGE TO CHANGE, β |
				Initial Student Grade Level 3 vs. 6	Teacher Context Slope × Grade Level 3 vs. 6	Dependent Variable Intercept × Grade Level 3 vs. 6		
ConMax	.37	.82***	(−.84)	.00	−.39***	(.56)	.48***	.44***
Promote	.28	.77***	(−.88)	.00	−.38***	(.69)	.44***	.39***
Undermine	.42	−.71***	(−1.02)	.00	.34***	(.59)	−.41***	−.38***
Strategy	.20	.54***	(−1.02)	.00	−.27***	(1.04)	.29***	.31***
Capacity	.38	.76***	(−.89)	.00	−.30***	(.61)	.51***	.45***
Control beliefs	.11	.26**	(.69)	.01	−.05	(−.55)	.25***	.19***
Strategy:								
Effort	.14	.08	(−1.02)	.01	.03	(.85)	.08*	.17***
Ability	.15	−.25**	(−1.01)	.01	.17*	(.77)	−.11**	−.08*
Powerful others	.53	−.71***	(−1.64)	.01	.46***	(1.18)	−.32***	−.32***
Unknown	.33	−.53***	(−.98)	.00	.35***	(.50)	−.23***	−.21***
Capacity:								
Effort	.25	.68***	(−.73)	−.01	−.39***	(.40)	.38***	.23***
Ability	.14	.58***	(−.12)	.00	−.30***	(−.07)	.34***	.26***
Powerful others	.42	.69***	(−1.03)	.01	−.22***	(.73)	.50***	.47***

NOTE.—Analyses were weighted by the number of times of measurement of children's perceived control. Teacher context was reported by students. N ranged from 1,333 to 1,382. Third-grade model N ranged from 727 to 746. Sixth-grade model N ranged from 606 to 637.

* $p < .05$.
** $p < .01$.
*** $p < .001$.

133

respectively, for ability (βs $= -.14$, $p < .001$, and .02, N.S.), powerful others (βs $-.31$, $p < .001$, and $-.12$, $p < .01$), and unknown (βs $-.26$, $p < .001$, and $-.09$, $p < .01$). In each case, the effects for the younger children were significant at the .001 level, and the effects for the older children were either nonsignificant or significant at the .01 level. In general, teacher context was more important in supporting the slopes of 2-year trajectories of uncontrollable strategy beliefs for younger children.

Effects of Achievement on Two-Year Slopes of Perceived Control

In these analyses, we examined the effects of previous performance (for third graders, school grades up to grade 2; for sixth graders, school grades up to grade 5) on the development of different aspects of children's control. Main effects are summarized in Table 43. The effects of achievement on the development of control over 2 years looked similar to the effects over 5 years. Previous achievement had an effect on the development of children's beliefs about control, capacities for effort and ability, and unknown strategy beliefs. Children with higher previous grades continued to show more positive 2-year slopes of control beliefs and beliefs about capacity effort and ability; children with lower grades showed more maladaptive trajectories of beliefs about unknown strategies.

Unique Effects of Teacher Context and Achievement on Two-Year Slopes of Perceived Control

In the last set of regression analyses, we examined the unique effects of students' reports of teacher context and previous performance on the development of children's control. Unique main effects and interactions with age are summarized in Table 44 (ambient level of teacher context) and Table 45 (change to change). In these regressions, of interest was the interaction of the independent variables with initial grade, which would indicate that predictors of the development of perceived control differed as a function of children's grade (grades 3–4 as opposed to grades 6–7).

Examination of the unique main effects of teacher context (both ambient-level and change-to-change variables) and previous achievement on the development of different aspects of control shows that, for the most part, the effects of context and achievement were additive. Almost all the effects of students' ratings of teacher context remained significant, even when controlling for achievement; the same is true for the age interactions involving context.

An examination of the significant age interactions reveals several interesting effects. First, age differences in the effects of ambient level of teacher

TABLE 43

EFFECT OF STUDENT ACHIEVEMENT ON 2-YEAR SLOPES OF THE GROWTH CURVES OF CHILDREN'S PERCEIVED CONTROL (Grades 3–4 and Grades 6–7)

Dependent Variables	R^2	Average Achievement, β	Dependent Variable Intercept, β	3rd-Grade Model, Average Achievement, β	6th-Grade Model, Average Achievement, β
ConMax	.22	.24***	(−.50)	.20***	.30***
Promote	.15	.18***	(−.41)	.15*	.24**
Undermine	.32	−.25***	(−.60)	−.21***	−.29**
Strategy	.08	.24***	(−.25)	.23***	.23**
Capacity	.22	.22***	(−.50)	.16**	.31***
Control beliefs	.08	.29***	(−.02)	.19**	.38***
Strategy:					
Effort	.14	.13**	(−.37)	.15**	.09
Ability	.14	.03	(−.37)	−.02	.20**
Powerful others	.31	−.06	(−.57)	−.06	−.16*
Unknown	.39	−.25***	(−.64)	−.26***	−.18**
Capacity:					
Effort	.21	.20***	(−.50)	.19**	.20**
Ability	.06	.18***	(−.25)	.18**	.16*
Powerful others	.23	.11*	(−.49)	−.01	.30***

NOTE.—Analyses were weighted by the number of times of measurements of children's perceived control. Average achievement = average achievement prior to the 2-year trajectory. N ranged from 424 to 433. Third-grade model N = 236. Sixth-grade model N ranges from 188 to 197.

* $p < .05$.
** $p < .01$.
*** $p < .001$.

TABLE 44

UNIQUE EFFECTS OF THE AMBIENT LEVEL OF TEACHER CONTEXT AND STUDENT ACHIEVEMENT ON 2-YEAR SLOPES OF THE GROWTH CURVES OF CHILDREN'S PERCEIVED CONTROL (Grades 3–4 and Grades 6–7) AND GRADE LEVEL INTERACTIONS

					GRADE LEVEL AND INTERACTIONS, β							
									3D-Grade Model		6th-Grade Model	
DEPENDENT VARIABLES	R^2	TEACHER CONTEXT AMBIENT LEVEL, β	AVE. ACH., β	DEPENDENT VARIABLE INTERCEPT, β	Initial Student Grade Level 3 vs. 6	Teacher Context Ambient Level × Grade Level 3 vs. 6	Ave. Ach. × Grade Level 3 vs. 6	Dependent Variable Intercept × Grade Level 3 vs. 6	Teacher Context Ambient Level, β	Ave. Ach., β	Teacher Context Ambient Level, β	Ave. Ach., β
ConMax	.41	.72***	.11	(−1.56)	.26	−.40	.23	.77***	.52***	.18***	.51***	.31***
Promote	.35	.61***	.08	(−1.42)	.16	−.28	.14	.78***	.45***	.12*	.50***	.21**
Undermine	.43	−.50***	−.14	(−1.41)	−.16	.27	−.16	.63***	−.36***	−.18***	−.37***	−.29***
Strategy	.26	.37***	.29*	(−1.47)	.57†	−.37	−.21	1.24***	.20***	.19**	.17*	.21**
Capacity	.42	.55***	−.06	(−1.41)	−.42	−.02	.53*	.59***	.52***	.13*	.55***	.32***
Control beliefs	.15	−.15	−.17	(.51)	−1.52***	.76*	.90**	−.70***	.12	.19*	.29***	.37***
Strategy:												
Effort	.24	−.06	.25†	(−1.18)	−.10	.42	−.31	.84***	.13*	.07	.26***	.03
Ability	.26	−.41***	−.06	(−1.38)	−.87***	.67*	.19	1.04***	−.15*	.01	.08	.17*
Powerful others	.54	−.79***	.04	(−1.96)	−1.06***	1.20***	−.17	1.38***	−.30***	−.02	.05	−.17*
Unknown	.49	−.63***	−.45***	(−1.63)	−1.38***	.88***	.54*	.95***	−.26***	−.21***	−.09	−.17*
Capacity:												
Effort	.31	.32*	.18	(−1.20)	−.09	.09	.02	.51*	.33***	.18***	.41***	.20**
Ability	.09	.20	.18	(−.30)	.08	−.02	−.03	−.05	.18*	.16*	.20*	.16*
Powerful others	.47	.59***	−.31**	(−1.33)	−.51	−.07	.72**	.56***	.55***	−.05	.54***	.20**

NOTE.—Analyses were weighted by the number of times of measurement of children's perceived control. Teacher context was reported by students. Ave. ach. = average achievement prior to the 2-year trajectory. N ranged from 424 to 433. Third-grade model $N = 236$. Sixth-grade model N ranged from 188 to 197.

* $p < .05$.
** $p < .01$.
*** $p < .001$.
† $p < .10$.

TABLE 45

UNIQUE EFFECTS OF THE 2-YEAR SLOPES OF TEACHER CONTEXT AND STUDENT ACHIEVEMENT ON 2-YEAR SLOPES OF THE GROWTH CURVES OF CHILDREN'S PERCEIVED CONTROL (Grades 3–4 and Grades 6–7) AND GRADE LEVEL INTERACTIONS

		TEACHER CONTEXT SLOPE; CHANGE TO CHANGE, β	AVE. ACH., β	DEPENDENT VARIABLE INTERCEPT, β	GRADE LEVEL AND INTERACTIONS, β				3D-GRADE MODEL		6TH-GRADE MODEL	
DEPENDENT VARIABLES	R^2				Initial Student Grade Level 3 vs. 6	Teacher Context Slope × Grade Level 3 vs. 6	Ave. Ach. × Grade Level 3 vs. 6	Dependent Variable Intercept × Grade Level 3 vs. 6	Teacher Context Slope, β	Ave. Ach., β	Teacher Context Slope, β	Ave. Ach., β
ConMax	.43	.68***	.19	(−1.07)	−.03	−.28*	−.01	.64***	.42***	.17***	.43***	.20**
Promote	.36	.65***	.13	(−1.12)	−.09	−.29*	.01	.78***	.39***	.12*	.39***	.16*
Undermine	.49	−.56***	−.24*	(−1.17)	−.05	.20†	.11	.63***	−.36***	−.19***	−.41***	−.19**
Strategy	.28	.34*	.36**	(−1.37)	.28	−.11	−.34	1.21***	.21***	.20***	.33***	.16*
Capacity	.46	.60***	.06	(−1.06)	−.25	−.16	.19	.65***	.45***	.13*	.47***	.19***
Control beliefs	.14	.22	−.14	(.38)	−.75**	−.04	.82**	−.43***	.22***	.19**	.16*	.35***
Strategy:												
Effort	.24	−.15	.27*	(−1.26)	.29	.27*	−.32	.96***	.02	.15*	.26***	.05
Ability	.25	−.33*	−.13	(−1.33)	−.31	.25†	.32	1.00***	−.13*	−.02	−.03	.20**
Powerful others	.57	−.77***	−.01	(−1.68)	.08	.53***	−.07	1.18***	−.32***	−.03	−.24***	−.13†
Unknown	.49	−.46***	−.55***	(−1.39)	−.62**	.30**	.68**	.81***	−.20***	−.25***	−.22***	−.14*
Capacity:												
Effort	.31	.54***	.21	(−.94)	.02	−.27*	−.08	.48***	.32***	.17**	.24***	.15*
Ability	.14	.38**	.24	(−.17)	.17	−.12	−.19	−.07	.27***	.17**	.28***	.11
Powerful others	.50	.63***	−.29**	(−1.14)	−.69**	−.16	.72***	.76***	.48***	−.04	.48***	.21***

NOTE.—Analyses were weighted by the number of times of measurement of children's perceived control. Teacher context was reported by students. Ave. ach. = average achievement prior to the 2-year trajectory. N ranged from 424 to 433. Third-grade model N = 236. Sixth-grade model N ranged from 188 to 197.

* p < .05.
** p < .01.
*** p < .001.
† p < .10.

137

context on the development of children's beliefs about uncontrollable strategies were magnified when the effects of previous achievement were controlled. For children initially in grade 3, ambient level of teacher context was a significantly greater predictor of the trajectories of strategy beliefs for ability ($\beta = -.15$, $p < .05$), powerful others ($\beta = -.30$, $p < .001$), and unknown ($\beta = -.26$, $p < .001$) than it was for older children (βs $= .08$, $.05$, and $-.09$, N.S., for ability, powerful others, and unknown, respectively).

Second, the effects of achievement on the development of perceived control differed by grade for three sets of beliefs. As predicted, previous achievement was a significantly greater unique predictor of trajectories of control beliefs for the older (than for the younger) children. Unexpectedly, previous achievement was also a greater unique predictor of changes in capacity beliefs about powerful others for the older (than for the younger) children. In fact, achievement was *not* a significant predictor of the development of capacity powerful others beliefs for younger children. It seems possible that, for older children, good school performance is one route toward perceiving oneself as increasingly effective in obtaining teachers' approval and liking. Although this effect was unpredicted, it was consistent with the general notion that individual performance would become a stronger predictor of the development of control as children became older.

The final age difference was not predicted and also was not consistent with the general viewpoint that individual achievement would be a stronger predictor of control for older children. It was found for unknown strategy beliefs. In this effect, achievement was a greater unique predictor of the development of unknown strategy beliefs for younger (than for older) children. This effect could reflect the greater centrality of unknown strategy beliefs in young children's views of control. For unknown, age interactions were significant and indicated that effects were stronger for younger than for older children. However, follow-ups separately by age revealed that the unique effects of achievement on the development of unknown strategy beliefs were also significant for older children.

Summary of the Results on Age Differences in the Predictors of Two-Year Trajectories

Although exploratory, these analyses were informative, more in terms of their overall pattern than in terms of any specific age interaction. In general, these models differed from the analyses of predictors of 5-year trajectories in that 2-year trajectories were not predicted solely by change-to-change models; in addition, both launch and ambient-level models also provided good accounts of the predictors of differential development.

In terms of the predictors of individual differences in the development of children's engagement, an overall age trend was found in which strategy beliefs were more important in launching younger children's engagement trajectories (compared to those of older children), whereas capacity beliefs were more important in shaping the development of engagement for older than for younger children. When individual beliefs were considered, both similarities and age differences in the effects of control on children's trajectories of engagement were suggested. For children of both ages, 2-year trajectories of engagement were launched and shaped by control beliefs and by capacity beliefs for ability. Beginning at both the third and the sixth grades, children who showed initially higher beliefs in their control and ability were more likely to show adaptive trends in their classroom engagement over the subsequent 2 years, whereas children who initially doubted their control and ability were more likely to show a pattern of increasing disaffection. Moreover, individual differences in changes in children's beliefs about control and ability also predicted changes in their engagement. These effects were more pronounced for younger children.

In addition, for younger children, trajectories of engagement were more closely related to strategy beliefs for external causes (powerful others and unknown) and capacity beliefs for effort. For older children, the only strategy beliefs that were significantly related to trajectories of engagement were unknown strategy beliefs. Individual differences in unknown strategy beliefs at the transition to middle school at the beginning of the sixth grade launched children's engagement trajectories for the next 2 years. For older children, these trajectories were also launched by effort capacity beliefs and shaped by capacity beliefs for powerful others. Relative to the younger children, older children showed a significantly greater change-to-change effect between their capacity to influence powerful others and their engagement over 2 years.

In terms of the effects of teacher context and achievement on individual differences in trajectories of control, exploratory analyses detected several interesting effects. First, at all ages, teacher context seemed to exert its effects on the development of children's beliefs about powerful others—both strategy and capacity beliefs. In addition, teacher context had a strong effect on the development of children's beliefs about their effort capacity and unknown strategy beliefs. Children who reported a supportive teacher context were more likely to show adaptive trajectories of beliefs about their capacities to exert effort and influence powerful others and less likely to develop maladaptive trajectories of beliefs that powerful others were the only route to school success and that the causes of school performance were unknown. For 2-year trajectories of control, both ambient-level and change-to-change models of the relations between teacher context and the development of these aspects of control were consistent with the data.

In terms of age differences, only one pattern was found for teacher context. In the ambient-level models, teacher context (students' reports) had a more pronounced effect on the development of beliefs about uncontrollable strategies (ability, powerful others, and unknown) for the younger children. These age differences were even more pronounced in regressions in which the effects of previous achievement were controlled.

In terms of the effects of achievement on the development of control, analyses of the 2-year trajectories revealed findings similar to those obtained from analyses of the 5-year trajectories—that achievement exerted effects on the development of children's beliefs about their control and capacity ability. Age differences in the effects of achievement showed, as predicted, that individual performance was a more important predictor of the development of control for older children, although these effects were not extremely strong. For older (compared to younger) children, previous achievement was a greater (positive) predictor of children's 2-year trajectories of beliefs about control and also about powerful others capacity. For younger (compared to older) children, previous achievement was also a greater (negative) predictor of children's 2-year trajectories of beliefs about unknown strategy beliefs.

VI. DISCUSSION

A great deal is known about the impact of individual differences in children's perceived control on their academic performance. Much has also been discovered about normative developmental changes in the processes by which children perceive and interpret control experiences. However, this *Monograph* describes one of the few studies that examines the interaction of individual differences and developmental change (Brandtstaedter, 1984; Gatz & Karel, 1993; Rholes et al., 1980; Shell et al., 1995; Stipek & MacIver, 1989). Taken together, the findings reveal much about the development of children's perceived control, its consequences for children's engagement in the classroom, and its antecedents in academic performance and in interactions with teachers. We summarize and integrate the findings of the study, analyze its limitations, and then discuss its implications for theories of control, for research examining both individual differences and development, and for interventions designed to optimize control and engagement.

INTEGRATION OF THE RESULTS ANALYZING INDIVIDUAL DIFFERENCES AND DEVELOPMENTAL CHANGE

The research had two main goals. First, we wanted to examine the antecedents and consequences of individual differences in perceived control in the academic domain in middle childhood and to investigate whether these antecedents and consequences changed for children of different ages. Second, we wanted to examine individual differences in the developmental trajectories of children's perceived control and to determine whether their relations to teacher context and students' engagement and performance could be best characterized as *launch, ambient level,* or *change to change.* Additional exploratory analyses investigated whether the predictors of individual differences in development differed for children of different ages.

In examining these issues within the longitudinal data set, different analytic procedures were used to address different facets of these questions successively. Structural equation modeling was used to test mediational hypotheses; time-lagged multiple regressions examined whether individual links were consistent with causal predictions; concurrent multiple regressions determined the unique contributions of different aspects of control and examined age interactions in these relations; analyses of growth curves used HLM to identify normative trends for context, self, and action over 5 years; and individual estimates output from these models were used to examine the predictors of individual differences in developmental trajectories. The findings from each of these analyses are presented in Table 46 and summarized in chart form in Figure 27; both the table and the figure indicate which findings were consistent with hypotheses and which were unexpected.

Cycles of Beliefs and Performance

As a first step, we wanted to examine the cyclic model of beliefs and performance in the academic domain during the elementary school years. We wondered whether the longitudinal data would be consistent with cycles in which children starting out "rich" in self-confidence and achievement in the third grade would get "richer" over time and children beginning their school careers "poor," that is, low in self-efficacy and academic attainment, would become "poorer" from the third to the seventh grade.

Findings were consistent with the motivational model of context, self, action, and outcomes (Connell & Wellborn, 1991; Skinner, 1991, 1995). Students' reports of teacher context predicted children's perceptions of control, which in turn predicted children's engagement versus disaffection in the classroom; engagement had an effect on children's actual performance, which in turn altered their subsequent perceptions of control.

Specifically, the structural equation modeling and time-lagged and concurrent multiple regressions indicated that children who experienced more structured and warm interactions with their teachers were more likely to believe that they could produce success and avoid failure in school, whereas children whose interactions with teachers were experienced as cold and inconsistent were more likely to doubt their own capacities and to expect success and failure to be contingent on powerful others and luck or simply on unknown factors. Although both structured and warm interactions with teachers were positively related to children's beliefs about their own capacities, children's strategy beliefs seemed to be especially shaped by the amount of structure that teachers provided; children who experienced teachers as chaotic and noncontingent were more likely to endorse *external* factors (such as powerful others, luck, and unknown) as causes of their success or failure in school.

In turn, children's convictions about the causes of school performance

TABLE 46

FINDINGS ABOUT INDIVIDUAL DIFFERENCES AND DEVELOPMENT

FINDINGS ABOUT INDIVIDUAL DIFFERENCES

Functional Model: Mediational Findings (from Structural Equation Modeling)

1.* Children's perceived control mediated the effects of teacher context on children's subsequent engagement in the classroom.
2.* Children's engagement mediated the effects of their perceived control on school performance.
3.* Children's school performance fed back into their perceptions of control.

Functional Model: Findings Consistent with a Causal Interpretation
(from Time-Lag Regressions)

4.* Teacher context (structure and involvement combined) predicted changes in children's perceptions of control from the fall to the spring.
5.* Children's perceptions of control predicted changes in their engagement in the classroom from the fall to the spring.
6.* Children's school performances predicted changes in their perceptions of control from the fall to the spring.

Effects of Context and Performance on Different Aspects of Control
(from Multiple Regressions)

7. Teacher involvement and structure (combined) showed unique effects on all aspects of children's perceived control, especially powerful others strategy and capacity beliefs; there were also strong effects on unknown strategy beliefs and control and capacity beliefs.
8. Children's academic performance showed unique feedback effects on all aspects of their perceived control (except strategy and capacity luck). Strongest feedback effects were found on control and on capacity effort and ability beliefs.

Effects of Different Aspects of Perceived Control on Engagement (from Correlations and Multiple Regressions)

9.* Children's engagement was predicted uniquely and positively by beliefs in control and capacities.
10.* Children's engagement was undermined by beliefs in "external" strategies (including powerful others, luck, and unknown factors).
11. Beliefs in *effort* as a strategy:
   a)* were positively correlated with beliefs about control and capacities;
   b) were positively correlated with ability strategy beliefs;
   c) were not related to external strategy beliefs (these relations became more negative with age);
   d)* were positive correlates of engagement and grades;
   e)* *showed a weak positive unique contribution to engagement overall when controlling for other beliefs.*
12. Beliefs in *ability* as a strategy:
   a)* were positively related to beliefs about effort as a strategy (this relation decreased linearly with age);
   b) were also positively related to beliefs about "external" strategies (powerful others, luck, and unknown) and negatively related to control and capacity beliefs;
   c) *were negatively predicted by teacher context;*
   d) *were weakly positively predicted by grades;*
   e) *were weak negative correlates of engagement;*
   f)* showed no unique effects on engagement overall.

TABLE 46 (*Continued*)

Functional Model: Age Differences in Effects of Control on Engagement
(from Age Interactions from Multiple Regressions)

13.* Control beliefs made a unique contribution to engagement for children all across the age range.

14.* Not only strategy but also *capacity* beliefs showed different unique effects depending on the age of the child:

    a)* For the youngest children (ages 8 and 9), beliefs about effort, not as a strategy, but as a *capacity* as well as unknown strategy beliefs were stronger unique predictors of engagement.

    b)* For the oldest children (ages 12 and 13), beliefs about ability, not as a strategy, but as a *capacity* were a stronger predictor of engagement.

    c) *In addition, beliefs about capacity powerful others were a unique significant predictor of children's engagement; unknown strategy beliefs also became significant again.*

    d) Age differences in luck as a unique predictor could not be tested.

Functional Model: Age Differences in Effects of Context on Control (from Age Interactions in the Multiple Regressions)

15. *Teacher context did not become less important to children's perceived control. Teacher context became increasingly important to beliefs about effort strategy from grade 5 to grade 7.*

16. Predictions about the differential effects of teacher involvement and structure could not be tested (owing to their high intercorrelation).

Functional Model: Age Differences in Effects of Performance on Control
(from Age Interactions in the Path Analyses and Multiple Regressions)

17.* Children's academic performances fed back to perceptions of control all across the age range.

18.* Performance showed an increasingly stronger unique feedback effect on capacity ability beliefs from grade 3 to grade 7.

FINDINGS ABOUT INDIVIDUAL DIFFERENCES IN DEVELOPMENT

Normative Changes in Context, Self, Action, and Outcomes from Age 8 to Age 13
(from Growth Curve Analyses and Dependent *t* Tests)

19. *Engagement did not decline steadily over this age range. It showed a curvilinear relation with age, remaining relatively steady and even increasing until the spring of grade 5 and then following the transition to middle school, showing more decline.*

20. *Teacher context did decline over age, but a distinct pattern of within-year declines was accompanied by slight recovery between years in grades 3, 4, and 5; however, starting between grades 5 and 6, no more between-year recoveries were seen, and context declined steadily.*

21. Different aspects of perceived control showed different developmental trajectories:

    a)* Overall, profiles of control (ConMax) showed a curvilinear relation with age, increasing slightly until the fall of grade 5, and then declining sharply.

    b)* Control and capacity beliefs remained relatively stable, especially control. All capacity beliefs declined slightly, the sharpest decline being for capacity luck.

    c) *Strategy beliefs did not seem to become more differentiated from each other over time:*

        i)* Strategy effort beliefs were high and stable.

        ii) *Strategy ability beliefs were lower but also stable; they did not decline starting in fifth grade.*

        iii) *Strategy beliefs for powerful others and luck did decline more rapidly and starting earlier; but they began to increase again in grade 5.*

        iv)* Strategy unknown did decline and did increase again (but only slightly) starting about grade 5.

        v) *Strategy beliefs for both powerful others and unknown showed some within-year improvements (declines) in grades 3 and 4, accompanied by between-year relapses for grades 3, 4, and 5.*

TABLE 46 (*Continued*)

Predictors of Individual Differences in Development (from Multiple Regressions
on Individual Estimates of Growth Curve Parameters)

Overall, They Will Be the Same as Predictors of Individual Differences

22.* The development of perceived control across 5 years was promoted by a more supportive teacher context and higher individual academic performances.

23.* Trajectories of teacher context uniquely predicted trajectories of all aspects of control, and previous academic performance uniquely predicted control and capacity
ability *as well as strategy beliefs for luck and unknown*. The development of powerful
others strategy and capacity were predicted only by teacher context.

24.* The development of engagement across 5 years was promoted by control and capacity beliefs and undermined by strategy beliefs about "external" causes (powerful others, luck, and unknown factors).

Comparison of Models

25. Ambient level *and* launch *models could not be compared (owing to the high correlations between average levels and intercepts).*

26.* Previous academic performance (grades prior to the third grade) *launched* individual trajectories of perceived control.

27. Not only was *ambient level* of context likely to support individual trajectories of perceived control; *in addition, unique (and often stronger) effects for* change-to-change
variables were also found.

28. *Stronger effects of ambient level of teacher context were found on the development of external
strategy beliefs for boys.*

29.* The relation between trajectories of perceived control and engagement was more
consistent with a *change-to-change* model; *however, some aspects of perceived control (especially external strategy beliefs) were also found to* launch *engagement trajectories*.

30. *Stronger effects on the development of engagement were found for* unknown strategy beliefs
for boys *and for* effort strategy beliefs for girls.

Predictors of Individual Differences in Development: Age Differences
(from Age Interactions in Multiple Regressions on Individual Estimates
of Parameters for 2-Year Growth Curves)

Effects of Teacher Context and Performance on the Development of Perceived
Control

31.* Both teacher involvement and structure (combined) and previous performance
predicted individual differences in 2-year trajectories of control. As with 5-year
trajectories, 2-year trajectories of teacher context uniquely predicted trajectories
of all aspects of control; in addition, performance uniquely predicted control and
ability capacity beliefs as well as strategy beliefs for luck and unknown.

32. *The development of powerful others strategy and capacity beliefs were predicted only by teacher
context.*

33. *Ambient level of teacher context was a stronger predictor of the development of uncontrollable
strategy beliefs for the youngest children (relative to the oldest children).*

34.* Achievement was a stronger predictor of the development of control and capacity
ability for older than for younger children. *Achievement was a stronger predictor of the
development of unknown strategy beliefs for younger than for older children.*

35. *Predictions about the differential effects of teacher involvement and structure could not be
tested (owing to their high intercorrelation).*

TABLE 46 (*Continued*)

Effects of Control on the Development of Engagement

36.* Control, capacity, and unknown strategy beliefs predicted individual differences in the development of engagement across 2 years. All children's engagement slopes were launched and shaped by their control and ability capacity beliefs.

37.* Relative to the oldest children, the youngest children's 2-year trajectories of engagement were launched more strongly by their beliefs in powerful others as a strategy. (*Unknown strategies were not a stronger predictor of the development of engagement at this age.*)

38. Relative to the youngest children, the oldest children's trajectories of engagement were influenced more strongly by trajectories of their beliefs in their capacity to influence powerful others. (*Ability strategy was not a stronger predictor at this age.*)

Comparison of Models

39. Compared to the 5-year trajectories, 2-year trajectories were more often predicted by *launch* variables.

40. More launch predictors were also found for 2-year trajectories starting closer to their absolute beginning (the fall of grade 3 vs. the fall of grade 6).

NOTE.—Findings largely or wholly consistent with hypotheses are marked by an asterisk. Unexpected findings and findings that contradict hypothesis are given in italics.

and about their own capacities to access those causes predicted their emotions and behavior in the classroom. Children with profiles reflecting high control were more likely to exert effort, pay attention, and persist in the face of failure, remaining optimistic and interested in academic activities. In contrast, children who perceived school outcomes as due to factors beyond their control and who doubted their own capacities were more likely to give up in the face of challenges, to become discouraged, anxious, and passive, and to simply go through the motions of school participation.

Not surprisingly, these differential patterns of action also produced different kinds of academic performances, with engaged children succeeding and disaffected children doing more poorly in school. These academic outcomes, in turn, influenced children's perceptions of control and especially their estimates of overall control, of their own ability, and of their capacity to exert effort. Hence, the very performances that were created in part by children's differential beliefs and patterns of action in the classroom were used to confirm these initial perceptions. This general picture of cycles of beliefs and performance (graphically depicted in Figure 28) is consistent with a body of research examining the effects of perceived control in the classroom (Schmitz & Skinner, 1993) as well as in other settings (for a review, see Skinner, 1995).

Beliefs-Performance Cycles and the Development of Individual Differences

As predicted, the effects of these cycles were not limited to concurrent beliefs and engagement or even change over a school year. They extended across the elementary school years. For each link in the cyclic model, we

Functional Model			
	Teacher Context to Control	Control to Engagement	Engagement to Performance	Performance to Control
Structural Equation Modeling	Control mediated effects of context on subsequent engagement.	Engagement mediated effects of control on performance.	Engagement predicted performance.	Performance had an effect on subsequent perceived control.
Time-lag Regression	Teacher context predicted changes in control.	Control predicted changes in engagement.		Performance predicted changes in control.
Multiple Regression	Teacher context especially strong to control, capacities, and external strategies.	Control and capacity beliefs promoted engagement. External strategies undermined engagement.		Performance especially fed back to control and capacity effort and ability. It also had an effect on external strategy beliefs.
Age Interactions	*Teacher context a stronger predictor of effort strategy beliefs as children go from grades 5 to 7.*	Strategy and *Capacity* Beliefs Youngest: *Capacity* effort and unknown. Oldest: *Capacity* ability and powerful others.		Performance had a stronger effect for older children, especially on their ability capacity beliefs.

Developmental Model			
	Teacher Context to Control	Control to Engagement	Engagement to Performance	Performance to Control
Group Growth Curves	Teacher context declines: *regular within year declines and between year recoveries (grades 3, 4, 5). Then declines.*	Control and capacity beliefs high and stable. Strategy and capacity luck decreases. Effort strategy high and stable. Ability strategy lower and stable. Powerful others and unknown strategies lower and decreasing until grade 6, then increases.	Engagement stable; decline starting at transition to middle school.	
Individual Growth Curves	Ambient Level *and Change-to-Change* Model Slope and average teacher context uniquely predicted development of control.	*Launch and* Change-to-change Model Changes in control predicted changes in engagement. *External strategy beliefs launched engagement.*		Launch Model Early performance influenced development of control.
Multiple Regressions of Predictors of Individual Growth Curves	*Development of powerful others strategy and capacity predicted only by teacher context.*	Development of engagement launched by external strategy beliefs. Improvements in engagement predicted by improvements in control and capacities. Declines in engagement predicted by increases in external strategies.		Early performance especially important to development of control, ability capacity, *strategy for luck and unknown.*
Age Interactions in Predictors of Individual Growth Curves	Ambient level of teacher context predicts development of beliefs about uncontrollable strategies more strongly for youngest and oldest children.	Two-year engagement slopes launched by control and capacity beliefs and shaped by capacity ability and unknown strategy beliefs. Youngest children's engagement launched more by powerful others strategies. Oldest children's engagement shaped more by changes in capacity powerful others.		Previous grades a stronger predictor of the development of control and capacity beliefs about powerful others for older children. Previous grades a stronger predictor of the development of unknown strategy beliefs for younger children.

FIGURE 27.—Summary of findings about individual differences and development. Findings largely or wholly consistent with hypotheses are printed in regular type. Unexpected findings are in italics.

found evidence that antecedents both launched and shaped individual differences in developmental trajectories over the 5 years examined in the study, from the third to the seventh grade.

Effects of Perceived Control on the Development of Engagement

Children's perceptions of control predicted individual differences in their 5-year trajectories of engagement. Trajectories of engagement were

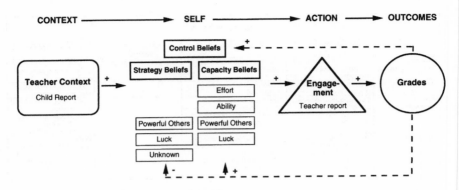

FIGURE 28.—A summary of the findings for beliefs-performance cycles from Tables 12, 13, and 16 above. Dashed lines are feedback loops.

launched by students' early beliefs about external causes as strategies for success and failure in school, including powerful others, luck, and unknown factors. Children who, at the beginning of third grade, reported that the causes of school performance were more external were more likely to develop maladaptive patterns of increasing disaffection in the classroom as their trajectories unfolded across 5 subsequent years.

More central as predictors of engagement trajectories, however, were *trajectories* of perceived control. Children whose trajectories of perceived control remained high or even increased slightly over time also sustained their initially high levels of engagement, whereas children whose perceived control was declining from third to seventh grade showed corresponding patterns of deteriorating engagement in the classroom. When children were selected on the basis of their trajectories of perceived control, and when the average engagement curves were plotted for children in the highest and the lowest 10% of control profiles, the engagement curves of the two groups did not touch over the 5 years of the study; in fact, they became increasingly divergent starting in about the fifth grade.

Individual differences in the development of control and capacity beliefs were especially strong predictors of corresponding trajectories of engagement. And individual differences in the development of external strategy beliefs were especially strong predictors of declines in engagement across 5 years. An interesting pattern of sex differences was also found. Effort strategy beliefs were a stronger predictor of the development of engagement for girls than for boys; however, unknown strategy beliefs were a stronger predictor of the development of engagement for boys than for girls.

These findings suggest that individual perceptions of perceived control

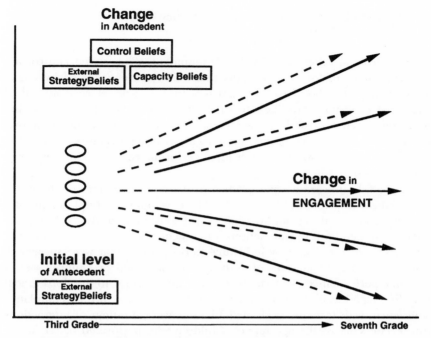

Perceived Control to Engagement
LAUNCH and CHANGE-TO-CHANGE MODELS

FIGURE 29.—A summary of the findings of the analyses of the effects of children's perceived control on individual differences in the development of their engagement (from Table 25 above).

laid down by the third grade, especially perceptions that reflect a pessimistic view about the strategies needed to succeed in school, can shape the development of children's engagement for years to come. In addition, the significant change-to-change relations are consistent with the notion of perceived control and engagement as parts of dynamic cycles in which perceived control influences engagement and is in turn influenced by the performances that result. This pattern is pictured graphically in Figure 29. The findings are all the more striking because developmental trends of engagement for individual children were composed of ratings from (up to) three different teachers in as many years and were nevertheless systematically related to individual differences in the self-reports of children.

Effects of Context and Achievement on the Development of Perceived Control

If individual differences in the development of perceived control are such central predictors of the paths that children's engagement will take across their early school years, then it is natural to wonder what individual and social conditions are likely to foster the optimal development of children's perceived control. In these analyses, we considered two potential predictors: children's reports of their teachers as providing structure and involvement and children's own prior individual performance in school (as indexed by their school grades).

Indeed, both were unique predictors of the development of children's perceived control from age 8 to age 13. The development of optimal profiles of perceived control, starting in grade 3 and continuing to the end of grade 7, was promoted both by interactions with teachers who were experienced as warm and structured and by individual performances that were successful. Children's 5-year trajectories of control were launched by children's early academic performances, as indexed by their grades prior to the third grade. In addition, children's trajectories of control were shaped by their cumulative experiences with teachers (as indexed by the average ratings of interactions with teachers across the age range). Children who performed better in the second grade and who had consistently more supportive interactions with their teachers were more likely to show positive trajectories of control from grade 3 to grade 7; in contrast, children who initially performed poorly and who reported nonsupportive interactions with teachers showed negative trajectories of perceived control across this age range.

The launch effects for initial achievement seemed to be played out as expected through the effects of early performance on the trajectories of children's ability capacity and control beliefs. In addition, poor performance prior to the third grade also predicted maladaptive trajectories of luck and unknown strategies. Children who started off with higher school grades showed more positive trajectories in the development of their convictions in their own control and ability; however, children who started out with lower grades came increasingly to believe that their school successes and failures were the result of luck and unknown factors. These findings are depicted graphically in Figure 30.

Children's experiences of their interactions with teachers seemed to play a role in the development of many aspects of their perceived control. Not surprisingly, children's reports of teacher context were the only strong unique predictors of the development of their beliefs about powerful others as a strategy and a capacity. Interestingly, the effects of teacher context were more pronounced for boys and affected the development of boys' beliefs about the effectiveness of "external" strategies more strongly. Boys who re-

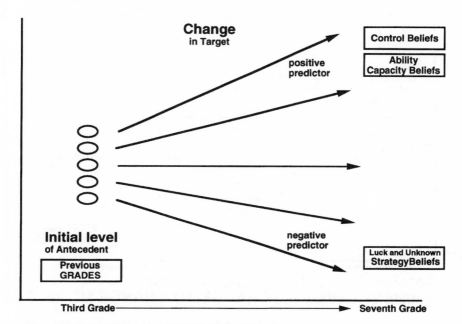

Grades to Perceived Control
LAUNCH MODEL

FIGURE 30.—A summary of the findings of the analyses of the unique effects of children's previous achievement on individual differences in the development of their perceived control (from Table 28 above). The effects of early grades on the development of effort strategy beliefs were significant for girls only. The effects of early grades on the development of unknown strategy beliefs were significant for boys only.

ported nonsupportive interactions with teachers were more likely to show maladaptive trajectories of control that emphasized the role of powerful others, luck, and unknown factors as causes of success and failure in school.

Throughout the age range examined in this study, namely, grades 3–7, teacher context also seemed to exert strong change-to-change effects on the development of children's control. Trajectories of context showed strong influences on all aspects of children's control beliefs, continuing to do so even when controlling for either of the other antecedent variables (children's "ambient level" of support from teachers or children's initial grades).

As mentioned briefly in Chapter V above, one explanation for the relatively strong, although unpredicted, effect of *changes* in teacher context on the development of perceived control refers to the normative pattern of change in children's experiences of their interactions with teachers. In general, children reported that these interactions became relatively *less* structured and involved over time. Hence, in addition to the overall average level

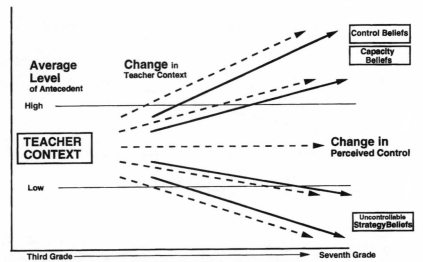

Teacher Context to Perceived Control
AMBIENT LEVEL and CHANGE-TO-CHANGE MODELS

FIGURE 31.—A summary of the findings of the analyses of the unique effects of teacher context on individual differences in the development of children's perceived control (from Table 26 above). The effects of ambient level of teacher context on the development of external strategy beliefs were greater for boys than for girls.

of support, children's experience of teachers as maintaining or decreasing their support over time was critical. No matter how high support was on the average, children's control declined when they experienced their interactions with teachers as deteriorating. A summary of these findings is presented graphically in Figure 31.

Age Differences in the Operation of the Beliefs-Performance Cycles

As a second step, we wanted to examine how the nature of beliefs-performance cycles might change as children developed cognitively and as they negotiated the transition to middle school in the sixth grade. We hypothesized that three characteristics of beliefs-performance cycles might change with age. The first was the kinds of beliefs that regulate engagement. We suggested that children's beliefs about effort and unknown causes might be more important at the youngest ages, whereas, when children grow older, beliefs about powerful others and ability may become successively more important predictors of their engagement in the classroom.

The second characteristic predicted to change with age was the extent to which cycles are open to influence from the outside, in this case from the context provided by teachers. We expected teacher context to be more important to the development of younger children's perceived control. The third aspect of beliefs-performance cycles hypothesized to change with age was the extent to which perceived control is tied to previous school performance. We expected that individual performances would exert a stronger feedback effect on the development of older (compared to younger) children's perceived control and that the effects of individual achievement would come to be increasingly focused on children's beliefs about their own ability. These hypotheses received only partial support.

Age Differences in the Effects of Perceived Control on Individual Differences and the Development of Engagement

The multiple regressions and exploratory analyses of 2-year trajectories did indeed reveal age differences in the kinds of beliefs that regulated children's engagement in the classroom in the third and the sixth grades. Relative to the older children, the youngest children's engagement was more strongly positively predicted by their beliefs about their own capacity to exert effort and more strongly negatively predicted by strategy beliefs organized around powerful others and unknown causes. In contrast, for the oldest (relative to the youngest) children, capacity beliefs were stronger predictors of subsequent engagement, especially beliefs about their own ability. In addition, for the older (compared to the younger) children, convictions about their capacity to influence powerful others emerged as a stronger predictor of engagement.

As expected, these age differences in the kinds of beliefs that regulate perceived control did not affect only children's concurrent levels of engagement in the classroom. Exploratory analyses revealed age differences in the predictors of children's engagement across 2 successive school years. These analyses compared the predictors of individual differences in the development of engagement during two points in its development: (1) from grade 3 to grade 4, when children were near the beginning of their school career and engagement was high and stable, and (2) from grade 6 to grade 7, when children had just completed the transition to middle school and engagement was declining.

Age differences in the predictors of 2-year trajectories of engagement suggested that, to some extent, the same beliefs that were central in predicting individual differences were also central in predicting developmental change. For the youngest children, engagement was launched more by strategy beliefs (relative to the older children), whereas capacity beliefs were more important in shaping trajectories of engagement for older (relative to younger) children.

Also similar to the concurrent effects, the development of younger children's engagement was predicted by their capacity effort and powerful others strategy beliefs; significant launch and change-to-change relations were found for both beliefs. For the older children, launch and change-to-change relations were found for powerful others capacity beliefs. And, for children of both ages, just as with individual differences in engagement, the development of engagement over 2 years was launched by control beliefs and predicted by changes in these beliefs. However, unlike the individual differences analyses, there was no increase with age in the importance of ability capacity beliefs as a predictor of the development of engagement. Ability capacity beliefs showed both launch and change-to-change effects for children's 2-year trajectories of engagement from third to fourth as well as from sixth to seventh grade.

Age Differences in the Unique Effects of Academic Performance on Individual Differences and the Development of Perceived Control

At the same time that children's beliefs about their capacities became more important in regulating their engagement in school, individual differences in school performance increased in importance as a source of information about control in general and one's own ability in particular. The feedback loop from grades to subsequent perceived control was more pronounced for seventh graders. At each age, individual performance (as indexed by school grades) had an effect on perceptions of control. However, the reciprocal effect of performance on beliefs was stronger for seventh graders than for third or fifth graders, suggesting that individual performance plays a more important role in the construction of control beliefs as children enter middle school.

At the same time, feedback effects from performance were being focused more narrowly on convictions about ability. At all ages, actual school success predicted higher beliefs about control and capacity effort, and poorer previous school performance predicted higher beliefs in external strategies. However, in addition, the feedback effect of previous performance on capacity beliefs about ability was found to increase linearly with age. This effect was not significant for third graders, but, by the time children reached the seventh grade, capacity ability registered the highest single feedback effect from achievement. At these older ages, children who earned lower grades were more likely to doubt, not only their capacity to exert effort, but also their own ability.

This pattern of age differences was also carried through, to some extent, in the effects of previous performance on the development of individual differences in perceived control. Older children (compared to the younger children) showed heightened effects of previous individual achievement on the development of their perceived control over 2 years, specifically, on the development of their control beliefs and of beliefs about their capacity to influence teachers. In addition, for the younger (relative to the older) children, poor previous individual achievement exerted a stronger effect on the development of unknown strategy beliefs. This latter effect was surprising since we did not expect individual performance to have a stronger effect on any aspect of perceived control for younger children. However, it is consistent with the overall notion that unknown strategy beliefs are a central aspect of control for younger children (Connell, 1985).

Age Differences in the Unique Effects of Teacher Context on Individual Differences and the Development of Perceived Control

Analyses of age differences in the concurrent relations between children's experiences of teachers and multiple aspects of perceived control did not reveal the hypothesized pattern of heightened effects of context for younger children. In general, almost all aspects of perceived control were related to students' reports of teacher context for children of both ages. In fact, the only age difference that was found suggested that teacher context was a more important predictor of children's strategy effort beliefs for older (as opposed to younger) children.

In contrast, the exploratory analyses examining teacher context as a predictor of the *development* of perceived control produced a clear pattern of findings suggesting that teacher context may play a more important role in the development of perceived control for younger than for older children. Younger children (compared to older children) showed a decisively stronger pattern of ambient-level effects from teacher context, especially of their effects on the development of strategy beliefs about uncontrollable causes (ability, powerful others, and unknown). Even in change-to-change analyses, the effects of teacher context were usually significantly higher for the younger children. Nevertheless, for children of both ages, changes in children's experiences with their teachers were a significant predictor of the development of their perceived control, especially as a positive predictor of the development of control and capacities and as a negative predictor of the development of maladaptive beliefs about external strategies.

Normative Development of Perceived Control

These shifts took place in the midst of cognitive developments and normative school transitions. Both normative trends and age differences in correlations suggested that children's perceptions of control underwent successive differentiation in terms of the causal categories considered as potential strategies for achieving school success and avoiding failure. Children's beliefs about luck, both capacity and strategy, declined markedly over this age range, at the same developmental periods during which children's conceptions of luck were differentiated from effort and other potentially controllable causes. These beliefs did not increase again, even during the transition to middle school.

Children's beliefs about the efficacy of effort were high and stable across this age range. However, analyses of age differences in the correlations among strategy beliefs revealed that, over time, beliefs about effort as a strategy were distinguished from beliefs about ability; effort and ability strategy beliefs showed linearly decreasing relations with age. Effort was also differentiated from external strategies. Effort strategy beliefs showed increasingly more negative relations to powerful others, luck, and unknown strategy beliefs all across the elementary school years, accompanied by increasingly more positive relations with control beliefs.

In contrast, beliefs about ability as a strategy did *not* show increasing differentiation from other potentially uncontrollable causes. As revealed by the correlational analyses, beliefs about ability as a strategy showed consistently high relations to strategy beliefs about powerful others, luck, and unknown strategy beliefs all across this age range. Although beliefs about ability as a strategy were shorn of their positive connection to effort, they still maintained close ties with other potentially uncontrollable strategy beliefs. This may be reflected in the pattern of slight increases in the negative correlations between ability strategy and control beliefs.

These normative age-graded trends in mean level and in correlational pattern of strategy beliefs are consistent with cross-national studies of the development of similar beliefs (Little & Lopez, 1997). This pattern is also consistent with underlying cognitive developments in this age range, in which children's conceptions of effort become differentiated from their understanding of ability (Nicholls, 1978, 1984) and other potentially uncontrollable causes (Weisz, 1983, 1986). Developmental shifts in the meaning of causal categories like effort and ability may provide a backdrop for changes in the aspects of children's perceived control that regulate and are, in turn, influenced by their school performances. The progressive differentiation of ability from effort has been shown to underlie shifts in the predictors of academic performance from effort to ability beliefs (Chapman & Skinner, 1989). As they successively differentiate causal categories, children may find it increasingly difficult to use the qualities of effort (as an internal, unstable, and potentially controllable cause) to buffer the effects of poor performance on their views about their own abilities.

Transition to Middle School

At the same time that children were shifting from effort to ability as central regulators of their engagement in school, they made the transition, at the beginning of the sixth grade, to middle school. The normative data suggest that generally this was not a pleasant experience. Children experienced their teachers as increasingly neglectful and chaotic; students' perceptions of teachers' support dropped about half a standard deviation from the spring of grade 5 to the spring of grade 7. These results are consistent with other studies of children's school experiences during the transition to middle school or junior high, in which children report decreasing support from teachers (Eccles et al., in press; Roeser et al., 1996) accompanied by increasing academic pressures (Harter et al., 1992).

The effects of this transition were also reflected in normative patterns of change in children's beliefs about powerful others and unknown strategies. Despite normative declines in these maladaptive beliefs across the school year starting in grade 3, both sets of beliefs (which are some of the strongest predictors of disaffection) began to rise again after the transition to middle school. These beliefs seemed to reflect children's growing uncertainty about the causes of good and bad school performance in this new, less supportive context, coupled with the dawning realization of the important role that teachers play in school success and failure. Not surprisingly, and consistent with other research, although children's engagement was high and stable from the beginning of the third to the end of the fifth grade, it was found to decrease sharply after the transition to middle school (Eccles et al., in press; Eccles et al., 1998; Harter et al., 1992; Roeser et al., 1996).

Developmental Differences in Cycles of Perceived Control and Performance

Both the individual differences and the developmental data were consistent with a model of context, self, action, and outcomes at a general level for children across the age range from 8 to 13. Together with the normative data, these findings suggest that such cycles may underlie differential patterns of developmental change, in which children who are initially optimistic are able to maintain their control and engagement over the challenging transition to middle school, whereas children who lack the resilience provided by control are thrown into patterns of ever more rapidly escalating discouragement and disaffection.

Self-confirming cycles of beliefs and performance unfolded in a developing individual and in a dynamic school context. Three characteristics of the competence system changed with age: (1) the kinds of control beliefs that influence engagement; (2) the extent to which perceived control is shaped by teacher context and individual performance; and (3) the kinds of beliefs that are influenced by individual achievement. If these age trends hold, it is possible that they represent changes in developing competence systems that make them less resilient with age.

Early Cycles of Beliefs and Performance

At the youngest ages included in this study (ages 8 and 9), cycles of beliefs and performance were organized around effort and strategy beliefs. Children's engagement was more strongly influenced by beliefs about effort as a capacity and strategy beliefs for powerful others and unknown. In turn, children's individual performances fed back into these beliefs. In addition, teacher context was an important predictor of perceived control and was an especially decisive factor in the development of beliefs about uncontrollable strategies, including ability, powerful others, and unknown.

The fact that younger children's explanations for school performance revolve around effort and strategy beliefs may offer them some advantages. Interpreting performances as providing information about causes operating in the school environment (i.e., strategies) may deflect the effects of failure away from beliefs about one's own capacities. Strategies may be more unstable and modifiable and so open to future improvements.

Children's perceived control did seem to be open to influence, especially from teacher context, and especially in terms of the development of beliefs about the role of uncontrollable strategies. Although students' reports of teacher context were closely linked to their perceptions of control at all ages, ambient level of teacher context played a heightened role in the development of younger children's maladaptive beliefs about ability, powerful others, and unknown strategies (relative to those of older children). If the development of younger children's perceived control is more open to input from the social context, then supportive teachers may be better able to modify children's maladaptive beliefs about the causes of school success and failure.

In addition, in grades 3 and 4, the capacity beliefs that were most important in regulating engagement involved *effort*. Reliance on effort suggests a focus on a potentially modifiable cause, thus allowing children to believe that and examine whether additional voluntary inputs, such as practice, studying, specific techniques, concentration, or exertion, can improve school performance. Because effort is a low inferential cause (since it can be directly experienced by children), it may also be easier for the social context to modify effort and to demonstrate to children that its modifications have the desired effects on outcomes. Evidence of the protective functions of these beliefs can be found in the fact that, in grade 3, children's academic achievement showed no unique feedback effects on their beliefs about their own ability as a capacity. If children do not use school performance as direct information about their level of ability, then students should be better able to recover from setbacks and failures.

The resilience of this system may also be reflected in the combined patterns of normative within- and between-year changes in context, self, and action over grades 3 and 4. In each school year, children's perceptions of teachers' involvement and the structure that they provided deteriorated slightly from the fall to the spring. However, students' perceptions of their interactions with teachers improved again at the start of each new school year. In addition, although children's maladaptive beliefs about powerful others and unknown strategies rose at each transition, that is, at the beginning of each new school year, these same beliefs also declined *during* the school year as students gained more confidence about the causes of school success and failure.

Another indicator of resilience can be seen in the normative patterns for beliefs about effort and for children's engagement in the classroom. Despite the demands of each new school year apparent in students' views of teachers and of unknown causes, children did not give up on the notion of effort. Children's beliefs about their own capacities to exert effort remained normatively stable across the third and fourth grades, and their beliefs about effort as a strategy even improved slightly. Active engagement in school may be one product of this resilient and perhaps even self-correcting system. Students' emotional and behavioral engagement in the classroom remained high and stable in these early years of elementary school.

Later Cycles of Beliefs and Performance

By the time children made the transition to middle school (ages 12 and 13), their cycles of beliefs and performance were organized around their capacities, especially their capacity to influence powerful others (teachers) and estimates of their own ability. Both these capacity beliefs exerted a stronger effect on engagement (relative to younger children), and poor school performance was more likely to lead older children to doubt their own capacities, especially their ability. Capacity effort no longer was a concurrent predictor of engagement. At the same time, children's strategy beliefs about the causes of school success and failure were becoming more differentiated, as the characteristics of effort (controllability and modifiability) were successively removed from ability. Nevertheless, ability strategy remained closely allied with other potentially uncontrollable causes, such as powerful others and luck.

If older children's performances are influenced more by beliefs about ability, and if, in turn, their academic successes and failures are more concentrated in their effects on estimates of ability, then children have less room to influence performance through effort and increased engagement. Increases in effort may even lead children to infer lower levels of ability (Covington & Omelich, 1979). Because ability is such a highly inferential cause, it is more difficult for interventions to demonstrate convincingly to children that ability has been improved. Even if actual performance improves, children with low perceived control may interpret these improvements as due to luck or even unknown factors (Diener & Dweck, 1980). Hence, these beliefs, which generate confirming negative experiences, are also more insulated from possible disconfirming positive experiences.

The effects of relatively linear developments in beliefs-performance cycles can be seen in the abrupt pattern of changes during the transition to middle school, as students experienced normative declines in the quality of their relationships with teachers. Children's maladaptive beliefs about powerful others and unknown strategies, which had also shown increases at the beginning of previous school years, no longer improved (declined) during the school year and, hence, became steadily worse. Children's beliefs in their capacity to exert effort and influence powerful others began to falter. The cumulative effects can be seen in children's classroom behavior. Students became increasingly disaffected with learning during the years of the sixth and seventh grades (Eccles et al., in press; Eccles et al., 1998; Harter et al., 1992; Roeser et al., 1996).

Despite the normative decline in engagement, however, marked variation was found in the trajectories of individual children. A major finding of this study is that the way that children negotiated this transition depended in part on their beliefs about the efficaciousness of the self and the contingencies operating in school. By grade 5, these beliefs were themselves a marker of a history of school success and of supportive interactions with teachers. However, during the transition, they also played an active role in progressive cycles, shaping trajectories of engagement over the next 2 years. Discussion of the implications of these findings should be considered in the context of an understanding of the study's limitations. It is to this issue that we turn next.

LIMITATIONS OF THE STUDY

Three main limitations of the study can be noted. The first two center on the measurement of teacher context and academic performance. The third focuses on the explanation of underlying cognitive developments responsible for age changes in the functions of perceived control. Each of these limitations is described and then discussed with respect to (1) how it informs interpretations of the findings of this study, (2) the extent to which it can be offset by findings from other studies, and (3) how it suggests further research building on the current study.

Assessment of Teacher Context

A major limitation of the current research project was the use of children's reports to assess the extent to which students' interactions with their teachers were characterized by involvement and structure. This reliance had two drawbacks. First, the use of children's reports guaranteed that we would be capturing children's *perceptions* or experiences of their interactions with teachers rather than objective indicators of these constructs, such as might be available through direct classroom observations. Second, students' perceptions of interactions with teachers were not as differentiated as objective indicators.

Teacher Context versus Perceived Control

Although the close correspondence between teacher context and children's perceived control was usually couched as the effects of interactions with teachers on children's beliefs, it certainly also reflects, at least in part, the effects of children's perceptions of control on their interpretation of their interactions with teachers. Hence, this study is likely to overestimate the connection between teacher context and students' perceived control and is not definitive with respect to the direction of effects.

Teacher Structure versus Involvement

The second drawback to the use of children's reports of interactions with teachers is that children's perceptions of these interactions were not as differentiated as the constructs we wished to tap, namely, teachers' involvement and the structure that teachers provided. Although these two aspects of adult-child interactions have been distinguished in studies of parenting and teaching that rely on direct observation (e.g., Baumrind, 1977; Pintrich & Blumenfeld, 1985), children's reports did not show an analogous distinction. Although factor analytically distinct (Belmont et al., 1992), they were nevertheless highly intercorrelated.

As a result, it was not possible to test predictions about the differential effects of structure and involvement on different aspects of perceived control or to test predictions about age differences in the importance of these two features of teacher-student interaction. Some hints were found in the data that structure might be more important to strategy beliefs about external causes such as powerful others, luck, and unknown factors. However, defini-

161

tive analysis of this and other predictions requires a study in which structure and involvement are empirically distinguished.

Children's Experiences of Their Interactions with Teachers

Despite the drawbacks of the measure of teacher context, we did feel comfortable with this choice on at least one level. We assumed, along with many other theorists, that children's *experiences* of their interactions with the social and physical context are the proximal mediators of their perceptions of control (Bandura, 1986; Roeser et al., 1996; Skinner, 1995; Weiner, 1986; Weisz, 1983). Hence, children's perceptions are the appropriate "one theoretical step backward" in the antecedents of perceived control (Skinner, in press).

At the same time, however, they also lead to the next empirical question: What are the antecedents of these experiences of structure and involvement? In order to resolve this issue, future studies will need to include assessments of children's actual interactions with the social and physical context, including perhaps objective indicators of contingency, warmth, and inductive disciplinary techniques (Carton & Nowicki, 1994). These studies may also wish to include children's *experiences* of these interactions as a mediator between objective and subjective control (Skinner, 1985, 1995, in press).

Assessment of Academic Performance

The second major limitation in the current study was that achievement was assessed for only a subset of children and was examined only at the aggregate level. Research exploring the reciprocal relations between self-concept and academic achievement suggests that it may be important to distinguish between achievement test performance and school marks as indicators of performance (Helmke & van Aken, 1995). In addition, it would be helpful to have information about children's actual intelligence. It seems clear that perceived control (or self-concept of any type) has its main effect on school performance through its effects on motivation and volition, in that it allows children access to the full range of intellectual performances of which they are capable, the upper bound of which is set by intelligence.

Development of Causal Conceptions

A third major limitation of the study derives from the absence of information about the cognitive developments hypothesized as underlying mechanisms to explain age changes in the functioning of perceived control. Two mechanisms were proposed: (1) the developmental differentiation of effort from noncontingent causes such as luck or powerful others and (2) the developmental differentiation of effort from ability as causes of school performance. The former developmental change was proposed to underlie the shift from effort and unknown causes as predictors of academic engagement (in grade 3) to powerful others (in grade 5). The latter developmental change was proposed as an explanation for the shift from powerful others and effort as influential in classroom engagement (in grade 5) to ability (in grade 7).

Had measures of these cognitive shifts been included, it would have been possible to directly test the prediction that individual differences in a particular aspect of control would come to influence engagement only after the cognitive shift had occurred. In addition, it would have been possible to select a subsample of children of the same age who were in different phases of the cognitive shift and to examine whether changes in the predictors of engagement and performance were a function of the cognitive shift.

Several smaller-scale studies have accomplished this for the effort-ability differentiation (Chapman & Skinner, 1989; Miller, 1985; Skinner & Schmitz, 1998; Stipek, 1993). For example, in a direct test of this hypothesis in an earlier study (Chapman & Skinner, 1989), we showed that, across the four phases of the process of distinguishing ability from effort, the correlations between beliefs about effort and actual performance show a linear decrease, whereas the relations between beliefs about ability and actual performance show a corresponding increase. However, no parallel set of studies exists that examines the proposed cognitive mechanisms underlying the shift from effort and unknown to powerful others at about ages 8–9. Hence, the exploration of this mechanism is one important avenue for further study.

IMPLICATIONS OF THE FINDINGS

While keeping the limitations of the study in mind, we now turn to a brief discussion of its implications. We touch first on the very specific issues of developmental change in the functioning of individual differences in perceived control. Then we look more generally at the implications for theories of control, including self-efficacy and learned helplessness. Third, we consider the general implications of the design and analytic framework for the study of individual differences in development. We end by outlining the implications of the research project for interventions aimed at optimizing children's perceived control and engagement in school.

Causal Mechanisms

It is important to point out that, in any thorough examination of the factors responsible for age changes in the aspects of perceived control that regulate engagement, normative cognitive changes will not be the sole explanatory mechanism. As pointed out by many theorists (Chapman & Skinner, 1989; Dweck, 1991; Eccles et al., in press; Eccles et al., 1998; Dweck & Heckhausen, in press; Nicholls, 1984; Rosenholtz & Simpson, 1984; Skinner, 1995; Stipek, 1993), such shifts are the product of social factors as well. These have been specified most clearly in the work on ability conceptions. This work suggests that both conceptions of ability and social contextual factors in schools contribute to increasingly vulnerable perceptions of control. Each of these general contributors has been examined as both a normative change and an individual differences factor.

Conceptions of Ability

First, there are general normative societal beliefs about the nature of ability; these constitute culture-specific definitions of the characteristics of a "mature" ability conception. In our culture, the general conception is one of ability as a stable, enduring, fixed trait, the capacity of which sets permanent upper-bound limits on the level of performance that can be achieved with maximum effort. In our culture, definitions of *inborn talent* are especially noticeable in the areas of mathematics, music, the arts, and sports. These cultural beliefs make it much more likely that, when developmental changes proceed to the point at which a child is cognitively capable of distinguishing between effort and ability, they will do so and will apply the "mature" definition, which specifies an inverse compensatory relation between the two.

Even within a society that emphasizes the trait-like nature of ability, however, children manage to show differential conceptions (Dweck, 1991; Dweck & Leggett, 1988; Stipek & Gralinski, 1996). According to this work, some children show "entity" conceptions of their own ability—corresponding to cultural norms—and view it as a fixed attribute; other children view ability as "incremental," as a malleable and plastic attribute that can be greatly improved through effort and practice. Studies that identify the social and individual factors that support children in continuing to view their ability as modifiable (and hence potentially controllable) are critical in formulating interventions that allow children to weather the developmental transition of the effort-ability differentiation successfully.

Finally, this work points out that the group of children who are particularly vulnerable during this developmental transition are those whose estimations of their own ability are low. It is these children who suffer most when they view ability as a fixed trait (Dweck, 1991). Hence, factors that contribute to children's perceptions of themselves as incompetent are implicated in this process as well. They include the social messages that are given to children as individuals and in subgroups (most noticeably by race, ethnicity, class, and

gender) about their own levels of ability and the causes of their own performances (Blumenfeld et al., 1982; Brophy, 1983; Eccles & Wigfield, 1985).

School Characteristics

Among the most interesting factors studied as potential contributors to
the development of maladaptive conceptions of ability are the characteristics
of schools and classrooms, for example, the extent to which a child's "ability"
is publicly assessed, compared, communicated, and used as a basis for differential treatment (Stevenson, Chen, & Lee, 1993; Oettingen, 1995; Oettingen
et al., 1994; Roeser et al., 1996). It would be interesting to document the
social factors involved in shaping children's conceptions, not just of their own
ability, but of effort, powerful others, and luck as well. The results of this
research would be very informative about the effects of such factors on the
development of children's perceptions of control.

Independent of any individual developments, researchers have documented normative age-graded changes in the social contexts of schools themselves and are examining the role that they play in the drop in children's
engagement and intrinsic interest in learning from the fifth to the seventh
grade and beyond (Eccles & Midgley, 1989; Eccles et al., 1984; Eccles, Midgley, et al., 1993). These researchers suggest that changes in the school system
usually introduced in middle school or junior high seem to result in simulta-
neous decreases in teachers' involvement with individual students and increases in the coerciveness of school rules and personnel. They point out that
these changes (part of which this study also picked up in children's perceptions) run directly counter to the developmental needs of early adolescents
(Eccles, Midgley, et al., 1993). These general trends will also be experienced
differentially, as teachers come to spend even less time with and become even
more coercive with students whose motivation and interest are deteriorating
(Skinner & Belmont, 1993).

In sum, the mechanisms underlying the age changes described in this
study will probably include normative developmental changes in both children's cognitive processes and the social contexts of their schools as well as
differential treatment from their teachers, some of which may be in response
to children's differential motivation and action. Future research, perhaps focusing on effort, powerful others, and luck as factors in school performance
in addition to ability, will attempt to unravel and detect the interactions
among these social and individual factors as both change across time.

Developmental Changes in the Functions of Perceived Control

It is easy to be skeptical about claims that the aspects of perceived control
that regulate children's engagement change with age. On the one hand, as

mentioned in Chapter I, decades of research have shown that perceptions of control exert effects on motivation and emotion, at all points in the life span (Baltes & Baltes, 1986; Brim, 1974; Rodin, 1986; Steitz, 1982; Watson, 1966). Hence, the effects of control seem invariant across age. In addition, many researchers, ourselves included, may have overstated the case for change, implying, for example, that young children are immune to the effects of helplessness (e.g., Rholes et al., 1980; Skinner, 1991; cf. Burhans & Dweck, 1995; Heyman, Dweck, & Cain, 1992).

On the other hand, however, decades of research also exist demonstrating normative developmental changes in many of the processes that underlie the perception and interpretation of control experiences. Children change in the strategies they use to detect covariation (Shaklee & Mims, 1981), in their use of causal schema (Shultz et al., 1975), in their conceptions of causes (Nicholls, 1978; Weisz, 1983), and in their very understanding of the nature of the self and competence (Heckhausen, 1982, 1984; for reviews, see Flammer, 1995; Skinner, 1995).

Continuity and Change in the Functioning of Individual Differences

Accepting the validity of both these bodies of research seems paradoxical only until one realizes that perceptions of control are multidimensional. The aspects of perceived control that are invariant in their effects across age are those that refer to convictions that the self can produce desired and prevent undesired events. These beliefs, which have been studied under many different labels, such as *sense of control, control expectations, perceived competence,* and sometimes *self-efficacy,* have been shown empirically to have almost uniform positive effects (Skinner, 1996). In the current study, this was also found to be the case. Across the age range considered, children's "control beliefs" (e.g., "If I want to, I can do well in school") were uniformly strong predictors of both individual differences and developmental improvements in children's academic engagement.

At the same time that a sense of control seems developmentally invariant in its effects on motivation and action, nevertheless, it seems clear that the causal processes that children use to interpret control experiences do show regular normative changes with age. What is the significance of changes, say, in the kinds of performances that lead to attributions of ability as opposed to effort? Two points can be highlighted. First, these interpretations are the basis for children's construction (and reevaluation) of their sense of control. As demonstrated by Miller (1985), for example, the very same experiences (e.g., failure on a normatively easy task despite high effort) can have very different effects on performance (i.e., helplessness or mastery) depending on how they are interpreted. So, through its effects on causal reasoning, development should change the effect of certain experiences on a child's sense of control.

Second, these causal reasoning processes are one critical avenue for intervention in the cycles of beliefs and performance that can bolster or undermine the development of engagement and control over time. Attribution retraining (Foersterling, 1985), and other attempts to influence children's interpretations of their interactions with the social and physical context (such as persuasion; Bandura, 1986), must rely on a solid understanding of the factors that contribute to these interpretations; these include both the developmental level of the reasoning processes and the individual biases introduced by prior beliefs.

Developmental Conceptions of Perceived Control

The findings of this study point out the advantages of a multidimensional conceptualization and measure of perceived control (Connell, 1985; Gurin & Brim, 1984; Lachman, 1986; Little et al., 1995; Weisz & Stipek, 1982). First, this study replicated the findings of early research that the many different aspects of perceived control assessed in this study are not redundant in their effects on individual differences and the development of children's engagement in school. Despite their empirical overlap, eight of the 10 aspects of control made unique contributions to engagement; the two aspects that did not show unique main effects (effort and ability strategy) did make unique contributions at different ages.

Second, this study demonstrates that assessing only a single aspect of perceived control precludes the detection of age changes in the aspects of control that regulate engagement and performance. If, in a given study, the single aspect of control that is assessed corresponds to the construct *control beliefs*, then such a study would conclude that the effects of perceived control are invariant over age. And, in fact, studies of these constructs, such as self-efficacy, do show such findings.

In contrast, studies that focus on the aspects of beliefs that reflect causal reasoning, such as causal attributions, strategy beliefs, or even locus of control, reveal systematic age differences in these beliefs as predictors of motivation, emotion, and academic performance (Barker & Graham, 1987; Findley & Cooper, 1983; Weiner, Kun, & Benesh-Weiner, 1980). However, these studies have sometimes been the basis for conclusions that young children's beliefs do not regulate their behavior (e.g., Rholes et al., 1980) when, of course, it is only fair to conclude that the aspects of control assessed in the specific study do not regulate younger children's action. Only with studies in which multiple aspects are assessed, including control beliefs and also beliefs about specific causes, will it be possible to identify which beliefs are constant in their effects across age and which beliefs change in their centrality as children develop.

It is also worth noting that research that examines age differences in the zero-order relations between one aspect of control and behavior or action will also tend to underestimate age changes. In some cases, only by examining the unique contributions of different aspects can age changes be detected. The reason is that developmental shifts in causal conceptions do not cause causal labels to appear and disappear but rather result in changes in the meaning that children assign to the causal label. For example, when a child has not yet differentiated ability from effort, beliefs about both effort and ability refer to causes that are malleable and controllable. Hence, zero-order correlations with engagement will be found for *both* effort and ability beliefs. However, for a child at this level, the effects of ability on engagement will disappear when effort is controlled for, revealing that the part of ability that was regulating engagement was the part that overlapped with effort.

The Analysis of Individual Differences in Development

This study illustrates the advantages of hierarchical linear modeling procedures for analyzing individual differences in the developmental trajectories of perceived control. The current study benefited from many aspects of the procedure's flexibility, including estimating missing data, empirically identifying the appropriate shape of the growth function for a given variable, determining whether the individual variation in growth curves was significant, and estimating individual growth curves while controlling for any group factors that might influence their shape (e.g., in our case, small curvilinearity and wave effects). The overall procedure provided a powerful method for calculating individual estimates of growth curve parameters for key variables and using them in analyzing multiple predictors of individual differences in growth curves, including individual differences in the growth curves of other variables.

Models of Individual Differences in Development

We were able to build on the features of this method in two small ways. First, we suggested three conceptual models that can be used to identify predictors of individual differences in development (Connell & Skinner, 1990). As described previously, these include the launch model, which looks at how the initial level of a predictor may influence the trajectory of a target outcome. This is the most commonly used model in developmental studies (Connell & Skinner, 1990; Kindermann & Skinner, 1992), even though in the current study it was not the most appropriate account of all the relations that we examined.

The second, ambient-level model looked at the effects of the average level of a predictor on the trajectory as it unfolded. We argued that this model may be a valuable one for understanding the effects of the social context (e.g., parents and teachers) on individual development. However, the current study suggested that it may not be a good fit if the social context itself is undergoing systematic changes (as was the case with our changing students' reports of teachers).

In our study, we found some evidence that different conceptual models were better accounts of different kinds of relations. Children's initial grades launched the development of their perceived control. Ambient level of context was a unique predictor of the development of control, especially for boys, and especially for the development of beliefs in external strategies. And change to change characterized most relations, but especially the strong ones between control beliefs and engagement. This model is consistent with the notion of reciprocal interaction over time. In addition, we found that, even within the same links (e.g., from control to engagement), different aspects were better described by different models. For example, external strategies (e.g., powerful others and unknown) acted to launch the development of engagement, whereas the contributions of capacity beliefs to engagement were best described as change to change.

We also learned that many factors can influence the fit of different models, including the shape and length of the normative trajectory and its distance from the absolute beginning of the trajectory. For example, more ambient-level effects of teacher context on the development of children's perceived control were found when 2- instead of 5-year trajectories were examined. And more launch effects were found for younger children, who were also closer to the beginning of their trajectories of engagement in the classroom.

We also realized that, although ambient-level models might in principle provide a valid account of many contributions of contextual factors to development, we did not anticipate an important qualifier. Social contextual factors may not need to improve over time to support optimal development (as would be implied by a change-to-change model), but they must remain above a threshold to do so. In the case of children's experiences of their interactions with teachers, the normative decline in children's perceptions provides one explanation for why *changes* (rather than ambient level) in teacher context were better predictors of the development of children's control. When trajectories are declining, slopes may be better markers than ambient levels of when a threshold has been crossed.

The use of the HLM procedures also made us aware of the disadvantages of the method, at least with respect to the data that we were analyzing. For example, although these procedures allowed us to identify variables for which higher-order (e.g., curvilinear) curves were appropriate depictions of the population slope, little consensus exists about what to do with these parameter estimates. In our data, we had to be satisfied with controlling for them in creating individual estimates. We were also disappointed that the developmental trajectories for several variables were so "flat" that intercepts and average levels were highly intercorrelated. This meant that we were unable to compare launch and ambient-level models in the same regression equation. Hence, in this study, what are referred to as *launch* effects may be ambient-level effects, or vice versa. This will be a problem for other individual difference variables that do not show marked normative change. In such cases, it may be more appropriate to calculate the two models separately and then to compare the relevant coefficients directly (see Zimmer-Gembeck, 1997; and Appendix B).

Developmental Differences in Models of Individual Change

Our second extension of the HLM procedures involved the exploratory analyses of 2-year trajectories. With HLM, it is common to use as outcomes the entire trajectory that can be estimated with the data available. However, by segmenting our 5-year, 10-point data into two 2-year, four-point data groups based on children's initial grade level, we were able to examine whether the predictors of individual differences in development of control and engagement were different for children of different ages and at different points in the trajectory. At least in this study, it turned out that they were. In developmental and applied work, when the outcome is improvement on some target variable over time, such a design may be used to determine whether the program elements that support progress at the beginning of the program are the same as the ones that support positive change later in the program.

We also discovered two important design features for making such comparisons theoretically useful. First, it is important that the trajectories of the target age groups do not overlap. In our study, even though we had 2-year trajectories for children initially in the third, fourth, fifth, and sixth grades, we compared only children who were initially in the third and the sixth grades. Had we compared all the groups, each group would have shared half its trajectory with the adjacent groups (e.g., at the last two points of the third graders' 2-year trajectories, children are the same age as the fourth graders at the first two points of their trajectories). Second, target trajectories should not span points at which the predictors (or consequences) of development are expected to shift. Again, in our study, we chose to compare third and sixth graders. This allowed us to obtain a clean picture of developmental differences.

Finally, the exploratory analyses also pointed out the difficulties of making statistically meaningful comparisons between age groups. It is precisely because the patterns of change were different between children at the beginning and near the middle of their trajectories of engagement that comparisons were appealing. However, those same differences translated into different patterns of interrelations among individual growth curve parameter estimates and so resulted in difficulties in interpreting age interactions in predictors of individual development. For example, even though teachers' ratings of engagement were similar in level for children in grades 3–4 and in grades 6–7, the correlations between intercepts and slopes were very different. This made it difficult to test age interactions in predictors of engagement slopes.

Integrating Individual Differences and Individual Development

The attempt to integrate findings from the typical multiple regressions and the HLM analyses reinforced the notion that all analyses of individual differences are actually analyses of portions of individual change (Baltes et al., 1977). That is, individual differences at any age represent the outcome of individual differences either in initial level or in patterns of change over time. Individual differences at any age can be linked to individual differences at each adjacent age, eventually forming individual trajectories over time.

When viewed from that perspective, all the correlational analyses could be characterized as subsets of the analyses of individual differences in individual development over 5 years. The exploratory analyses examined differences between predictors of 2-year (four time points) portions of the trajectories. The time-lagged regressions examined predictors of 1-year (two time points) portions of the trajectories. And even the analyses of the concurrent correlations at different ages were simply analyses of the part of the developmental trajectory that was captured for one time point at each successive age. In effect, individual differences at any age both reflected the cumulative development that preceded it and could serve as potential launch points for the next set of trajectories. If individual differences at one time point are like a "snapshot" of previous quantitative development, then a developmental trajectory is more like a "moving picture," although it may better be described as a "moving window" since there are always likely to be more past and more future changes than can be captured in most longitudinal studies.

Developmental Time versus Causal Time

The biggest drawback for us was apparent when we tried to use HLM to analyze a theoretical model that is process oriented (i.e., mediational and causal) yet also has as its outcomes individual differences in development. We had to be satisfied with different analytic procedures to examine different facets of the model (e.g., time-lagged regressions for causal hypotheses and structural equation modeling for mediational hypotheses). Fortunately, the results of these different analyses converged. However, it would have been more powerful and parsimonious had we been able to examine them all simultaneously.

We also came face to face with a problem that is not caused by HLM procedures but is highlighted by them. The span of time needed to identify a "developmental trajectory" is at least months and often years. For example, in the current study, developmental trajectories were estimated over fall and spring of 5 consecutive years. However, the time lags appropriate for a detailed study of process (causal and mediational) are much shorter, sometimes taking place over days or weeks. (For discussions of these issues, see Schmitz, 1987; or Turkewitz & Devenny, 1993.)

In the case of perceived control and engagement in school, we found the right time unit for the cyclic process in the time-series study described in Chapter I (Schmitz & Skinner, 1993); it was almost daily and was organized around children's graded performances (homework and tests) in the classroom. Within this time frame, it was possible to examine how children's beliefs (along with the difficulty of the assignment) regulated both the quantity and the quality of their subsequent engagement; how this engagement affected the level of the individual performance; how success or failure shaped children's causal interpretations of their performances; and how these interpretations influenced revision (or confirmation) of children's expectations for future control. However, although these daily assessments were useful in forming interindividual and average intraindividual maps of the processes connecting beliefs, engagement, and performance, they were not conducted over a time span sufficient to produce "development"; hence, we could not examine individual differences in development as one outcome of these mediational processes.

Although the simple combination of these two time scales is desirable in principle, it is difficult to accomplish in practice. We had enough difficulty maintaining the time-series sample in conducting daily assessments over a period of 5 months, and we had enough difficulty maintaining the involvement of the longitudinal sample over 4 years when we requested participation only twice a year. However, the juxtaposition of the results of these two kinds of studies suggests a theoretically valid integration of the two designs. Longitudinal studies can be used to identify narrower periods or "windows" of time during which specific developmental processes seem to be particularly active (Kindermann & Skinner, 1992). For example, in the present study, the fifth to the sixth grade was a time when engagement (normatively) starts a precipitous decline. A time-series study conducted during this period might reveal a great deal about the processes underlying this development. If it were complemented by just a few follow-up assessments, spaced perhaps 6 months apart, then individual differences in process could be used to predict individual differences in development. And, learning from the omissions of this study, if assessments of the developmental changes thought to underlie changes in these processes (e.g., effort-ability differentiation or curricular shifts) were included, then the normative changes hypothesized to be responsible for creating the window in the first place could be identified.

OPTIMIZATION OF PERCEIVED CONTROL AND ENGAGEMENT

Because children's perceived control has been found to be such a powerful predictor of their motivation, behavior, and performance, a great deal of study has been devoted to determining how to promote optimal control beliefs. Although this literature will not be reviewed here (but see Ames & Ames, 1985; Skinner, 1995; Stipek, 1993), the implications drawn from the results of this study will be discussed in light of that literature. Accordingly, any new insights or any implications that contradict this literature will be especially highlighted.

Target Outcomes of Interventions

Development as an Outcome

The first major implication involves the conceptualization of "optimal" perceived control and engagement. The present study suggests that, instead of focusing, as is typically the case, on individual differences in a particular outcome, interventions should aim to optimize individual *trajectories* of control and engagement. Furthermore, rather than focusing on a single aspect of control, such as effort versus ability attributions or self-efficacy, it may be more useful to consider a *profile* of control-related beliefs. Figure 19 above contains a graphic representation of the variation in control trajectories. The variable ConMax consists of a combination of control, capacity, and strategy beliefs, each of which were shown to exert unique effects on children's classroom engagement. Despite the fact that, over the age range depicted in Figure 19, perceived control is normatively declining, this figure shows that some trajectories of control are nevertheless being maintained over time at their initial optimistic levels and a few are actually increasing. For perceived control and engagement, the optimization of interindividual differences in intraindividual change over time (Baltes et al., 1977) would have as its goal, not just increasing their mean levels at one point in time, but also maintaining or improving children's control and action over time.

Age-Graded Target Outcomes

The findings of this study also suggest that the specific aspects of perceived control that are targeted in interventions may change with age. In the third grade, interventions may be especially tuned to the kinds of experiences that promote children's beliefs in the effectiveness of their own effort and that prevent children from concluding that the causes of school success and failure are unknown.

In terms of unknown strategies, this study provided a few indications that children's beliefs about whether the causes of school performance are unknown may be influenced by the amount of structure provided by teachers. Although the empirical support for this link was not definitive, it was consistent with the expectation that children express more certainty about "what it takes" to do well in school when teachers are consistent and contingent, when they explain the reasons for discipline and rules, when they outline the steps in solving problems, and when they monitor children's progress. In addition, the analysis of developmental change showed that poor performances feed back into the development of unknown strategy beliefs, especially for younger children.

In terms of effort, the findings of this study point out that interventions that target only effort attributions may need to be expanded. Children's beliefs about effort as a strategy were not the primary predictors of their engagement. Instead, children's effort capacity beliefs were strong predictors of their engagement and its development starting in the third grade. This point is important because many interventions focus on attribution retraining (e.g., Foersterling, 1985), in which children are persuaded that the primary cause of school failure is simply lack of effort. However, if in response to these interventions children increase their effort and still are not able to succeed, these very strong beliefs about the potency of effort may lead them to conclude that they themselves are simply not capable of exerting appropriate effort (low capacity beliefs).

For children who are in the fifth grade (ages 10–11), the current study suggests that interventions may want to add a focus on beliefs about the role of powerful others (in this case, teachers) in children's school performance. Whether because of normative changes in causal conceptions, in which children distinguish effort from luck and chance factors, or because of normative changes in the school system, it seems that children at this age increasingly come to realize that teachers play a role in their successes and failures. According to the present study, increases in the role assigned to powerful others will create a barrier to engagement especially for children who also believe that they do not have the capacity to influence them. The results of the present study suggest that both teachers' provision of structure and their involvement may be important to the development of children's beliefs that "powerful others" are a benign force that operates with rather than against them.

Finally, when considering children in the seventh grade (ages 12–13), this study is consistent with other research that concludes that, if interventions wish to improve children's school performance by changing their control beliefs, they will have to work through children's beliefs about ability (Stipek, 1993). Findings in the current study suggest that supportive teachers convince children not only that high ability is not a necessary condition for school success (low ability strategy beliefs) but also that the children themselves possess high ability. The findings also suggest that, any time that children go through transitions, unknown strategy beliefs may again surface as a target for interventions.

It should be noted that, as mentioned previously, because in this study teachers' provision of structure and their involvement were assessed using students' reports, no firm prescriptions can be derived about how interventions should change objective conditions of teacher-student interactions. However, because of the close relation between students' reports of teacher context and children's perceptions of control, it may be fair to conclude that, whatever steps are taken to improve student-teacher relations, these changes in objective conditions will not register on children's beliefs about control unless they also change students' experiences of interactions. Hence, at the very least, the results suggest that, as a "manipulation check" on interventions designed to increase objective teacher structure and involvement, it may make sense to gauge their effects on students' experiences of these interaction characteristics.

Individual Performance as a Predictor of Control

Throughout the study, it was also clear that, although teachers may play a unique role in shaping children's beliefs about control, children are nevertheless also using information about their own school performances and grades to (re)estimate their control and capacity beliefs. Starting already in the second grade, early successes predict 5-year trajectories of control and ability capacity beliefs, whereas early failures predict trajectories of luck and unknown strategy beliefs.

The feedback loop from performance to perceptions of control was present even in the third grade, but it was especially pronounced for seventh graders. The launch effects of early performance on control, together with the increasing relations between grades and capacity beliefs, may reflect the

175

increasing difficulty of maintaining optimistic control beliefs in the face of failure. When children are in the third grade, even if they are not doing well at the present time, they can continue to believe that they *can* do well in school. By the seventh grade, however, a record of cumulative failure (probably accompanied by increasingly differential treatment from teachers) makes it nearly impossible to maintain a sense of control.

These findings suggest that interventions will also have to attend to the factors that actually improve children's performances. This study and others document that engagement improves performance. In addition, work in the areas of metacognition (Borkowski, Carr, Rellinger, & Pressley, 1990; Kurtz & Borkowski, 1984; Paris & Oka, 1986; Schneider, 1985), action regulation (Kuhl, 1984; Schunk, 1991; Zimmerman, 1986), and coping (Skinner & Wellborn, 1994) have revealed a set of strategies that allow children to get the most out of the effort they exert, by helping them, for example, monitor their progress, check their strategy steps, diagnose when outside help is needed, etc. In addition to improving performance, the teaching of these strategies conveys to children that they have an active role in guiding their own actions toward success. These messages, accompanied by interactions in which effort actually is effective in producing desired outcomes, are prototypes of control experience.

Interventions into the Competence System

Timing of Interventions

This study reveals that typical interventions, which often aim for a single time point and have the goal of raising the mean level of perceived control, may be disappointed by the effects that any launch variable can exert on a developmental trajectory that continues very far out into the future. The powerful change-to-change effects suggest that more than "one-shot inoculations" may be needed. It is for future research to determine whether interventions that target multiple time points are best organized as longer-term interventions, as "booster" interventions, or as interventions that make permanent changes in the teacher context, with the result that the interventions themselves are continuously changing.

The longitudinal study also offers some specific suggestions about the timing of interventions with respect to the developmental shifts in the predictors of engagement. In specific, it seems that grades 3 and 5 include age ranges during which shifts in causal conceptions have the potential to translate into periods of "risk" for developing maladaptive control beliefs. For example, in grade 3, interventions should lay the foundation for maintaining beliefs in the importance of effort; lack of teacher support at this age launches trajectories of strategy beliefs about the potency of external factors, like powerful others, luck, and unknown causes.

At each age transition, the general principle would be that, as strategies that compete with effort are emphasized (specifically, powerful others and then ability), interventions should attempt to facilitate contexts that not only minimize their importance but also compensate for their normative emergence by encouraging children to develop confidence in their corresponding capacities. Hence, although interventions would not necessarily be limited to these developmental windows, it seems that they might wish to include them in any comprehensive attempt to improve perceived control and engagement.

In terms of age-graded interventions, this study also points out that, because of the discontinuity between the beliefs that predict engagement in earlier and those that predict engagement in later grades, beliefs that are "fixed" by interventions at one age may not stay "fixed" following a developmental transition. For example, if an intervention succeeds in helping a child focus more on effort (as a strategy and a capacity) at younger ages, this nevertheless cannot ensure that, when effort is differentiated from ability, the child will continue to view effort (and not ability) as the primary source of school performance. Hence, it seems that there may be no substitute for interventions that address the entire sequence of developmental transitions.

This does not mean, of course, that early interventions should ignore what the findings of this study foreshadow about later transitions. For example, even though emphasizing a child's ability may have a positive effect at younger ages (when ability is seen as a malleable and controllable cause), interventions may decide to discourage these practices because they may result in the formation of beliefs (such as the conviction that ability is an important cause of school success and failure) that are potentially maladaptive at later ages (Skinner, 1991). Likewise, typical intervention strategies that seek to increase success experiences by presenting children with easier tasks will backfire when children begin using social comparison as a basis for estimating ability (Ruble, 1983). The same kinds of tasks that communicated high control in grade 3 will communicate low ability in grade 6.

It should also be pointed out that, although not examined in this study, there is no reason to believe that intervention efforts should stop in grade 7. On the contrary, work on perceived control suggests that it exerts effects over the life span. Especially important to target would be times of transition since these involve new contingencies, new strategies, false starts, and heightened probability of failure. In the academic domain, these would include changes in schools and transitions to high school, college, graduate school, and first jobs. Any time that control beliefs are recalibrated, the possibility exists that people will conclude that, although they did well up to this point, new skills are required for success in the current situation. Their beliefs about whether they possess those capacities may prove to be a critical factor in en-

gagement and actual performances, which in turn may influence the development of future beliefs.

Not Just Perceived Control

The implications for intervention that can be derived from this study
focus on the process of improving children's perceived control in order to
optimize their engagement in the classroom. However, perceived control is
not the only self-system process that influences engagement. Research shows
that, in addition to a sense of control, children are more engaged in learning
activities when they experience themselves as autonomous and as belonging
to the classroom and school (Blumenfeld, 1992; Connell, 1990; Connell &
Wellborn, 1991; Cordova & Lepper, 1996; DeCharms, 1981; Deci, Connell, &
Ryan, 1985; Deci & Ryan, 1985; Roeser et al., 1996; Vallerand, Fortier, & Guay,
1997; Wentzel, 1997). For example, in an earlier study (Patrick, Skinner, &
Connell, 1993), our findings showed that, despite the strong effects of perceived control, children's autonomy in learning made a significant unique
contribution to their engagement in the classroom, a contribution that was
especially strong to children's emotional engagement. Children who were
more autonomous were more likely to be interested, enthusiastic, and enjoy
learning activities, whereas children who were less autonomous were more
likely to be bored, anxious, and even angry in the classroom.

Such findings suggest three qualifiers for discussion of interventions to
optimize children's engagement. First, a range of self-system processes, in
addition to control, can be considered. Second, interventions to improve control should proceed with care in order not to impinge on children's other
self-system processes. For example, as important as teachers' provision of
structure may be to a child's sense of control in the academic domain, that
structure, if administered without warmth and caring, may be experienced
by children as coercive and, instead of promoting engagement by supporting
control, may therefore undermine engagement by eroding children's sense
of autonomy (Ryan, 1982). Third, the self-systems that are the most influential for engagement may change with development.

Reorganization of the Competence System

The final implication for optimization efforts is a very general one. It
points out that children's beliefs and behaviors are not just isolated elements
that can be removed from their context, "fixed," and then "reinserted."
Instead, the entire program of research suggests that these are part of a system in which beliefs influence action, which influences performance, which
feeds back into beliefs and contextual reactions. The effects of changing any

one element must be considered in the context of the whole system, both as it reaffirms and readjusts itself over time and as the entire system may undergo qualitative changes with age. From this perspective, the overarching goal of interventions is to provide developmentally appropriate support for the reorganization of the competence system. Then, long after the intervention is completed, the entire system will continue to "intervene on its own behalf" so that optimistic beliefs can support active meaningful engagement and coping, which in turn lead to real learning and better performances, which provoke warmth and structure from the social context and confirm a developing sense of control.

THE STUDENT PERCEPTIONS OF CONTROL QUESTIONNAIRE (SPOCQ): A NEW MEASURE OF PERCEIVED CONTROL IN CHILDREN IN THE ACADEMIC DOMAIN (FULL SCALE)

James G. Wellborn, James P. Connell, and Ellen A. Skinner

The present study used a shortened version of the SPOCQ. Asterisks indicate the items included in the shortened version. Because higher reliability is obtained with scales that contain more items, we recommend the use of the complete scales. Item numbers are taken from the administration version of the scale.

THE STUDENT PERCEPTIONS OF CONTROL QUESTIONNAIRE (SPOCQ), FULL SCALE

Control Beliefs

35.*	If I decide to learn something hard, I can.	ASCNP01
50.*	I can do well in school if I want to.	ASCNP02
58.*	I can get good grades in school.	ASCNP03
10.*	I can't get good grades, no matter what I do.	ASCNN01
5.*	I can't stop myself from doing poorly in school.	ASCNN02
14.*	I can't do well in school, even if I want to.	ASCNN03

Strategy Beliefs

Effort

54.	For me to do well in school, all I have to do is work hard.	ASSEP01
22.*	If I want to do well on my schoolwork, I just need to try hard.	ASSEP02
25.*	The best way for me to get good grades is to work hard.	ASSEP03
39.*	If I don't do well in school, it's because I didn't work hard enough.	ASSEN01
43.*	If I get bad grades, it's because I didn't try hard enough.	ASSEN02
37.*	If I don't do well on my schoolwork, it's because I didn't try hard enough.	ASSEN03

Attributes (Ability)

46.*	I have to be smart to get good grades in school.	ASSAP01
15.	Getting good grades depends on how smart I am.	ASSAP02
55.*	If I want to do well in school, I have to be smart.	ASSAP03
33.*	If I'm not smart, I won't get good grades.	ASSAN01
41.	If I'm not already good in a school subject, I won't do well at it.	ASSAN02
29.*	If I'm not smart in a school subject, I won't do well at it.	ASSAN03

Powerful Others

48.*	To do well in school, I just have to get my teacher to like me.	ASSOP01
59.	The best way for me to get good grades is to get my teacher to like me.	ASSOP02
51.*	If I want to get good grades in a subject, I have to get along with my teacher.	ASSOP03
53.*	I won't do well in school if my teacher doesn't like me.	ASSON01
38.	If my teacher doesn't like me, I won't do well in that class.	ASSON02
34.*	If I get bad grades, it's because I don't get along with my teacher.	ASSON03

Luck

20.	Getting good grades for me is a matter of luck.	ASSLP01
16.*	To do well in school, I have to be lucky.	ASSLP02
32.*	If I get good grades, it's because I'm lucky.	ASSLP03
49.*	If I get good grades, it's because I'm unlucky.	ASSLN01
56.*	If I don't get good grades in class, it is because of bad luck.	ASSLN02
1.	When I don't do well in a subject, it's because of bad luck.	ASSLN03

Unknown

36.*	When I do well in school, I usually can't figure out why.	ASSUP01
44.*	I don't know what it takes for me to get good grades in school.	ASSUP02
23.	If I get a good grade on a test, I usually don't know why.	ASSUP03
27.*	When I do badly in school, I usually can't figure out why.	ASSUN01
26.*	I don't know how to keep myself from getting bad grades.	ASSUN02
40.	If I get a bad grade in school, I usually don't understand why I got it.	ASSUN03

Capacity Beliefs

Effort

24.*	When I'm in class, I can work hard.	ASYEP01
28.*	I can work really hard in school.	ASYEP02
3.*	When I'm doing classwork, I can really work hard on it.	ASYEP03
57.*	I can't seem to try very hard in school.	ASYEN01
6.*	When I'm in class, I can't seem to work very hard.	ASYEN02
4.*	I have trouble working hard in school.	ASYEN03

Attributes (Ability)

12.*	I think I'm pretty smart in school.	ASYAP01
19.*	When it comes to school, I'm pretty smart.	ASYAP02

42.	I would say I'm pretty smart in school.	ASYAP03
2.*	I don't have the brains to do well in school.	ASYAN01
31.*	I'm not very smart when it comes to schoolwork.	ASYAN02
52.	When it comes to schoolwork, I don't think I'm very smart.	ASYAN03

Powerful Others

47.*	I am able to get my teacher to like me.	ASYOP01
17.*	I can get my teacher to like me.	ASYOP02
8.	I can get along with my teacher.	ASYOP03
18.	I can't get my teacher to like me.	ASYON01
21.*	I don't seem to be able to get my teacher to like me.	ASYON02
13.*	I'm just not able to get along with my teacher.	ASYON03

Luck

45.*	I am lucky in school.	ASYLP01
7.*	I'm pretty lucky when it comes to getting grades.	ASYLP02
11.*	As far as doing well in school goes, I'm pretty lucky.	ASYLP03
30.*	I am unlucky when it comes to schoolwork.	ASYLN01
9.*	When it comes to grades, I'm unlucky.	ASYLN02
60.*	I'm unlucky at school work.	ASYLN03

COMPUTING SCORES FOR THE SPOCQ, FULL SCALE

Key to Coding

Column 1, Domain: Academic
Column 2, Reporter: Student
Column 3, Scale: CN = control, S = strategy, Y = capacity
Column 4, Causal category: Effort, attributes, powerful others, luck, unknown
Column 5, Valence: Positive, negative
Column 6, Item number

Computing Subscale and Scale Scores

Control Beliefs

Positive events	$CONp = (ASCNP01 + ASCNP02 + ASCNP03)/3$
Negative events	$CONn = (ASCNN01 + ASCNN02 + ASCNN03)/3$
Total	$CON = (CONp + [5\text{-}CONn])/2$

Strategy Beliefs

Effort:

Positive events	$STeffp = (ASSEP01 + ASSEP02 + ASSEP03)/3$
Negative events	$STeffn = (ASSEN01 + ASSEN02 + ASSEN03)/3$
Total	$STeff = (STeffp + STeffn)/2$

Attributes (ability):

Positive events	$STattp = (ASSAP01 + ASSAP02 + ASSAP03)/3$
Negative events	$STattn = (ASSAN01 + ASSAN02 + ASSAN03)/3$
Total	$STatt = (STattp + STattn)/2$

Powerful others:

Positive events	$STothp = (ASSOP01 + ASSOP02 + ASSOP03)/3$
Negative events	$STothn = (ASSON01 + ASSON02 + ASSON03)/3$
Total	$SToth = (STothp + STothn)/2$

Luck:

Positive events	$STlucp = (ASSLP01 + ASSLP02 + ASSLP03)/3$
Negative events	$STlucn = (ASSLN01 + ASSLN02 + ASSLN03)/3$
Total	$STluc = (STlucp + STlucn)/2$

Unknown:

Positive events	$STunkp = (ASSUP01 + ASSUP02 + ASSUP03)/3$
Negative events	$STunkn = (ASSUN01 + ASSUN02 + ASSUN03)/3$
Total	$STunk = (STunkp + STunkn)/2$

Capacity Beliefs

Effort:

Positive events	$CPeffp = (ASYEP01 + ASYEP02 + ASYEP03)/3$
Negative events	$CPeffn = (ASYEN01 + ASYEN02 + ASYEN03)/3$
Total	$CPeff = (CPeffp + [5-CPeffn])/2$

Attributes (ability):

Positive events	$CPattp = (ASYAP01 + ASYAP02 + ASYAP03)/3$
Negative events	$CPattn = (ASYAN01 + ASYAN02 + ASYAN03)/3$
Total	$CPatt = (CPattp + [5-CPattn])/2$

Powerful others:

Positive events	$CPothp = (ASYOP01 + ASYOP02 + ASYOP03)/3$
Negative events	$CPothn = (ASYON01 + ASYON02 + ASYON03)/3$
Total	$CPoth = (CPothp + [5-CPothn])/2$

Luck:

Positive events	$CPlucp = (ASYLP01 + ASYLP02 + ASYLP03)/3$
Negative events	$CPlucn = (ASYLN01 + ASYLN02 + ASYLN03)/3$
Total	$CPluc = (CPlucp + [5-CPlucn])/2$

Resultant Scales

SCALE NAME	SCALE LABEL	RANGE	HIGHER SCORES INDICATE:
1. CON	Control beliefs	(1–4)	More control
2. STeff	Strategy beliefs for effort	(1–4)	Effort is more effective
3. STatt	Strategy beliefs for attributes (ability)	(1–4)	Ability is more effective
4. SToth	Strategy beliefs for powerful others	(1–4)	Powerful others are more effective
5. STluc	Strategy beliefs for luck	(1–4)	Luck is more effective
6. STunk	Strategy beliefs for unknown factors	(1–4)	Less is known about causes

7. CPeff	Capacity beliefs for effort	(1–4)	Effort is more accessible
8. CPatt	Capacity beliefs for attributes	(1–4)	Attributes are more accessible
9. CPoth	Capacity beliefs for powerful others	(1–4)	Powerful others are more accessible
10. CPluc	Capacity beliefs for luck	(1–4)	Luck is more accessible

Computing Interaction Scores and Summary Scores

Interaction of Strategy and Capacity Beliefs

Effort	$INTeff = STeff \times CPeff$
Attributes (ability)	$INTatt = (5\text{-}STatt) \times CPatt$
Powerful others	$INToth = SToth \times (5\text{-}CPoth)$
Luck	$INTluc = STluc = STluc \times (5\text{-}CPluc)$

Cumulative Effects on Motivation and Performance

Promote
$$Promote = (CON \times 4) + (Steff \times CPeffp) \\ + ([5\text{-}STatt] \times CPattp) \\ + (CPothp \times 4) + (CPlucp \times 4)$$

Undermine
$$Undermine = (STunk \times 4) + (CPeffn \times 4) \\ + (CPattn \times 4) \\ + (SToth \times CPothn) \\ + (STluc \times CPlucn)$$

Maximum control
$$ConMax = Promote - Undermine$$

USING HIERARCHICAL LINEAR MODELING AND SAS PROC MIXED TO INVESTIGATE LAUNCH, AMBIENT-LEVEL, AND CHANGE-TO-CHANGE RELATIONS

Melanie J. Zimmer-Gembeck

INTRODUCTION

Most fundamental questions in the study of development involve describing and predicting change processes. Traditionally, these questions have reflected the desire to understand the basics of development and the nature of systematic age-graded change. However, those interested in development have come increasingly to recognize that, in addition to issues of normative change, an understanding of development also involves the study of differential change. In the literature on developmental psychology and education, these change processes are often labeled *developmental growth curves* or *trajectories*. A key issue in the study of individual differences in development is the examination of the antecedents, outcomes, and correlates of interindividual differences in trajectories.

The study of developmental growth curves is evolving. Currently, the literature often describes and applies methods that can be used to study normative change, for example, by describing a particular growth curve for a population or comparing the average growth curve of one group to that of another group (e.g., an intervention group and a control group; Bailey et al., 1993; Francis et al., 1991; Singer, 1997; Willett et al., 1991). However, there are other applications of this methodology that appear less frequently. These applications attempt to answer questions about interindividual differences in intraindividual development. In these analyses, the target of study is variation among individuals in their patterns of change over time. Sample questions include asking whether the initial level of an antecedent variable launches the developmental trajectory of a second construct (a launch relation), determining whether a measured variable must be maintained at some level to promote a more positive change pattern in other constructs (an ambient-level relation), or understanding the relation between multiple change processes occurring simultaneously (a change-to-change relation; Connell & Skinner, 1990; Skinner, Zimmer-Gembeck, & Connell, 1995; Zimmer-Gembeck, 1997).

The purpose of this appendix is to describe one set of procedures that can be used to estimate parameters representing characteristics of individual trajectories and to examine the antecedents and correlates of individual differences in developmental trajectories. The first two sections provide an overview of the procedure and explain how it is typically used. In the first section, a short introduction to a set of procedures that can be used to investigate these hypotheses will be presented, specifically, hierarchical linear modeling (HLM) using the MIXED procedure available in SAS/STAT software (SAS PROC MIXED; SAS Institute, Inc., Cary, NC). In the second section, examples of using SAS PROC MIXED to test some commonly proposed hypotheses about development will be presented.

The last two sections describe in detail how to use and interpret SAS PROC MIXED to answer launch, ambient-level, and change-to-change research questions. The third section defines launch, ambient-level, and change-to-change hypotheses and describes how the components of the hypothesized associations can be operationalized. The fourth section describes how these hypotheses can be tested using SAS PROC MIXED combined with simple linear or multiple regression analysis. The mathematics of HLM will not be described. Interested readers should refer to Bryk and Raudenbush (1992) and Littell, Milliken, Stroup, and Wolfinger (1996).

INTRODUCTION TO HLM USING SAS PROC MIXED

HLM is a generalization of the standard linear model and is sometimes called a *general linear mixed model,* a *multilevel model,* or a *growth model* (Bailey et al., 1993; Bryk & Raudenbush, 1992; Burchinal & Appelbaum, 1991; Francis et al., 1991; Singer, 1997; Willet et al., 1991). The *hierarchical* in HLM comes from the hierarchical structure of the data. Clusters of data are nested within other variables, forming a hierarchy. In the case of repeated measures of constructs, times of measurement are nested within subjects. HLM can be used to test many hypotheses that focus on change over time and, hence, involve repeated measures of constructs. For example, HLM allows the assessment of the shape of the developmental trajectory of a population, can be used to test differences between the trajectories of two or more groups, allows the testing of the association between independent and dependent variables that have been repeatedly measured, and provides estimates of parameters that describe participants' individual growth trajectories.

SAS PROC MIXED is a powerful procedure to complete HLM. This procedure can be used to specify both fixed and random effects, and these effects are then estimated simultaneously. Fixed effects are those variables that are assumed to represent all possibilities in the entire population of interest (e.g., sex). Fixed effects are predictor variables as typically used in multiple linear regression. When using SAS PROC MIXED with multiwave data, fixed effects can define populations for which growth curves will be estimated.

Random effects are those that are assumed to have been randomly selected from all possibilities. For example, with repeated measures of data, times of measurement are assumed to have been randomly selected from the entire set of available times of measurement. In SAS PROC MIXED, random effects can be specified to estimate individual growth trajectories. Missing data are then estimated for individuals on the basis of available data for those individuals and the populations to which they belong, and growth trajectories for all individuals are estimated with respect to the population trajectory.

Although examples are provided later in this appendix in which analyses were conducted outside the framework of HLM, it is always preferable to test as many hypotheses as possible within this framework. In the example presented here, the additional analyses were conducted because the specific hypotheses described could not be tested within a single mixed model. It should also be noted that there are a number of preliminary analyses and decisions that were completed before proceeding through the steps presented here. These initial steps focused on analyses to determine the shape of the growth curve to be specified for each variable, including analyses to select the shape of the population growth curve, to detect differences between slopes as a function of different group characteristics (e.g., sex, wave), and to examine the extent to which that shape of the slope for different individuals deviated from the population shape.

We also examined several features of the data that influenced the quality of group and individual estimates, such as the sample size at each time of measurement (cross-sectional sample sizes) and the numbers of participants who were present for one, two, three, etc. times of measurement (longitudinal sample sizes). To determine the viability of using individual estimates in subsequent analyses, we then assessed standard errors of estimates of individual parameters and the accuracy of our models as done when using simple linear or multiple regression analyses. Finally, as a cross-check on the accuracy of estimates of the slopes of individual growth curves, we compared estimates of individual parameters obtained from mixed models to beta parameter estimates obtained from regressing each participant's repeated observed scores of a variable onto time of measurement.

SUBNUM	SEX	WAVE	GRADE	TIME	CONMAX
4410	2	1	.	1	.
4410	2	1	.	2	.
4410	2	1	.	3	.
4410	2	1	.	4	.
4410	2	1	5	5	33.00
4410	2	1	.	6	.
4410	2	1	6	7	30.11
4410	2	1	6	8	31.39
4410	2	1	.	9	.
4410	2	1	7	10	34.42
8360	1	2	3	1	28.25
8360	1	2	3	2	22.46
8360	1	2	4	3	39.00
8360	1	2	4	4	21.67
8360	1	2	.	5	.
8360	1	2	.	6	.
8360	1	2	.	7	.
8360	1	2	.	8	.
ETC . . .					

FIGURE B1.—Data prepared for use with SAS PROC MIXED

OVERVIEW OF HLM AND ILLUSTRATIONS OF PROCEDURES TO TEST COMMON HYPOTHESES

Assessing the Population Trajectory and between-Group Differences in Trajectories

Applications of HLM are increasingly familiar to researchers. The most basic applications describe patterns of change in constructs over time within populations and test differences in the trajectories of change between two or more groups (e.g., males and females or intervention group and control group). A good example of these uses of HLM is described by Bailey et al. (1993), and a useful introduction to using SAS PROC MIXED for testing group differences in growth curves is provided by Singer (1997). Other software packages also provide powerful tools for conducting these types of growth curve analyses. In this section, an example is provided to demonstrate how SAS PROC MIXED can be used to examine differences in growth curves between males and females. The example tests differences in growth trajectories of perceived control (CONMAX) between the third and the seventh grades.

In order to use SAS PROC MIXED to estimate the population trajectory of CONMAX and trajectories of subgroups, the data were structured as in Figure B1. Figure B1 shows a record for each subject at each of 10 times of measurement from the fall of grade 3 to the spring of grade 7. In this set of data, not all participants were present at all times of measurement. In fact, it was not possible for any participant to be present at all times of measurement since students completed measures a maximum of six consecutive times.

```
PROC MIXED DATA=SASUSER.ALLDATGC NOCLPRINT;                    #1
CLASS SUBNUM SEX WAVE;                                         #2
MODEL CONMAX=TIME SEX WAVE TIME*SEX TIME*WAVE /               #3
  SOLUTION CHISQ;
RANDOM INTERCEPT TIME / TYPE=UN SUBJECT=SUBNUM;               #4
RUN;
```

FIGURE B2.—Example of an SAS Program using the MIXED procedure

Variables included in the data set were SUBNUM, SEX, WAVE, GRADE, TIME, and CONMAX. SUBNUM indicated each participant's identification number. SEX and WAVE were nominal variables that identified each participant's sex (1 = male, 2 = female) and whether they began the study in the first or second wave of data collection. TIME indicated the time of measurement and was coded 1 for a measurement in the fall of the third grade, 2 for a measurement in the spring of the third grade, and 3–10 for measurements in the fall and spring of the fourth, fifth, sixth, and seventh grades. CONMAX was an aggregate measurement of the optimal profile of perceived control (see Appendix A; as well as Skinner, 1995; Wellborn et al., 1989).

SAS Program

Figure B2 provides an example of an SAS program using the MIXED procedure. Rows in Figure B2 were numbered on the right to provide points of reference. In row 1, the SAS data set to be used was specified and the NOCLPRINT option was used. NOCLPRINT suppresses the printing of CLASS variables (e.g., the printing of subject identification numbers; see row 2). In row 2, SUBNUM, SEX, and WAVE were specified as CLASS variables. This statement identified these variables as nominal variables. Dummy variables were then automatically constructed by the SAS procedure.

Row 3 contained the MODEL statement. CONMAX (children's perceived control) was the dependent variable. CONMAX had been repeatedly measured. Therefore, an independent variable specified in the model was TIME of measurement. SEX and WAVE were additional independent variables. The main effects of SEX and WAVE were tests of whether the *level* of the trajectories of perceived control differed between participants grouped by sex or wave. TIME*SEX and TIME*WAVE were interaction effects that were tests of whether *linear rates of change* in perceived control over time (slopes) differed by sex or by wave.

The SOLUTION option requested that a solution for the fixed effects of TIME, SEX, WAVE, SEX*TIME, and WAVE*TIME be calculated and output. The CHISQ option requested that chi-square tests of these effects be calculated in addition to the default F test. Although not included in the example, higher-order effects may also be added to test whether the shape

191

of the developmental trajectory is quadratic, cubic, etc. For example, to test a quadratic shape, TIME*TIME (TIMESQ) could be included as a covariate in the model. A SEX*TIMESQ interaction could be included in order to test sex differences in the quadratic shape of trajectories of perceived control.

Row 4 contained the RANDOM statement. This statement indicated that intercept and time were random effects in the model. TYPE allowed for selection of the covariance structure of random effects. TYPE=UN requested that the variance-covariance matrix for the intercepts and slopes be unstructured. The variances of the intercepts and slopes were allowed to have no structure and to differ, and the covariance between them was not restricted to have a particular structure. SUBJECT=SUBNUM identified the individual subjects in the database. An alternative to the RANDOM statement used in this example is the REPEATED statement. Some statisticians prefer this statement when analyzing repeated-measures data (see version 6.09 of the SAS/STAT manual, SAS Institute, Inc., Cary, NC; Littell et al., 1996; Singer, 1997).

SAS Output

Partial output from this MIXED procedure is shown in Figure B3. The *covariance parameter estimates* were computed using the default residual maximum likelihood method (REML). UN(1,1) gives the estimated variance of the intercepts of CONMAX trajectories. The Wald Z test was performed to test whether this variance was significantly different from zero. As can be seen in the section of Figure B3 titled *Covariance Parameter Estimates,* the estimate of the variance of the intercepts [INTERCEPT UN(1,1)] of the individual developmental trajectories of CONMAX was 149.268, and the Wald Z test was significant ($p < .05$). Therefore, the variance of the intercepts of CONMAX was significantly different from zero.

UN(2,2) in the *Covariance Parameter Estimates* section of Figure B3 reports the estimated variance of the individual slopes of the developmental trajectories of CONMAX and was a test of whether the variance was significantly different from zero. The estimated variance of the slopes was 3.220. There was significant variation in the slopes of the trajectories of CONMAX since the Wald Z test was significant ($p < .05$). In sum, participants began at different levels of CONMAX and had varying rates of linear change. Establishing the presence of significant variation in intercepts and slopes was an important condition preceding the use of estimated individual intercepts and slopes of CONMAX as individual difference variables.

In Figure B3, the section titled *Model Fitting Information for CONMAX* details various pieces of information on the fit of the model, including the number of observations (3,537), the residual variance estimate (73.28), and the square root of this estimate (8.56). The model fitting information was valu-

Covariance Parameter Estimates (REML)

Cov Parm	Ratio	Estimate	Std Error	Z	Pr > |Z|
INTERCEPT UN(1,1)	2.037	149.268	17.372	8.59	0.0001
UN(2,1)	−0.123	−9.030	2.950	−3.06	0.0022
UN(2,2)	0.044	3.220	0.590	5.46	0.0001
Residual	1.000	73.284	2.563	28.60	0.0000

Model Fitting Information for CONMAX

Description	Value
Observations	3537.000
Variance Estimate	73.2840
Standard Deviation Estimate	8.5606
REML Log Likelihood	−13905.0
Akaike's Information Criterion	−13909.0
Schwarz's Bayesian Criterion	−13921.3
−2 REML Log Likelihood	27810.01
Null Model LRT Chi-Square	1496.106
Null Model LRT DF	3.0000
Null Model LRT P-Value	0.0000

Solution for Fixed Effects

Parameter	Estimate	Std Error	DDF	T	Pr > |T|
INTERCEPT	27.84558858	1.15501576	1371	24.11	0.0001
TIME	−0.81089296	0.20353164	1014	−3.98	0.0001
SEX 1	−0.19219962	1.25612969	1146	−0.15	0.8784
SEX 2	0.00000000	.	.	.	.
WAVE 1	−4.89374893	1.28511818	1146	−3.81	0.0001
WAVE 2	0.00000000	.	.	.	.
TIME*SEX 1	−0.80432672	0.22459966	1146	−3.58	0.0004
TIME*SEX 2	0.00000000	.	.	.	.
TIME*WAVE 1	0.98868675	0.23000283	1146	4.30	0.0001
TIME*WAVE 2	0.00000000	.	.	.	.

Tests of Fixed Effects

Source	NDF	DDF	Type III ChiSq	Type III F	Pr > ChiSq	Pr > F
TIME	1	1014	39.07	39.07	0.0001	0.0001
SEX	1	1146	0.02	0.02	0.8784	0.8784
WAVE	1	1146	14.50	14.50	0.0001	0.0001
TIME*SEX	1	1146	12.82	12.82	0.0003	0.0004
TIME*WAVE	1	1146	18.48	18.48	0.0001	0.0001

FIGURE B3.—Example of Output from SAS PROC MIXED

able when comparing this model to other nested models and when comparing this model to the same model with different assumptions about the variance-covariance matrix (for more details, see Littell et al., 1996).

The *Solution for Fixed Effects* section of Figure B3 provides information on the estimated intercepts and slopes of the population trajectories of CONMAX. All estimates for subgroups (e.g., SEX or WAVE groups) were calculated with respect to the estimates for INTERCEPT and TIME. For example, the intercept of the CONMAX trajectory of SEX 2 in WAVE 2 was the INTERCEPT estimate (27.846) plus the estimate for SEX 2 (0.000) plus the estimate for WAVE 2 (0.000). Adding these three values resulted in an estimated intercept for SEX 2 in WAVE 2 of 27.846. Further, the intercept for SEX 1 in WAVE 2 was the intercept estimate (27.846) plus the estimate for SEX 1 (-0.192) plus the estimate of WAVE 2 (0.000). Therefore, the intercept for SEX 1 in WAVE 2 was 27.654.

Similar calculations can be conducted to obtain estimates of the linear slopes of CONMAX for particular groups. The parameter estimate of the TIME effect equals -0.811, so the estimate of the slope of the CONMAX trajectory of SEX 2 in WAVE 2 was -0.811 plus the estimate of TIME*SEX 2 (0.000) plus the estimate of TIME*WAVE 2 (0.000), resulting in a slope of SEX 2 in WAVE 2 of -0.811. The slope for SEX 1 in WAVE 2 was -0.811 plus the estimate of TIME*SEX 1 (-0.804) plus the estimate of TIME*WAVE 2 (0.000), resulting in a slope of CONMAX for SEX 1 in WAVE 2 of -1.615. In summary, although both sexes in WAVE 2 started with about the same initial level of CONMAX (27.846 and 27.654), SEX 1 (males) declined significantly more rapidly (-1.615) than SEX 2 (females; -0.811).

The *Tests of Fixed Effects* section of Figure B3 reports the tests of the unique fixed effects. The effect of TIME was significant ($p < .05$), indicating that there was a significant linear rate of change in CONMAX from the third to the seventh grade level (see Pr $>$ ChiSq and Pr $> F$). Further, since the estimate for TIME was negative (-0.811), there was a significant linear decline in CONMAX from the third to the seventh grade in this population. The main effect of SEX was not significant, indicating that there was no significant difference between the initial levels of the CONMAX trajectories of participants grouped by SEX. The main effect of WAVE was significant, indicating that there was a difference in the initial levels of CONMAX when comparing the two WAVE groups. Both the TIME*SEX interaction and the TIME*WAVE interaction were significant. These findings indicated that there were significant differences in the slopes of CONMAX between participants grouped by SEX or WAVE.

Independent and Dependent Variables with Repeated Measures

The application of HLM described previously involved the examination of patterns of change over time in a single variable, either for an entire group or as a function of membership in two (or more) groups. The next set of applications is slightly more complex because it involves the examination of the relation between two variables repeatedly measured over time. This can either be examined directly or be used to describe the shape of the population trajectory of one variable after partialing out the effects of a covariate with repeated measures. These can be investigated within a single random effects mixed model using SAS PROC MIXED.

SUBNUM	SEX	WAVE	GRADE	TIME	CONMAX	TENG
4410	2	1	.	1	.	.
4410	2	1	.	2	.	.
4410	2	1	.	3	.	.
4410	2	1	.	4	.	.
4410	2	1	5	5	33.00	3.67
4410	2	1	5	6	.	3.66
4410	2	1	6	7	30.11	3.56
4410	2	1	6	8	31.39	3.42
4410	2	1	7	9	.	3.40
4410	2	1	7	10	34.42	3.40
8360	1	2	3	1	28.25	3.65
8360	1	2	3	2	22.46	3.55
8360	1	2	4	3	39.00	3.44
8360	1	2	4	4	21.67	3.32
8360	1	2	5	5	.	3.33
8360	1	2	5	6	.	3.40
8360	1	2	.	7	.	.
8360	1	2	.	8	.	.
8360	1	2	.	9	.	.
8360	1	2	.	10	.	. ETC. . .

FIGURE B4.—Sample data including TENG prepared for use with SAS PROC MIXED

Figure B4 shows the same data presented in Figure B1 above with one additional variable, TENG (teacher-reported students' engagement in school). TENG has been repeatedly measured for each student. The data in Figure B4 were used in the SAS MIXED procedure shown in Figure B5. This procedure was designed to test the association between a time-varying independent variable (CONMAX) and a time-varying dependent variable (TENG).

The output obtained from this SAS program is shown in Figure B6. The association between the main effect of CONMAX and TENG was significant (see the main effect of CONMAX in the *Tests of Fixed Effects* section of Figure B6; Pr > F was < .05). The main effect of CONMAX was a test of the relation between CONMAX and the initial level of TENG after partialing out changes over time in TENG and the effects of SEX and WAVE. The interaction between CONMAX and TIME was not significant (see CONMAX*TIME in the *Tests of Fixed Effects* section of Figure B6). Therefore, there was no association between CONMAX and the rate of linear change of TENG. For every

```
PROC MIXED DATA=SASUSER.ALLDATGC NOCLPRINT;
CLASS SUBNUM SEX WAVE;
MODEL TENG=TIME SEX WAVE TIME*SEX TIME*WAVE CONMAX
   CONMAX*TIME / SOLUTION CHISQ;
RANDOM INTERCEPT TIME / TYPE=UN SUBJECT=SUBNUM;
RUN;
```

FIGURE B5.—Example of an SAS program using the MIXED procedure to determine the association between two variables with repeated measures.

Covariance Parameter Estimates (REML)

Cov Parm		Ratio	Estimate	Std Error	Z	Pr > |Z|
INTERCEPT	UN(1,1)	1.934	0.263	0.0367	7.25	0.0001
	UN(2,1)	−0.183	−0.025	0.0063	−3.99	0.0001
	UN(2,2)	0.034	0.005	0.0011	4.15	0.0001
Residual		1.000	0.138	0.0059	23.53	0.0001

Model Fitting Information for TENG

Description	Value
Observations	2677.000
Variance Estimate	0.1377
Standard Deviation Estimate	0.3711
REML Log Likelihood	−1934.44
Akaike's Information Criterion	−1938.44
Schwarz's Bayesian Criterion	−1950.22
−2 REML Log Likelihood	3868.871
Null Model LRT Chi-Square	454.4360
Null Model LRT DF	3.0000
Null Model LRT P-Value	0.0000

Solution for Fixed Effects

Parameter	Estimate	Std Error	DDF	T	Pr > |T|
INTERCEPT	3.01240436	0.05048224	1182	59.67	0.0001
TIME	−0.01269591	0.00713026	789	−1.78	0.0754
SEX 1	−0.10434076	0.02822920	698	−3.70	0.0002
SEX 2	0.00000000	.	.	.	.
WAVE 1	−0.10721330	0.02843241	698	−3.77	0.0002
WAVE 2	0.00000000	.	.	.	.
CONMAX	0.01179038	0.00163691	698	7.20	0.0001
CONMAX*TIME	0.00005993	0.00026496	698	0.23	0.8211

Tests of Fixed Effects

Source	NDF	DDF	Type III ChiSq	Type III F	Pr > ChiSq	Pr > F
TIME	1	791	3.17	3.17	0.0750	0.0754
SEX	1	698	13.66	13.66	0.0002	0.0002
WAVE	1	698	14.22	14.22	0.0002	0.0002
CONMAX	1	698	51.88	51.88	0.0001	0.0001
CONMAX*TIME	1	698	0.05	0.05	0.8211	0.8211

FIGURE B6.—Example of output from SAS PROC MIXED testing the association between time-varying independent and dependent variables.

increase of 1.0 in CONMAX, the growth rate of TENG increased (nonsignificantly) by .00006 after accounting for SEX and WAVE (see the estimate of CONMAX*TIME in the *Solution for Fixed Effects* section of Figure B6). Further, the trajectory of TENG did not have a linear slope that was significantly different from zero (TIME was not significant in the *Tests of Fixed Effects* section of Figure B6) after partialing out the effects of CONMAX, SEX, WAVE, and CONMAX*TIME.

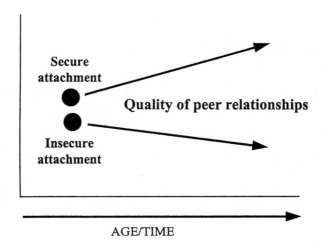

FIGURE B7.—Example of a launch relation: individual differences in attachment at 18 months of age launch the trajectory of the quality of relationships with peers throughout life.

LAUNCH, AMBIENT-LEVEL, AND CHANGE-TO-CHANGE HYPOTHESES

Definitions of Launch, Ambient-Level, and Change-to-Change Models

These last two sections describe and illustrate procedures for testing three specific models of the predictors of individual differences in developmental change (Connell & Skinner, 1990). A launch hypothesis predicts that differences in the rate of change of a target variable are predicted from individual differences in the *initial level* of an antecedent variable. Therefore, the target of analysis is the rate of change of the outcome and the predictor is the initial level of the antecedent variable. For example, a launch hypothesis might state that individual differences in attachment at 18 months of age *launches* the trajectory of the quality of relationships with peers throughout life (see Figure B7).

An ambient-level hypothesis predicts that individual differences in the average level of an antecedent variable present across time are important for shaping individual differences in the rate of change in a target variable. The target in this case is also the rate of change of the outcome, but the predictor is the average level of the antecedent variable. For example, an ambient-level hypothesis might hold that maintaining some threshold of parental warmth is necessary for optimal development of an aspect of the psychosocial functioning of a child (see Figure B8).

Finally, a change-to-change hypothesis predicts that individual differences in the *pattern* or *rate of change* of an antecedent variable predict individ-

197

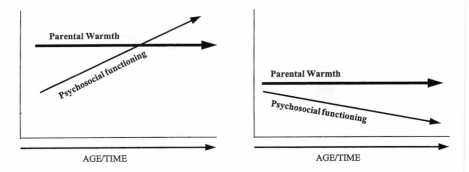

FIGURE B8.—Example of an ambient-level relation: a certain ambient level of parental warmth is necessary for optimal development of the psychosocial functioning of a child. Increases in parental warmth are not necessary, but decreasing parental warmth may be detrimental.

ual differences in the pattern or rate of change of a target variable. The target is the rate of change of the outcome, and the predictor is the rate of change of the antecedent variable. For example, a change-to-change hypothesis might state that it is the pattern of change in self-esteem that predicts the pattern of change in positive affect. As self-esteem improves, positive affect also improves. As self-esteem decays, positive affect also decays (see Figure B9).

Estimation of Launch, Ambient-Level, and Change-to-Change Indicators

The intercept of the developmental trajectory of an antecedent variable is the indicator of a launch variable (see Figure B10). The slope of the developmental trajectory of an antecedent or target variable is the indicator of

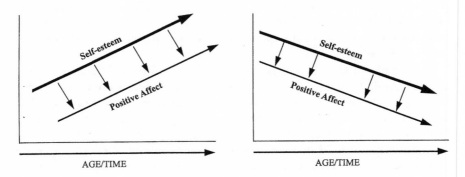

FIGURE B9.—Example of a change-to-change relation: as self-esteem improves, positive affect also improves. As self-esteem decays, positive affect also decays. It is the pattern of change in self-esteem that predicts positive affect.

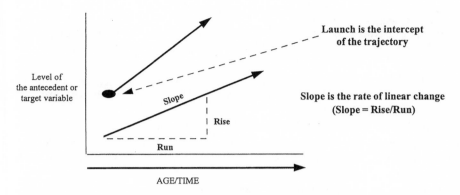

FIGURE B10.—Definition of the intercept of a developmental trajectory

"change" (see Figure B10). The slope is the rate of change of a trajectory and is defined as the "rise" of the trajectory divided by the "run" of the trajectory. Finally, the level of the antecedent variable averaged across time is the indicator of "ambient level."

In order to generate intercepts, ambient level, and slopes of developmental trajectories, there are at least three data requirements. First, longitudinal data are necessary since the focus is on change over time. Second, at least three times of measurement are needed (Rogosa, 1988). The actual shape of the trajectory may not be adequately described with only two times of measurement. Third, estimates of the intercept, slope, and ambient level of the trajectories of antecedent and target variables are needed for each study participant.

When the intercept and time of measurement are specified as random effects in SAS PROC MIXED, estimates of the intercept and slope of the developmental trajectory of the dependent variable for each study participant are calculated. These estimates are based on information available about the average population trajectory and the individual's own observed repeated measures of the variable of interest. Therefore, individuals with more complete data carry more weight in the estimation.

Using SAS PROC MIXED to Test Launch, Ambient-Level, and Change-to-Change Hypotheses

The following example describes how to use SAS PROC MIXED to calculate and output variables that can be used to test launch and change-to-change hypotheses. SAS PROC MIXED was used to output estimates of the intercept and slope of each individual's developmental trajectory of CONMAX and TENG. These variables were then used in an analysis of in-

```
PROC MIXED DATA=SASUSER.ALLDATGC NOCLPRINT;
CLASS SUBNUM SEX WAVE;
MODEL CONMAX=TIME SEX WAVE TIME*SEX TIME*WAVE / SOLUTION CHISQ;
RANDOM INTERCEPT TIME / TYPE=UN SUBJECT=SUBNUM SOLUTION;
RUN;
```

FIGURE B11.—Example of an SAS program using the MIXED procedure to print the estimated intercept and slope of the trajectory of CONMAX for each study participant.

terindividual differences. The example will describe how to output estimates of intercepts and slopes of CONMAX for each student. The example also describes how to output values of CONMAX predicted by the model for each participant at each time of measurement.

In order to output the estimates of intercept and slope of each individual's developmental trajectory of CONMAX, an additional option, SOLUTION, was added to the RANDOM statement in the SAS PROC MIXED program (see Figure B11). When INTERCEPT and TIME were specified as random effects, the SOLUTION option resulted in output containing estimated intercepts and slopes of trajectories of the specified dependent variable for all study participants.

Including the SOLUTION option (as well as some additional programming to output the information to a file) resulted in the output shown in Figure B12. INTERCEPT was the estimated intercept of each participant's CONMAX trajectory. TIME was the estimated slope of the trajectory of CONMAX for each individual. For example, the developmental trajectory of CONMAX for SUBNUM 4410 had an estimated intercept of 4.94 and an estimated slope of 2.00. These individual estimates were expressed as deviations from the estimates of the population trajectory. To get the actual intercept and slope values, individual estimates were added to the INTERCEPT estimate and the TIME estimate; these estimates were available in the *Solution for Fixed Effects* section of the SAS PROC MIXED output. INTSE and TIMESE shown in Figure B12 were the standard errors of the intercept and slope estimates, respectively, for each subject. Figure 19 above illustrates the trajectories of CONMAX for nine participants and the estimates of the slopes of their trajectories.

The intercepts and slopes can, in principle, be used as individual difference variables. However, before proceeding to the step using intercept and

SUBNUM	INTERCEPT	INTSE	TIME	TIMESE
4410	4.93949332	6.80477868	2.00358954	2.38626018
6340	4.44533301	6.76336746	−0.60975877	2.33977441
7598	6.79776566	9.50030688	−2.52123912	2.83436687
8360	10.50907960	6.76349884	1.14906584	2.33977923
ETC . . .				

FIGURE B12.—Output from the RANDOM statement with the SOLUTION option in SAS PROC MIXED.

TABLE B1

RESULTS OF A LINEAR REGRESSION EXAMINING LAUNCH AND CHANGE-TO-CHANGE RELATIONS
BETWEEN TRAJECTORIES OF CHILDREN'S PERCEIVED CONTROL AND TRAJECTORIES
OF STUDENT ENGAGEMENT (Dependent Variable: Slope of the Growth
Curve of Student Engagement [Teacher Report])

Independent Variable	R^2	Perceived Control Intercept; Launch, β	Perceived Control Slope; Change to Change, β	Student Engagement Intercept (Teacher Report), β
ConMax	.16	.03	.22***	(−.40)

NOTE.—The model was weighted by the number of times of measurement of teacher-reported student engagement.
$N = 1,258$.
*** $p < .001$.

slope estimates as individual difference variables in other analyses, it was critical to assess the precision of the estimates. This was done by examining the
standard error of the estimates as well as by examining the predicted values
and the residuals of the predicted values (see below). Further, adequate data
were available to provide fairly precise estimates before conducting these
analyses. This was a large sample (over 1,600 students and their teachers),
which allowed for more confidence in the estimates. Even so, there were con-
cerns that some of the estimated parameters describing individual trajectories
may not be precise. For example, estimates of the slopes of trajectories for
students who were present at only three times of measurement may have been
less precise than estimates for students who were present at six times of measurement. Therefore, in the regression analysis in Table B1, each participant's data were weighted by the number of times of measurement of the
dependent variable to partially account for this possibility. Once these conditions are met, intercept and slope estimates can be used in more traditional
correlation or regression analyses. For example, multiple linear regression
was used to examine the relation between interindividual differences in the
intercepts and slopes of the trajectories of CONMAX and the slopes of TENG
(see Table B1).

The regression results indicated that there was no launch relation between CONMAX (children's perceptions of perceived control in the academic domain) and TENG (engagement in the classroom; β = .03). However, there was a change-to-change relation (β = .22, $p < .001$). Note that,
in this analysis, the intercept of the trajectory of engagement in the classroom
was included as an independent variable. This variable was included to account for possible ceiling effects (the intercept and slope of engagement were
negatively correlated, indicating that children who started higher were likely
to show a greater decline in engagement over time), and to determine the
unique launch and change-to-change relations between children's perceived

```
PROC MIXED DATA=SASUSER.ALLDATGC NOCLPRINT;
CLASS SUBNUM SEX WAVE;
MODEL CONMAX=TIME SEX WAVE TIME*SEX TIME*WAVE / SOLUTION CHISQ
    PREDICTED;
RANDOM INTERCEPT TIME / TYPE=UN SUBJECT=SUBNUM;
ID SUBNUM TIME;
MAKE PREDICTED OUT=SASUSER.CONPRED;
RUN;
```

FIGURE B13.—Example of an SAS program using the MIXED procedure to output estimated values of CONMAX for each participant at each time of measurement.

control and engagement after partialing out individual differences in the initial level of engagement.

VALUES OF CONMAX ESTIMATED BY USING SAS PROC MIXED

SAS PROC MIXED can be used to output estimated values of the dependent variable for all participants at each time of measurement. These estimated values were obtained by adding the PREDICTED option to the MODEL statement and adding the ID and MAKE statements to the SAS MIXED procedure (see Figure B13).

The PREDICTED option requested estimated values of the dependent variable for each subject at each time of measurement. The input data set must include a record for each subject and time for which one wants to output predicted values (e.g., see SUBNUM 4410 in Figure B1 above). The ID statement specified that each record in the output data set contain the listed variables (SUBNUM and TIME) for identification. The MAKE statement requested that the predicted values of the dependent variable be output to a data set named CONPRED.

Figure B14 provides an example of the output received by including the PREDICTED option, ID statement, and MAKE statement in SAS PROC MIXED. CONMAOBS in Figure B14 was the actual (observed) score for CONMAX, and CONMPRED was the value estimated (predicted) by the model. In addition, the variance of each estimated value, the standard error of each estimated value, the lower and upper 95% confidence interval of each estimated value, and the residual were included in the output data set. These estimated values were then used to plot complete trajectories of CONMAX from the fall of the third grade to the spring of the seventh grade whether or not a participant had missing data (e.g., see Figure 14 above). These estimates could also be used to compute ambient levels. The ambient level for each participant would be the average of his or her 10 estimated values of CONMAX. Alternatively, ambient levels can be computed on the basis of observed values of CONMAX.

SUBNUM	TIME	CONMAOBS	CONMPRED	CONMV_PR	CONMSE_P	CONL95M	CONU95M	CONMARES
4410	1	.	35.01	2.05				
4410	2	.	35.06	1.54	ETC			
4410	3	34.42	34.32	2.34				
4410	4	32.14	32.25	2.21				
4410	5	23.58	26.45	2.10				
4410	6	19.10	19.13	1.78				
4410	7	.	18.67	1.79				
4410	8	18.00	18.10	1.87				
4410	9	.	18.25	1.76				
4410	10	18.50	18.43	1.87				

FIGURE B14.—Example of output produced by including the PREDICTED option in the MODEL statement, the ID statement, and the MAKE statement in SAS PROC MIXED.

CONCLUSION

The purpose of this appendix was to describe and illustrate one method of investigating hypotheses regarding processes of group and individual change. It was shown that SAS PROC MIXED is a powerful tool for assessing quantitative repeated-measures data. The inclusion of this procedure in a widely available software package makes it possible to describe developmental trajectories, test interindividual differences in intraindividual change, and determine the nature of launch, ambient-level, and change-to-change relations.

REFERENCES

Abramson, L. Y., Seligman, M. E. P., & Teasdale, J. D. (1978). Learned helplessness in humans. *Journal of Abnormal Psychology, 87,* 49–74.

Ainsworth, M. D. S. (1979). Infant-mother attachment. *American Psychologist, 34*(10), 932–937.

Alloy, L. B., & Abramson, L. Y. (1979). Judgment of contingency in depressed and nondepressed students: Sadder but wiser? *Journal of Experimental Psychology: General, 18,* 441–485.

Ames, C., & Ames, R. (1985). *Research on motivation in education: Vol. 2. The classroom milieu.* San Diego: Academic.

Anderman, E. M., & Maeher, M. L. (1994). Motivation and schooling in the middle grades. *Review of Educational Research, 64,* 287–309.

Bailey, D. B., Jr., Burchinal, M. R., & McWilliam, R. A. (1993). Age of peers and early childhood development. *Child Development, 64,* 848–862.

Baltes, M. M., & Baltes, P. B. (1986). *The psychology of control and aging.* Hillsdale, NJ: Erlbaum.

Baltes, P. B. (1987). Theoretical propositions of life-span developmental psychology: On the dynamics between growth and decline. *Developmental Psychology, 23,* 611–626.

Baltes, P. B., Cornelius, S. W., & Nesselroade, J. R. (1980). Cohort effects in developmental psychology. In J. R. Nesselroade & P. B. Baltes (Eds.), *Longitudinal research in the study of behavior and development.* New York: Academic.

Baltes, P. B., Lindenberger, U., & Staudinger, U. M. (1998). Life-span theory in developmental psychology. In R. M. Lerner (Ed.), W. Damon (Series Ed.), *Handbook of child psychology: Vol. 1. Theoretical models of human development.* New York: Wiley.

Baltes, P. B., Reese, H. W., & Nesselroade, J. R. (1977). *Life-span developmental psychology: Introduction to research methods.* Monterey, CA: Brooks/Cole.

Bandura, A. (1977). Self-efficacy: Toward a unified theory of behavioral change. *Psychological Review, 84,* 191–215.

Bandura, A. (1986). *The social foundations of thought and action: A social cognitive theory.* Englewood Cliffs, NJ: Prentice-Hall.

Bandura, A. (1989). Human agency in social cognitive theory. *American Psychologist, 44*(9), 1175–1184.

Bandura, A. (1991). Self-regulation of motivation through anticipatory and self-regulatory mechanisms. In R. A. Dienstbier (Ed.), *Perspectives on motivation: Nebraska symposium on motivation* (Vol. 38). Lincoln: University of Nebraska Press.

Bandura, A. (1996). *Self-efficacy: The exercise of control.* New York: Freeman.

Bandura, A., Barbaranelli, C., Caprara, G. V., & Pastorelli, C. (1996). Multi-faceted impact of self-efficacy beliefs on academic functioning. *Child Development, 67,* 1206–1222.

Bandura, A., & Schunk, D. H. (1981). Cultivating competence, self-efficacy, and intrinsic interest through proximal self-motivation. *Journal of Personality and Social Psychology*, **41**, 586–598.

Barker, G. P., & Graham, S. (1987). Developmental study of praise and blame as attributional cues. *Journal of Educational Psychology*, **79**, 62–66.

Baumrind, D. (1977, April). *Socialization determinants of personal agency*. Paper presented at the meeting of the Society for Research in Child Development, New Orleans.

Belmont, M., Skinner, E., Wellborn, J., & Connell, J. (1992). *Teacher as Social Context (TASC): Two measures of teacher provision of involvement, structure, and autonomy support: Student report measure* (Tech. Rep.). Rochester, NY: University of Rochester.

Berry, J. M., & West, R. L. (1993). Cognitive self-efficacy in relation to personal mastery and goal setting across the life span. *International Journal of Behavioral Development*, **16**(2), 351–379.

Beyer, S. (1995). Maternal employment and children's academic achievement: Parenting styles as mediating variables. *Development Review*, **15**, 212–253.

Bialer, I. (1961). Conceptualization of success and failure in mentally retarded and normal children. *Journal of Personality*, **29**, 303–320.

Birch, S. H., & Ladd, G. W. (1997). The teacher-child relationship and children's early school adjustment. *Journal of School Psychology*, **35**, 61–79.

Blumenfeld, P. C. (1992). Classroom learning and motivation: Clarifying and expanding goal theory. *Journal of Educational Psychology*, **84**, 272–281.

Blumenfeld, P., Pintrich, P., & Hamilton, V. (1986). Children's concept of ability, effort, and conduct. *American Educational Research Journal*, **23**, 95–104.

Blumenfeld, P. C., Pintrich, P., Meece, J., & Wessels, K. (1982). The formation and role of self-perceptions of ability in elementary school classrooms. *Elementary School Journal*, **82**, 401–420.

Boggiano, A. K., Main, D. S., & Katz, P. A. (1988). Children's preference for challenge: The role of perceived competence and control. *Journal of Personality and Social Psychology*, **54**, 134–141.

Borkowski, J. G., Carr, M., Rellinger, E., & Pressley, M. (1990). Self-regulated cognition: Interdependence of metacognition, attributions, and self-esteem. In B. Jones & L. Idol (Eds.), *Dimensions of thinking*. Hillsdale, NJ: Erlbaum.

Bouffard-Bouchard, T. (1989). Influence of self-efficacy on performance in a cognitive task. *Journal of Social Psychology*, **130**, 353–363.

Bouffard-Bouchard, T., Parent, S., & Larivee, S. (1991). Influence of self-efficacy on self-regulation and performance among junior and senior high school–age students. *International Journal of Behavioral Development*, **14**, 153–164.

Bradley, R. H., & Caldwell, B. M. (1979). Home environment and locus of control. *Journal of Clinical Child Psychology*, **8**, 107–111.

Brandtstaedter, J. (1984). Personal and social control over development: Some implications of an action perspective in life-span developmental psychology. In P. B. Baltes & O. G. Brim (Eds.), *Life-span development and behavior*. New York: Academic.

Brandtstaedter, J. (1989). Personal self-regulation of development: Cross-sequential analyses of development-related control beliefs and emotions. *Developmental Psychology*, **25**, 96–108.

Brandtstaedter, J., Wentura, D., & Greve, W. (1993). Adaptive resources of the aging self: Outlines of an emergent perspective. *International Journal of Behavioral Development*, **16**(2), 323–349.

Brim, O. G. (1974, August). *The sense of personal control over one's life*. Invitational address presented at the annual convention of the American Psychological Association, New Orleans.

Brophy, J. E. (1983). Research on the self-fulfilling prophecy and teacher expectations. *Journal of Educational Psychology, 75,* 631–661.

Brown, A. L. (1984). Meta-cognition, executive control, self-regulation, and other even more mysterious mechanisms. In F. E. Weinert & R. H. Kluwe (Eds.), *Metacognition, motivation, and learning.* Stuttgart: Kuhlhammer.

Brunstein, J. C. (1994). Dispositional action control as a predictor of how people cope with academic failure. In J. Kuhl & J. Beckman (Eds.), *Volition and personality: Action versus state orientation.* Seattle: Hogrefe & Huber.

Brunstein, J. C., & Olbrich, E. (1985). Personal helplessness and action control: Analysis of achievement-related cognitions, self-assessments, and performance. *Journal of Personality and Social Psychology, 48,* 1540–1551.

Bryk, A. S., & Raudenbush, S. W. (1992). *Hierarchical linear models: Applications and data analysis methods.* Newbury Park, CA: Sage.

Bullock, M., Gelman, R., & Baillargeon, R. (1982). The development of causal reasoning. In W. Friedman (Ed.), *The developmental psychology of time.* New York: Academic.

Burchinal, M., & Appelbaum, M. I. (1991). Estimating individual developmental functions: Methods and their assumptions. *Child Development, 62,* 23–43.

Burhans, K. K., & Dweck, C. S. (1995). Helplessness in early childhood: The role of contingent worth. *Child Development, 66,* 1719–1738.

Byrne, B. M. (1989). *A primer of LISREL: Basic applications and programming for confirmatory factor analytic models.* New York: Springer.

Carton, J. S., & Nowicki, S. (1994). Antecedents of individual differences in locus of control of reinforcement: A critical review. *Genetic, Social, and General Psychology Monographs, 120,* 31–81.

Chance, J. E. (1972). Academic correlates and maternal antecedents of children's' belief in external or internal control of reinforcements. In J. B. Rotter, J. E. Chance, & E. J. Phares (Eds.), *Applications of a social learning theory of personality.* New York: Holt, Rinehart & Winston.

Chandler, T. A., Wolf, F. M., Cook, B., & Dugovics, D. (1980). Parental correlates of locus of control in fifth graders: An attempt at experimentation in the home. *Merrill-Palmer Quarterly, 26,* 183–195.

Chapman, M., & Skinner, E. A. (1989). Children's agency beliefs, cognitive performance and conceptions of effort and ability: Interaction of individual and developmental differences. *Child Development, 60,* 1229–1238.

Connell, J. P. (1985). A new multidimensional measure of children's perceptions of control. *Child Development, 56,* 1011–1018.

Connell, J. P. (1990). Context, self, and action: A motivational analysis of self-system processes across the life-span. In D. Cicchetti & M. Beeghly (Eds.), *The self in transition: From infancy to childhood.* Chicago: University of Chicago Press.

Connell, J. P., & Furman, W. (1984). Conceptual and methodological considerations in the study of transition. In R. Emde & R. Harmon (Eds.), *Continuities and discontinuities in development.* New York: Plenum.

Connell, J. P., & Skinner, E. A. (1990, April). Predicting trajectories of academic engagement: A growth curve analysis of children's motivation in school. In P. Wood (Chair), *Methodological advances in the study of change processes in education.* Symposium presented at the meeting of the American Educational Research Association, Boston.

Connell, J. P., & Wellborn, J. G. (1991). Competence, autonomy and relatedness: A motivational analysis of self-system processes. In M. Gunnar & L. A. Sroufe (Eds.), *Minnesota Symposium on Child Psychology* (Vol. **23**). Chicago: University of Chicago Press.

Cordova, D. I., & Lepper, M. R. (1996). Intrinsic motivation and the process of learning:

Beneficial effects of contextualization, personalization, and choice. *Journal of Educational Psychology,* **88,** 715–730.

Covington, M. V., & Omelich, C. L. (1979). Effort: The double-edged sword in school achievement. *Journal of Educational Psychology,* **71,** 169–182.

Covington, M. V., & Omelich, C. L. (1985). Ability and effort valuation among failure-avoiding and failure-accepting students. *Journal of Educational Psychology,* **77,** 446–459.

Crandall, V. C. (1967). Achievement behavior in young children. In W. W. Hartup & N. L. Smothergill (Eds.), *The young child.* Washington: Association for the Education of Young Children.

Crandall, V. C., & Crandall, B. W. (1983). Maternal and childhood behaviors as antecedents of internal-external control perceptions in young adulthood. In H. M. Lefcourt (Ed.), *Research with the locus of control construct: Vol. 2. Developments and social problems.* New York: Academic.

Crandall, V. C., Katkovsky, W., & Crandall, V. J. (1965). Children's beliefs in their control of reinforcement in intellectual academic achievement behaviors. *Child Development,* **36,** 91–109.

Crandall, V. J., Katkovsky, W., & Preston, A. (1962). Motivational and ability determinants of young children's intellectual achievement behaviors. *Child Development,* **33,** 643–661.

Crandall, V. J., & Rabson, A. (1960). Children's repetition choices in an intellectual achievement situation following success and failure. *Journal of Genetic Psychology,* **97,** 161–168.

Davis, W. L., & Phares, E. J. (1969). Parental antecedents of internal-external control of reinforcement. *Psychological Reports,* **24,** 427–436.

DeCharms, R. (1981). Personal causation and locus of control: Two different traditions and two uncorrelated constructs. In H. Lefcourt (Ed.), *Research with the locus of control construct* (Vol. 1). San Diego, CA: Academic.

Deci, E. L., Connell, J. P., & Ryan, R. M. (1985). A motivational analysis of self-determination and self-regulation in the classroom. In C. Ames & R. Ames (Eds.), *Research on motivation in education: Vol. 2. The classroom milieu.* San Diego: Academic.

Deci, E. L., & Ryan, R. M. (1985). *Intrinsic motivation and self-determination in human behavior.* New York: Plenum.

Diener, C. I., & Dweck, C. S. (1978). An analysis of learned helplessness: Continuous changes in performance, strategy, and achievement cognitions following failure. *Journal of Personality and Social Psychology,* **36,** 451–462.

Diener, C. I., & Dweck, C. S. (1980). An analysis of learned helplessness: 2. The processing of success. *Journal of Personality and Social Psychology,* **39,** 940–952.

Diethelm, K. (1991). *Mutter-Kind-Interaktion: Entwicklung von ersten Kontollueberzeugungen* [Mother-child interaction: Development of early control beliefs]. Bern: Huber.

Dix, T. (1991). The affective organization of parenting: Adaptive and maladaptive processes. *Psychological Bulletin,* **110,** 3–25.

Dweck, C. S. (1975). The role of expectations and attributions in the alleviation of learned helplessness. *Journal of Personality and Social Psychology,* **31,** 674–685.

Dweck, C. S. (1976). Children's interpretations of evaluative feedback: The effect of social cues on learned helplessness. *Merrill-Palmer Quarterly,* **22,** 105–109.

Dweck, C. S. (1991). Self-theories and goals: Their role in motivation, personality, and development. In R. A. Dienstbier (Ed.), *Perspectives on Motivation: Nebraska Symposium on Motivation* (Vol. 38). Lincoln: University of Nebraska Press.

Dweck, C. S., & Bush, E. S. (1976). Sex differences in learned helplessness: 1. Differential debilitation with peer and adult evaluators. *Developmental Psychology,* **12,** 147–156.

Dweck, C. S., Davidson, W., Nelson, S., & Enna, B. (1978). Sex differences in learned helplessness: 2. The contingencies of evaluative feedback in the classroom; 3. An experimental analysis. *Developmental Psychology,* **14,** 268–776.

Dweck, C. S., & Elliott, E. S. (1983). Achievement motivation. In E. M. Hetherington (Ed.), P. H. Mussen (Series Ed.), *Handbook of child psychology: Vol. 4. Socialization, personality, and social development*. New York: Wiley.

Dweck, C. S., & Gillard, D. (1975). Expectancy statements as determinants of reactions to failure: Sex differences in persistence and expectancy change. *Journal of Personality and Social Psychology, 32*, 1077–1084.

Dweck, C. S., & Heckhausen, J. (Eds.). (in press). *Life-span perspectives on motivation and control*. New York: Cambridge University Press.

Dweck, C. S., & Leggett, E. L. (1988). A social-cognitive approach to motivation and personality. *Psychological Review, 95*, 256–273.

Dweck, C. S., & Licht, B. G. (1980). Learned helplessness and academic achievement. In J. Garber & M. Seligman (Eds.), *Human helplessness: Theory and application*. New York: Academic.

Eccles, J. S., Adler, T. F., Futterman, R., Goff, S. B., Kaczala, C. M., Meece, J., & Midgley, C. (1983). Expectancies, values and academic behaviors. In J. T. Spence (Ed.), *Achievement and achievement motives*. San Francisco: Freeman.

Eccles, J. S., Lord, S. E., Roeser, R. W., Barber, B. L., & Jozefowicz, D. M. (in press). The association of school transitions in early adolescence with developmental trajectories through high school. In J. Schulenberg, J. Maggs, & K. Hurrelmann (Eds.), *Health risks and developmental transitions during adolescence*. New York: Cambridge University Press.

Eccles, J. S., & Midgley, C. (1989). Stage-environment fit: Developmentally appropriate classrooms for early adolescents. In R. E. Ames & C. Ames (Eds.), *Research on motivation in education: Vol. 3. Goals and cognitions*. New York: Academic.

Eccles, J. S., Midgley, A., & Adler, T. (1984). Grade-related changes in the school environment: Effects on achievement motivation. In J. G. Nicholls (Ed.), *The development of achievement motivation* (Vol. 3). Greenwich, CT: JAI.

Eccles, J. S., Midgley, C., Wigfield, A., Buchanan, C. M., Reuman, D., Flanagan, C., & MacIver, D. (1993). Development during adolescence: The impact of stage-environment fit on adolescents' experiences in schools and families. *American Psychologist, 48*, 90–101.

Eccles, J. S., & Wigfield, A. (1985). Teacher expectations and student motivation. In J. B. Dusek (Ed.), *Teacher expectations*. Hillsdale, NJ: Erlbaum.

Eccles, J., Wigfield, A., Harold, R. D., & Blumenfeld, P. (1993). Age and gender differences in children's self- and task perceptions during elementary school. *Child Development, 64*, 830–847.

Eccles, J. S., Wigfield, A., & Schiefele, U. (1998). Motivation. In N. Eisenberg (Ed.), W. Damon (Series Ed.), *Handbook of child psychology: Vol. 4. Social and personality development*. New York: Wiley.

Estrada, P., Arsenio, W. F., Hess, R. D., & Holloway, S. D. (1987). Affective quality of the mother-child relationship: Longitudinal consequences for children's school-relevant cognitive functioning. *Developmental Psychology, 23*, 210–215.

Fincham, F. D., & Cain, K. M. (1986). Learned helplessness in humans: A developmental analysis. *Developmental Review, 6*(4), 301–333.

Fincham, F., Hokoda, A., & Sanders, R. J. (1989). Learned helplessness, test anxiety, and academic achievement: A longitudinal analysis. *Child Development, 60*, 138–145.

Findley, M. J., & Cooper, H. M. (1983). Locus of control and academic achievement: A literature review. *Journal of Personality and Social Psychology, 44*(2), 419–427.

Finkelstein, N. W., & Ramey, C. T. (1977). Learning to control the environment in infancy. *Child Development, 48*, 806–819.

Flammer, A. (1995). Developmental analysis of control beliefs. In A. Bandura (Ed.), *Self-efficacy in changing societies*. New York: Cambridge University Press.

Foersterling, F. (1985). Attributional retraining: A review. *Psychological Bulletin, 98*, 495–512.

Francis, D. J., Fletcher, J. M., Steubing, K. K., Davidson, K. C., & Thompson, N. M. (1991). Analysis of change: Modeling individual growth. *Journal of Consulting and Clinical Psychology*, **59**, 27–37.

Frodi, A., Bridges, L., & Grolnick, W. S. (1985). Correlates of mastery-related behavior: A short-term longitudinal study of infants in their second year. *Child Development*, **56**, 1291–1298.

Gatz, M., & Karel, M. J. (1993). Individual change in perceived control over 20 years. *International Journal of Behavioral Development*, **16**(2), 305–322.

Gollwitzer, P. M. (1990). Action phases and mind states. In E. T. Higgins & R. M. Sorrentino (Eds.), *Handbook of motivation and cognition: Foundations of social behavior* (Vol. **2**). New York: Guilford.

Gordon, D., Nowicki, S., & Wichern, F. (1981). Observed maternal and child behavior in a dependency producing task as a function of children's locus of control orientation. *Merrill-Palmer Quarterly*, **27**, 43–51.

Graham, S. (1984). Communicating sympathy and anger to black and white children: The cognitive (attributional) consequences of affective cues. *Journal of Personality and Social Psychology*, **47**, 40–54.

Graham, S. (1990). Communicating low ability in the classroom: Bad things good teachers sometimes do. In S. Graham & V. S. Folkes (Eds.), *Attribution theory: Applications to achievement, mental health, and interpersonal conflict*. Hillsdale, NJ: Erlbaum.

Graham, S. (1991). A review of attribution theory in achievement contexts. *Educational Psychology Review*, **3**, 5–35.

Grob, A., Little, T., Wanner, B., Wearing, A., & Euronet. (1996). Adolescents' well-being and perceived control across 14 sociocultural contexts. *Journal of Personality and Social Psychology*, **71**, 785–795.

Grolnick, W. S., Frodi, A., & Bridges, L. B. (1984). Maternal control style and the mastery motivation of one-year-olds. *Infant Mental Health*, **5**, 77–82.

Grolnick, W. S., & Ryan, R. M. (1987). Autonomy support in education: Creating the facilitating environment. In N. Hastings & J. Schwieso (Eds.), *New directions in educational psychology: Vol. 2. Behavior and motivation in the classroom*. New York: Falmer.

Grolnick, W. S., & Ryan, R. M. (1989). Parent styles associated with children's self-regulation and competence: A social contextual perspective. *Journal of Educational Psychology*, **81**, 143–154.

Grolnick, W. S., & Ryan, R. M. (1992). Parental resources and the developing child in school. In M. E. Procidano & C. B. F. Fisher (Eds.), *Contemporary families: A handbook for school professionals*. New York: Teachers College Press.

Grolnick, W. S., Ryan, R. M., & Deci, E. L. (1991). Inner resources for school achievement: Motivational mediators of children's perceptions of their parents. *Journal of Educational Psychology*, **83**, 508–517.

Grolnick, W. S., & Slowiaczek, M. (1994). Parents' involvement in children's schooling: A multi-dimensional conceptualization and motivational model. *Child Development*, **65**, 237–252.

Gunnar, M. R. (1980). Contingent stimulation: A review of its role in early development. In S. Levine & H. Ursin (Eds.), *Coping and health*. New York: Plenum.

Gunnar, M. R. (1986). Human developmental psychoneuroendocrinology: A review of research on neuroendocrine responses to challenge and threat in infancy and childhood. In M. E. Lamb, A. L. Brun, & B. Nopeff (Eds.), *Advances in developmental psychology*. Hillsdale, NJ: Erlbaum.

Gurin, P., & Brim, O. G. (1984). Change in self in adulthood: The example of sense of control. In P. B. Baltes & O. G. Brim (Eds.), *Life-span development and behavior*. New York: Academic.

Halpin, B. M., & Ottinger, D. R. (1983). Children's locus of control scales: A reappraisal of reliability characteristics. *Child Development, 5,* 484–487.

Harter, S. (1978). Effectance motivation reconsidered: Toward a developmental model. *Human Development, 21,* 36–64.

Harter, S. (1981a). A model of mastery motivation in children: Individual differences and developmental change. In W. A. Collins (Ed.), *The Minnesota symposia on child psychology* (Vol. **14**). Hillsdale, NJ: Erlbaum.

Harter, S. (1981b). A new self-report scale of intrinsic versus extrinsic motivation in the classroom: Motivational and informational components. *Developmental Psychology, 17,* 300–312.

Harter, S. (1982). The perceived competence scale for children. *Child Development, 53,* 89–97.

Harter, S. (1983). Developmental perspectives on the self system. In E. M. Hetherington (Ed.), P. H. Mussen (Series Ed.), *Handbook of child psychology: Vol. 4. Socialization, personality, and social development.* New York: Wiley.

Harter, S., & Connell, J. P. (1984). A model of the relationships among children's academic achievement and their self-perceptions of competence, control, and motivational orientation. In J. Nicholls (Ed.), *The development of achievement motivation.* Greenwich, CT: JAI.

Harter, S., Whitesell, N., & Kowalski, P. (1992). Individual differences in the effects of educational transitions on young adolescent's perceptions of competence and motivational orientation. *American Educational Research Journal, 29,* 777–807.

Heckhausen, H. (1977). Achievement motivation and its constructs: A cognitive model. *Motivation and Emotion, 1,* 283–329.

Heckhausen, H. (1982). The development of achievement motivation. In W. W. Hartup (Ed.), *Reviews of child development research* (Vol. **6**). Chicago: University of Chicago Press.

Heckhausen, H. (1984). Emergent achievement behavior: Some early developments. In M. Haehr (Ed.), *Advances in motivation and achievement.* Greenwich, CT: JAI.

Heckhausen, H. (1991). *Motivation and action* (Peter K. Leppmann, Trans.). Berlin: Springer.

Heckhausen, H., & Gollwitzer, P. (1987). Thought contents and cognitive functioning in motivational vs. volitional states of mind. *Motivation and Emotion, 11,* 101–120.

Heckhausen, J. (1991). *CASE-A: Causality and Self-Efficacy in Adulthood Questionnaire.* Berlin: Max Planck Institute.

Helmke, A., & van Aken, M. (1995). The causal ordering of academic achievement and self-concept of ability during elementary school: A longitudinal study. *Journal of Educational Psychology, 87,* 624–637.

Heyman, G. D., Dweck, C. S., & Cain, K. M. (1992). Young children's vulnerability to self-blame and helplessness: Relationship to beliefs about goodness. *Child Development, 63,* 401–415.

Hirsch, B. J., & DuBois, D. L. (1991). Self-esteem in early adolescence: The identification and prediction of contrasting longitudinal trajectories. *Journal of Youth and Adolescence, 20,* 53–72.

Hokoda, A., & Fincham, F. D. (1995). Origins of children's helpless and mastery achievement patterns in the family. *Journal of Educational Psychology, 87,* 375–385.

Jennings, K. D., Harmon, R. J., Morgan, G. A., Gaiter, J. L., & Yarrow, L. J. (1979). Exploratory play as an index of mastery motivation: Relationships to persistence, cognitive functioning, and environmental measures. *Developmental Psychology, 15,* 386–394.

Karabenick, J., & Heller, K. (1976). A developmental study of effort and ability attributions. *Developmental Psychology, 12,* 559–560.

Kindermann, T. A., & Skinner, E. A. (1992). Modeling environmental development: Individual and contextual trajectories. In J. B. Asendorpf & J. Valsiner (Eds.), *Framing stability and change: An investigation into methodological issues.* Newbury Park, CA: Sage.

Koestner, R., & McClelland, D. C. (1990). Perspectives on competence motivation. In L. A. Pervin (Ed.), *Handbook of personality: Theory and research*. New York: Guilford.

Kofta, M. (1993). Uncertainty, mental models, and learned helplessness: An anatomy of control loss. In G. Weary, F. Gleicher, & K. Marsh (Eds.), *Control motivation and social cognition*. New York: Springer.

Kofta, M., & Sedek, G. (1989). Repeated failure: A source of helplessness or a factor irrelevant to its emergence? *Journal of Experimental Psychology: General*, 118(1), 3–12.

Krampen, G. (1987). Entwicklung von Kontrollueberzeugungen: Thesen zu Forschungsstand und Perspektiven. *Zeitschrift für Entwicklungspsychologie und Paedagogische Psychologie*, 19, 195–227.

Krampen, G. (1989). Perceived child-rearing practices and the development of locus of control in early adolescence. *International Journal of Behavioral Development*, 12, 177–193.

Krampen, G. (1994). Kontrollueberzeugungen in der Erziehung und Sozialisation [Control beliefs in education and socialization]. In K. A. Schneewind (Ed.), *Psychologie der Erziehung und Sozialisation: Enzyklopaedie der Psychologie: Paedagogische Psychologie* [Psychology of education and socialization: Encyclopedia of psychology: Educational psychology] (Vol. 1). Göttingen: Hogrefe.

Kuhl, J. (1981). Motivational and functional helplessness: The moderating effect of state versus action orientation. *Journal of Personality and Social Psychology*, 40(1), 155–170.

Kuhl, J. (1984). Volitional aspects of achievement motivation and learned helplessness: Toward a comprehensive theory of action control. In B. A. Maher & W. A. Maher (Eds.), *Progress in experimental personalities research*. New York: Academic.

Kuhl, J., & Beckman, J. (1985). *Action control: From cognition to behavior*. New York: Springer.

Kuhl, J., & Weiss, M. (1994). Performance deficits following uncontrollable failure: Impaired action control or global attributions and generalized expectancy deficits? In J. Kuhl & J. Beckman (Eds.), *Volition and personality: Action versus state orientation*. Seattle: Hogrefe & Huber.

Kun, A. (1977). Development of magnitude-covariation and compensation schemata in ability and effort attributions of performance. *Child Development*, 48, 862–973.

Kun, A., Parsons, J., & Ruble, D. (1974). Development of integration processes using ability and effort information to predict outcome. *Developmental Psychology*, 10, 721–732.

Kurtz, B. E., & Borkowski, J. G. (1984). Children's metacognition: Exploring relations between knowledge, process, and motivational variables. *Journal of Experimental Child Psychology*, 37, 335–354.

Lachman, M. E. (1986). Locus of control in aging research: A case for multidimensional and domain-specific assessment. *Psychology and Aging*, 1, 34–40.

Lefcourt, H. M. (1977). *Locus of control: Current trends in theory and research*. New York: Wiley.

Levenson, H. (1973). Perceived parental antecedents of internal, powerful others, and chance locus of control orientations. *Developmental Psychology*, 9, 260–265.

Lewis, M., & Brooks-Gunn, J. (1979). *Social cognition and the acquisition of self*. New York: Plenum.

Licht, B. G., & Dweck, C. S. (1984). Determinants of academic achievement: The interaction of children's achievement orientations with skill area. *Developmental Psychology*, 20, 628–636.

Littell, R. C., Milliken, G. A., Stroup, W. W., & Wolfinger, R. D. (1996). *SAS system for mixed models*. Cary, NC: SAS Institute.

Little, T. D. (in press). Sociocultural influences on the development of children's action-control beliefs. In J. Heckhausen & C. S. Dweck (Eds.), *Motivation and self-regulation across the life span*. New York: Cambridge University Press.

Little, T. D., & Lopez, D. F. (1997). Regularities in the development of children's causality beliefs about school performance across six sociocultural contexts. *Developmental Psychology*, **33**, 165–175.

Little, T. D., Oettingen, G., Stetsenko, A., & Baltes, P. B. (1995). *The revised Control, Agency, and Means-Ends Interview (CAMI): A multi-culture validity assessment using mean and covariance structures (MACS) analyses* (Materialen aus der Bildungsforschung, No. 49). Berlin: Max Planck Institute for Human Development and Education.

Loeb, R. C. (1975). Concomitants of boys' locus of control examined in parent-child interactions. *Developmental Psychology*, **11**, 353–358.

Lopez, D. F., Little, T. D., Oettingen, G., & Baltes, P. B. (in press). Action-control beliefs and self-regulated performance: Is there an optimal level of action-control. *Journal of Experimental Child Psychology*.

Lord, S., Eccles, J. S., & McCarthy, K. (1994). Risk and protective factors in the transition to junior high school. *Journal of Early Adolescence*, **14**, 162–199.

MacDonald, A. P. (1971). Internal-external locus of control: Parental antecedents. *Journal of Consulting and Clinical Psychology*, **37**, 141–147.

Marsh, H. W. (1984). Relationships among dimensions of selfattribution, dimensions of self-concept, and academic achievements. *Journal of Educational Psychology*, **76**, 1291–1308.

Meece, J. L., Wigfield, A., & Eccles, J. S. (1990). Predictors of math anxiety and its influence on young adolescents' course enrollment intentions and performance in mathematics. *Journal of Educational Psychology*, **82**, 60–70.

Miller, A. (1985). A developmental study of the cognitive basis of performance impairment after failure. *Journal of Personality and Social Psychology*, **49**, 529–538.

Mischel, W. R., Zeiss, A., & Zeiss, R. (1974). Internal-external control and persistence: Validation and implication of the Stanford preschool internal-external scale. *Journal of Personality and Social Psychology*, **29**, 265–270.

Miserandino, M. (1996). Children who do well in school: Individual differences in perceived competence and autonomy in above-average children. *Journal of Educational Psychology*, **88**, 203–214.

Morgan, G. A., & Harmon, R. A. (1984). Developmental transformations in mastery motivation: Measurement and validation. In R. N. Emde & R. J. Harmon (Eds.), *Continuities and discontinuities in development*. New York: Plenum.

Morgan, G. A., Harmon, R. J., & Maslin-Cole, C. A. (1990). Mastery motivation: Definition and measurement. *Early Education and Development*, **1**(5), 318–339.

Morgan, G. A., Maslin-Cole, C. A., Biringen, Z., & Harmon, R. (1991). Play assessment of mastery motivation in infants and young children. In C. E. Schaefer, K. Gitlin, & A. Sandgrund (Eds.), *Play diagnosis and assessment*. New York: Wiley.

Mullen, B., & Riordan, C. A. (1988). Self-serving attributions for performance in naturalistic settings: A meta-analytic review. *Journal of Applied Social Psychology*, **18**, 3–22.

Multon, K. D., Brown, S. D., & Lent, R. W. (1991). Relation of self-efficacy beliefs to academic outcomes: A meta-analytic investigation. *Journal of Counseling Psychology*, **18**, 30–38.

Nicholls, J. G. (1978). The development of the concepts of effort and ability, perception of academic attainment, and the understanding that difficult tasks require more ability. *Child Development*, **49**, 800–814.

Nicholls, J. G. (1980). The development of the concept of difficulty. *Merrill-Palmer Quarterly*, **26**, 271–281.

Nicholls, J. G. (1984). Achievement motivation: Conceptions of ability, subjective experience, task choice, and performance. *Psychological Review*, **91**, 328–346.

Nicholls, J. G., & Miller, A. T. (1985a). Development and its discontents: The differentiation of the concept of ability. In J. G. Nicholls (Ed.), *Advances in motivation and achievement: Vol. 3. The development of achievement motivation*. Greenwich, CT: JAI.

Nicholls, J. G., & Miller, A. T. (1985b). Differentiation of the concepts of luck and skill. *Developmental Psychology,* **21,** 76–82.

Nolen-Hoeksema, S., Girgus, J. S., & Seligman, M. E. P. (1986). Learned helplessness in children: A longitudinal study of depression, achievement, and explanatory style. *Journal of Personality and Social Psychology,* **51,** 435–442.

Nolen-Hoeksema, S., Girgus, J. S., & Seligman, M. E. P. (1992). Predictors and consequences of childhood depressive symptoms: A 5-year longitudinal study. *Journal of Abnormal Psychology,* **101,** 405–422.

Nolen-Hoeksema, S., Wolfson, A., Mumme, D., & Guskin, K. (1995). Helplessness in children of depressed and nondepressed mothers. *Developmental Psychology,* **31,** 377–387.

Nowicki, S., & Schneewind, K. A. (1982). Relation of family climate variables to locus of control in German and American students. *Journal of Genetic Psychology,* **141,** 277–286.

Nowicki, S., & Segal, W. (1974). Perceived parental characteristics, locus of control orientation, and behavioral correlates of locus of control. *Developmental Psychology,* **10,** 33–37.

Nowicki, S., & Strickland, B. R. (1973). A locus of control scale for children. *Journal of Consulting and Clinical Psychology,* **40,** 148–154.

Oettingen, G. (1995). Cross-cultural perspectives on self-efficacy. In A. Bandura (Ed.), *Self-efficacy in changing societies.* New York: Cambridge University Press.

Oettingen, G., Little, T. D., Lindenberger, U., & Baltes, P. B. (1994). Causality, agency, and control beliefs in East versus West Berlin children: A natural experiment on the role of context. *Journal of Personality and Social Psychology,* **66,** 579–595.

Orr, E., Assor, A., & Priel, B. P. (1989). Maternal attitudes and children's self-perceptions in three Israeli social contexts. *Genetic, Social, and General Psychology Monographs,* **115,** 7–24.

Pajares, F., & Miller, M. D. (1994). Role of self-efficacy and self-concept beliefs in math problem-solving: A path analysis. *Journal of Educational Psychology,* **86,** 193–203.

Paris, S. G., & Oka, E. R. (1986). Children's reading strategies, metacognition, and motivation. *Developmental Review,* **6,** 25–56.

Patrick, B. C., Skinner, E. A., & Connell, J. P. (1993). What motivates children's behavior and emotion? The joint effects of perceived control and autonomy in the academic domain. *Journal of Personality and Social Psychology,* **65**(4), 781–791.

Peterson, C., Maier, S. F., & Seligman, M. E. P. (1993). *Learned helplessness: A theory for the age of personal control.* New York: Oxford University Press.

Peterson, C., & Seligman, M. E. P. (1984). Causal explanations as a risk factor for depression: Theory and evidence. *Psychological Review,* **91,** 347–374.

Phillips, D. A. (1984). The illusion of incompetence among academically competent children. *Child Development,* **55,** 2000–2016.

Phillips, D. A. (1987). Socialization of perceived academic competence among highly competent children. *Child Development,* **58,** 1308–1320.

Phillips, D. A., & Zimmerman, M. (1990). The developmental course of perceived competence and incompetence among competent children. In R. J. Sternberg & J. Kolligian (Eds.), *Competence considered.* New Haven, CT: Yale University Press.

Pintrich, P. R., & Blumenfeld, P. C. (1985). Classroom experience and children's self-perceptions of ability, effort, and conduct. *Journal of Educational Psychology,* **77**(6), 646–657.

Pintrich, P. R., & De Groot, E. V. (1990). Motivational and self-regulated learning components of classroom academic performance. *Journal of Educational Psychology,* **82,** 33–40.

Redlich, J. D., Debus, R. L., & Walker, R. (1986). The mediating role of attribution and self-efficacy variables for treatment effects on achievement outcomes. *Contemporary Educational Psychology,* **11,** 195–216.

Rholes, W. S., Blackwell, J., Jordan, C., & Walters, C. (1980). A developmental study of learned helplessness. *Developmental Psychology,* **16,** 616–624.

Riksen-Walraven, J. M. (1978). Effects of caregiver behavior on habituation rate and self-efficacy in infants. *International Journal of Behavioural Development,* **1,** 105–130.

Rodin, J. (1986). Personal control through the life course. In R. Abeles (Ed.), *Implications of the life span perspective for social psychology.* Hillsdale, NJ: Erlbaum.

Roeser, R., Midgley, C., & Urdan, T. C. (1996). Perceptions of the school psychological environment and early adolescents' psychological and behavioral functioning in school: The mediating role of goals and belonging. *Journal of Educational Psychology,* **88,** 408–422.

Rogosa, D. (1988). Myths about longitudinal research. In K. W. Schaie, R. T. Campbell, W. Meredith, & S. C. Rawlings (Eds.), *Methodological issues in aging research.* New York: Springer.

Rosenholtz, S. J., & Simpson, C. (1984). The formation of ability conceptions: Developmental trend or social construction? *Review of Educational Research,* **54**(1), 31–63.

Rotter, B. (1966). Generalized expectancies for internal versus external control of reinforcement. *Psychological Monographs,* **80**(1, Whole No. 609).

Rotter, J. B. (1975). Some problems and misconceptions related to the construct of internal versus external control of reinforcement. *Journal of Consulting and Clinical Psychology,* **43,** 56–67.

Rotter, J. B. (1990). Internal versus external control of reinforcement: A case history of a variable. *American Psychologist,* **45**(4), 489–493.

Ruble, D. (1983). The development of social processes and their role in achievement-related self-socialization. In E. T. Higgins, D. N. Ruble, & W. W. Hartup (Eds.), *Social cognition and social development: A sociocultural perspective.* New York: Cambridge University Press.

Ryan, R. M. (1982). Control and information in the intrapersonal sphere: An extension of cognitive evaluation theory. *Journal of Personality and Social Psychology,* **43,** 450–461.

Schaffer, C. E., & Blatt, S. J. (1990). Interpersonal relationships and the experience of perceived efficacy. In R. J. Sternberg & J. Kolligian (Eds.), *Competence considered.* New Haven, CT: Yale University Press.

Schmitz, B. (1987). *Zeitreihenanlyse in der Psychologie: Verfahren zur Veraenderungsmessung und Prozessdiagnostik* [Time series analysis in psychology: Methods for the measurement of change and press in evaluation]. Weinheim: Beltz.

Schmitz, B., & Skinner, E. (1993). Perceived control, effort, and academic performance: Interindividual, intraindividual, and multivariate time-series analyses. *Journal of Personality and Social Psychology,* **64**(6), 1010–1028.

Schneewind, K. A. (1995). Impact of family processes on control beliefs. In A. Bandura (Ed.), *Self-efficacy in changing societies.* New York: Cambridge University Press.

Schneider, W. (1985). Developmental trends in the metamemory-memory behavior relationship: An integrative review. In D. L. Forrest-Pressley, G. E. MacKinnon, & T. G. Waller (Eds.), *Cognition, metacognition, and human performance.* New York: Academic.

Schunk, D. H. (1981). Modeling and attributional feedback effects on children's achievement: A self-efficacy analysis. *Journal of Educational Psychology,* **74,** 93–105.

Schunk, D. H. (1989). Self-efficacy and achievement behaviors. *Educational Psychology Review,* **1,** 173–182.

Schunk, D. H. (1991). Self-efficacy and academic motivation. *Educational Psychologist,* **26,** 207–231.

Schunk, D. H., & Cox, P. D. (1986). Strategy training and attributional feedback with learning-disabled students. *Journal of Educational Psychology,* **78,** 201–209.

Schunk, D. H., & Hanson, A. R. (1985). Peer models: Influence on children's self-efficacy and achievement behaviors. *Journal of Educational Psychology,* **77,** 313–322.

Schunk, D. H., & Swartz, C. W. (1991). Writing strategy instruction with gifted students: Effects of goals and feedback on self-efficacy and skills. *Roeper Review,* **15,** 225–230.

Sedek, G., & Kofta, M. (1990). When cognitive exertion does not yield cognitive gain: Toward an informational explanation of learned helplessness. *Journal of Personality and Social Psychology,* **58**(4), 729–743.

Sedek, G., Kofta, M., & Tyszka, T. (1993). Effects of uncontrollability on subsequent decision-making: Testing the cognitive exhaustion hypothesis. *Journal of Personality and Social Psychology,* **65**, 1270–1281.

Seligman, M. E. P. (1975). *Helplessness: On depression, development, and death.* San Francisco: Freeman.

Shaklee, H., & Mims, M. (1981). Development of rule use in judgments of covariation between events. *Child Development,* **52**, 317–325.

Shell, D. F., Colvin, C., & Bruning, R. H. (1995). Self-efficacy, attribution, and outcome expectancy mechanisms in reading and writing achievement: Grade-level and achievement-level differences. *Journal of Educational Psychology,* **87**, 386–398.

Shultz, T. R., Butkowsky, I., Pearce, J. W., & Shanfield, H. (1975). Development of schemes for the attribution of multiple psychological causes. *Developmental Psychology,* **11**(4), 502–510.

Sigel, I. E., Stinson, E. T., & Flaugher, J. (1989, May). *Family processes and school achievement.* Paper presented at the Fifth Summer Institute of the Family Research Consortium, Harwich Port, MA.

Singer, J. D. (1997). *Using SAS PROC MIXED to fit multilevel models, hierarchical models, and individual growth models.* Manuscript submitted for publication.

Skinner, E. A. (1985). Action, control judgments, and the structure of control experience. *Psychological Review,* **92**, 39–58.

Skinner, E. A. (1986). The origins of young children's perceived control: Caregiver contingent and sensitive behavior. *International Journal of Behavioral Development,* **9**, 359–382.

Skinner, E. A. (1990). Age differences in the dimensions of perceived control during middle childhood: Implications for developmental conceptualizations and research. *Child Development,* **61**, 1882–1890.

Skinner, E. A. (1991). Development and perceived control: A dynamic model of action in context. In M. Gunnar & L. A. Sroufe (Eds.), *Minnesota Symposium on Child Psychology* (Vol. **23**). Hillsdale, NJ: Erlbaum.

Skinner, E. A. (1995). *Perceived control, motivation, and coping.* Newbury Park, CA: Sage.

Skinner, E. A. (1996). A guide to constructs of control. *Journal of Personality and Social Psychology,* **71**, 549–570.

Skinner, E. A. (in press). Strategies for studying social influences on motivation. In C. Dweck & J. Heckhausen (Eds.), *Life-span perspectives on motivation and control.* New York: Cambridge University Press.

Skinner, E. A., & Belmont, M. J. (1993). Motivation in the classroom: Reciprocal effects of teacher behavior and student engagement across the school year. *Journal of Educational Psychology,* **85**, 571–581.

Skinner, E. A., Chapman, M., & Baltes, P. B. (1983). *The Control, Agency and Means-Ends Interview (CAMI)* (Tech. Rep. [in both English and German]). Berlin: Max Planck Institute.

Skinner, E. A., Chapman, M., & Baltes, P. B.. (1988a). Beliefs about control, means-ends, and agency: Developmental differences during middle childhood. *International Journal of Behavioural Development,* **11**, 369–388.

Skinner, E. A., Chapman, M., & Baltes, P. B. (1988b). Control, means-ends, and agency beliefs: A new conceptualization and its measurement during childhood. *Journal of Personality and Social Psychology,* **54**, 117–133.

Skinner, E. A., & Connell, J. P. (1986). Control understanding: Suggestions for a developmental framework. In M. M. Baltes & P. B. Baltes (Eds.), *The psychology of control and aging.* Hillsdale, NJ: Erlbaum.

216

Skinner, E. A., & Schmitz, B. (1998). *Intraindividual analysis of the causes of attributions: Covariation or beliefs?* Unpublished manuscript, Portland State University.

Skinner, E. A., & Wellborn, J. G. (1994). Coping during childhood and adolescence: A motivational perspective. In D. Featherman, R. Lerner, & M. Perlmutter (Eds.), *Life-span development and behavior*. Hillsdale, NJ: Erlbaum.

Skinner, E. A., Wellborn, J. G., & Connell, J. P. (1990). What it takes to do well in school and whether I've got it: The role of perceived control in children's engagement and school achievement. *Journal of Educational Psychology, 82,* 22–32.

Skinner, E. A., Zimmer-Gembeck, M. J., Connell, J. (1995, August). *Individual trajectories of perceived control across three years: Relations to context, action, and outcomes.* Poster presented at the conference of the Society of Research in Child Development, Indianapolis.

Steitz, J. A. (1982). Locus of control as a life-span developmental process: Revision of the construct. *International Journal of Behavioral Development, 5,* 299–316.

Stevenson, H. W., Chen, C., & Lee, S.-Y. (1993). Mathematics achievement of Chinese, Japanese, and American children: Ten years later. *Science, 259,* 53–58.

Stevenson, H. W., & Lee, S.-Y. (1990). Contexts of achievement: A study of American, Chinese, and Japanese children. *Monographs of the Society for Research in Child Development, 55*(1–2, Serial No. 221).

Stipek, D. J. (1980). A causal analysis of the relationship between locus of control and academic achievement in first grade. *Contemporary Educational Psychology, 5,* 90–99.

Stipek, D. J. (1984a). The development of achievement motivation. In C. Ames & R. Ames (Eds.), *Research on motivation and education: Student motivation* (Vol. 1). San Diego: Academic.

Stipek, D. J. (1984b). Young children's performance expectations: Logical analysis or wishful thinking? In M. Haehr (Ed.), *Advances in motivation and achievement.* Greenwich, CT: JAI.

Stipek, D. J. (1993). *Motivation to learn: From theory to practice* (2d ed.). Needham Heights, MA: Allyn & Bacon.

Stipek, D. J., & Daniels, D. H. (1988). Declining perceptions of competence: A consequence of changes in the child or in the educational environment? *Journal of Educational Psychology, 80,* 352–356.

Stipek, D., Feiler, R., Daniels, D., & Milburn, S. (1995). Effects of different instructional approaches on young children's achievement and motivation. *Child Development, 66,* 209–223.

Stipek, D., & Gralinski, J. H. (1996). Children's beliefs about intelligence and school performance. *Journal of Educational Psychology, 88,* 397–407.

Stipek, D. J., & Hoffman, J. M. (1980). Children's achievement-related expectancies as a function of academic performance histories and sex. *Journal of Educational Psychology, 72,* 861–865.

Stipek, D. J., & MacIver, D. (1989). Developmental change in children's assessment of intellectual competence. *Child Development, 60,* 521–538.

Stipek, D., Recchia, S., & McClintic, S. (1992). Self-evaluation in young children. *Monographs of the Society for Research in Child Development, 57*(1, Serial No. 226).

Stipek, D. J., & Weisz, J. R. (1981). Perceived personal control and academic achievement. *Review of Educational Research, 51,* 101–137.

Tennen, H., Drum, P., Gillen, R., & Stanton, A. (1982). Learned helplessness and the detection of contingency: A direct test. *Journal of Personality, 50*(4), 426–442.

Turkewitz, G., & Devenny, D. A. (Eds.). (1993). *Developmental time and timing.* Hillsdale, NJ: Erlbaum.

Vallerand, R. J., Fortier, M. S., & Guay, F. (1997). Self-determination and persistence in a real-life setting: Toward a motivational model of high school dropout. *Journal of Personality and Social Psychology, 72,* 1161–1176.

Vroom, V. H. (1964). *Work and motivation*. New York: Wiley.

Wagner, B. M., & Phillips, D. A. (1992). Beyond beliefs: Parent and child behaviors and children's perceived academic competence. *Child Development, 63,* 1380–1391.

Watson, J. S. (1966). The development and generalization of "contingency awareness" in early infancy: Some hypotheses. *Merrill-Palmer Quarterly, 12,* 123–135.

Watson, J. S. (1979). Perception of contingency as a determinant of social responsiveness. In E. G. Thoman (Ed.), *Origins of the infant's social responsiveness*. Hillsdale, NJ: Erlbaum.

Watson, J. S., & Ramey, C. T. (1972). Reactions to response-contingent stimulation in early infancy. *Merrill-Palmer Quarterly, 18,* 219–227.

Weiner, B. (1979). A theory of motivation for some classroom experiences. *Journal of Educational Psychology, 71,* 3–25.

Weiner, B. (1985a). An attributional theory of achievement motivation and emotion. *Psychological Review, 92,* 548–573.

Weiner, B. (1985b). "Spontaneous" causal thinking. *Psychological Bulletin, 97,* 74–84.

Weiner, B. (1986). *An attributional theory of motivation and emotion*. New York: Springer.

Weiner, B., Heckhausen, H., Meyer, W. U., & Cook, R. E. (1972). Causal ascriptions and achievement motivation. *Journal of Personality and Social Psychology, 21,* 239–248.

Weiner, B., Kun, A., & Benesh-Weiner, M. (1980). The development of mastery, emotions, and morality from an attributional perspective. In *Minnesota Symposium on Child Psychology*. Hillsdale, NJ: Erlbaum.

Weiner, B., Nierenberg, R., & Goldstein, M. (1976). Social learning (locus of control) versus attributional (causal stability) interpretations of expectancy of success. *Journal of Personality, 44,* 52–68.

Weisz, J. R. (1980). Developmental change in perceived control: Recognizing noncontingency in the laboratory and perceiving it in the world. *Developmental Psychology, 16,* 385–390.

Weisz, J. R. (1981). Illusory contingency in children at the state fair. *Developmental Psychology, 17,* 481–489.

Weisz, J. R. (1983). Can I control it? The pursuit of veridical answers across the life span. In P. B. Baltes & O. G. Brim Jr. (Eds.), *Life-span development and behavior*. New York: Academic.

Weisz, J. R. (1986). Understanding the developing understanding of control. In M. Perlmutter (Ed.), *Social cognition: Minnesota symposium on child psychology* (Vol. 18). Hillsdale, NJ: Erlbaum.

Weisz, J. R., & Stipek, D. J. (1982). Competence, contingency, and the development of perceived control. *Human Development, 25,* 250–281.

Wellborn, J. G. (1991). *Engaged and disaffected action: The conceptualization and measurement of motivation in the academic domain*. Unpublished doctoral dissertation, University of Rochester.

Wellborn, J. G., Connell, J. P., & Skinner, E. A. (1989). *The Student's Perceptions of Control Questionnaire (SPOCQ): Academic domain* (Tech. Rep.). Rochester, NY: University of Rochester.

Wentzel, K. R. (1997). Student motivation in middle school: The role of perceived pedagogical caring. *Journal of Educational Psychology, 89,* 411–419.

Whitbeck, L. B. (1987). Modeling efficacy: The effect of perceived parental efficacy on the self-efficacy of early adolescents. *Journal of Early Adolescence, 7,* 175–177.

White, R. W. (1959). Motivation reconsidered: The concept of competence. *Psychological Review, 66,* 297–333.

Whitley, B. E., & Frieze, I. H. (1985). Children's causal attributions for success and failure in achievement settings: A meta-analysis. *Journal of Educational Psychology, 77,* 211–220.

Wichern, F., & Nowicki, S. (1976). Independence training practices and locus of control orientation in children and adolescents. *Developmental Psychology, 12,* 65–77.

Wigfield, A., Eccles, J. S., MacIver, D., Reuman, D. A., & Midgley, C. (1991). Transitions during early adolescence: Changes in children's domain-specific self-perceptions and general self-esteem across the transition to junior high school. *Developmental Psychology,* 27(4), 552–565.

Willett, J. B., Ayoub, C. C., & Robinson, D. (1991). Using growth modeling to examine systematic differences in growth: An example of change in the functioning of families at risk of maladaptive parenting, child abuse, or neglect. *Journal of Consulting and Clinical Psychology, 59,* 38–47.

Yates, R., Kennelly, K., & Cox, S. (1975). Perceived contingency of parental reinforcements, parent-child relations and locus of control. *Psychological Reports, 36,* 139–146.

Zimmer-Gembeck, M. J. (1997, April). *Using hierarchical linear modeling to investigate launch, change-to-change, and ambient level relationships.* Poster presented at the meeting of the Society for Research in Child Development, Washington, DC.

Zimmerman, B. J. (1986). A social cognitive view of self-regulated learning. *Journal of Educational Psychology, 81,* 329–339.

Zimmerman, B. J. (1995). Self-efficacy and educational development. In A. Bandura (Ed.), *Self-efficacy in changing societies.* New York: Cambridge University Press.

Zimmerman, B. J., Bandura, A., & Martinez-Pons, M. (1992). Self-motivation for academic attainment: The role of self-efficacy and personal goal-setting. *American Educational Research Journal, 29,* 663–676.

Zimmerman, B. J., & Ringle, J. (1981). Effects of model persistence and statements of confidence on children's selfefficacy and problem solving. *Journal of Educational Psychology, 73,* 485–493.

ACKNOWLEDGMENTS

We thank the Brockport School District and its superintendent, principals, teachers, students, and parents for their generous participation in this research. We gratefully acknowledge the hard work and good spirits of the research team members, including Jeff Altman, Michael Belmont, Helen Dorsett, Jennifer Herman, Marianne Miserandino, Brian Patrick, Cara Regan, Hayley Sherwood, and Peter Usinger. We express our gratitude to the Motivation Research Group at the University of Rochester, especially Edward Deci, Richard Ryan, and James Wellborn. We thank Margaret Burchinal and Nancy Perrin, both of whom graciously consulted on some of the statistical procedures. We also appreciate the critiques provided by Jacquelynne Eccles, which benefited earlier drafts of this manuscript. We happily acknowledge support from the W. T. Grant Foundation, from Research Grant HD19914 from the National Institute of Child Health and Human Development, and from Training Grant 527594 from the National Institutes of Mental Health.

Direct all correspondence to Ellen Skinner, Psychology Department, Portland State University, PO Box 751, Portland OR 97207-0751; email: Ellen@ch1.ch.pdx.edu.

PERCEIVED CONTROL AND THE DEVELOPMENT
OF ACADEMIC MOTIVATION

Jacquelynne S. Eccles

It was with great pleasure that I accepted the charge to write the Commentary for this *Monograph.* I have followed the work of Ellen Skinner, James Connell, and their colleagues for many years with great enthusiasm because it has such strong theoretical and empirical grounding. This *Monograph* certainly reinforced this view. Rarely does one have the opportunity to praise a piece of work as a tour de force—such a characterization is fully warranted in this case. Skinner, Zimmer-Gembeck, and Connell have given the field a great gift—one that will serve as a model of longitudinal research and analysis for years to come.

The authors set out, and fully met, clear theoretical and empirical goals. In so doing, they provided the field with both a comprehensive account of the control-action theory of motivation and its link to attribution theory. The associations among their various constructs were thoroughly discussed, and a wide set of specific hypotheses were generated. Furthermore, the authors were quite clear about when their theoretical framework could lead to specific individual differences hypotheses and when it merely provided hints for exploratory empirical work.

In addition, the authors provided an excellent example of how to aggregate a set of constructs into a higher-order construct on the basis of differentiated patterns of responding rather than simple summary composites. Guided by both their theoretical framework and empirical findings from a variety of motivational perspectives, the authors specified exactly which patterns of beliefs would facilitate, and which would undermine, academic engagement. By and large, their predictions were confirmed, and these composites yielded the strongest relations. For example, the strongest evidence for their general motivational model came from LISREL and cross-time lagged analyses using these composite variables. In each case, the findings were consistent with their model of influences running from context to self-beliefs to action to outcomes.

Finally, the authors laid out a smaller set of specific developmental predictions based on a variety of other theoretical and empirical work. I found their explication of the launch, ambient, and change-to-change developmental models especially interesting. This distinction should facilitate thinking in the field about the need for proposing mathematically specific developmental models. However, given the current level of theorizing about developmental changes in these types of constructs, the authors were justifiably more cautious in making these predictions than they were in making the individual difference hypotheses derived from their own theoretical framework. Consequently, several of the more interesting patterns of developmental change were not predicted a priori. This was particularly true for the change-to-change model findings. The authors provided quite interesting post hoc explanations for these findings, along with a challenge to the field to replicate the findings and test the validity of their various possible explanations.

Given my theoretical biases, I was especially intrigued by both the data and the theorizing related to systematic grade-related changes in classroom contexts. As has been suggested by several researchers, including those working with me on our stage-environment fit theory of declining academic motivation (see Eccles, Wigfield, & Schiefele, 1998), these authors found evidence of a link between students' declining perceptions of their classroom context and negative changes in achievement-related beliefs (in this case, control beliefs), which, in turn, were linked to declining engagement. They also found that this pattern was particularly marked at the time of the transition into middle grades' educational settings.

I was, however, a bit surprised by the authors reluctance to make change-to-change predictions and by their suggestion that change-to-change models are rare in developmental work. I agree with them that this model is not incorporated into the design of longitudinal studies as much as it should be, given its relevance for all contextual-based developmental theories; and I applaud the authors for both pointing out the importance of such an approach and clearly demonstrating its power. There has, however, been a dramatic increase in the prevalence of these types of studies over the last 10–15 years. Furthermore, work in areas of prevention/intervention, operant conditioning, and time-series analyses have used these types of designs for a very long time (e.g., see Bronfenbrenner & Morris, 1998; Elder, 1998). Finally, prospective longitudinal studies of this type are quite common in studies of life span development (see, e.g., Baltes, Lindenberger, & Staudinger, 1998).

The contribution of this *Monograph* to our appreciation of the statistical methods available for longitudinal analyses is also quite impressive. The authors used several different statistical techniques both to test their various hypotheses and to perform their more exploratory analyses. Given the complexity of both their data set and their hypotheses, they had to make many decisions along the way—ranging from how to aggregate the participants into appropriate groups for the analyses to how best to present their findings. Through the use of multiple summaries, tables, and an extensive methodological appendix, the authors did a masterful job of explaining both the issues they had to confront and the rationale for their particular solution. They have done the field a great service by providing such a detailed discussion of their techniques, particularly their hierarchical linear modeling (HLM) analyses. The HLM method is emerging as a powerful tool in longitudinal analyses. Although it was originally developed to look at contextual influences in nested designs (such as students nested within classrooms), several statistical programs are being developed and refined for use in the longitudinal modeling of stability and change. This *Monograph* makes these new techniques accessible to developmentalists in a very concrete way.

In addition, this *Monograph* will certainly stimulate the debate about how best to deal with missing data and attrition in longitudinal studies. HLM provides one solution to this problem—it models the developmental trajectories of individuals using all available information. Although this approach is mathematically quite legitimate, I am sure that there are those of us who become increasingly uncomfortable with this strategy as the amount of missing data increases. Yet attrition is a fact of life in longitudinal work—at least given the current norms regarding funding levels for developmental research. Studies such as this one are needed to find the optimal mix of "real" data with modeled "data" for understanding development.

The authors have also provided a model of the importance of internal replication. Since their data are correlational in nature, it is impossible to draw firm causal inferences. Instead, correlational studies need to be evaluated on the consistency of the empirical evidence with specific causal models. Providing congruent evidence from several different analytic techniques and from various subpopulations within the sample bolsters our confidence that the findings are not an artifact of either the methods used or the particular sample studied. This *Monograph* includes several examples of this type of internal replication. Given these methodological strengths, it would be quite appropriate to use this *Monograph* in graduate developmental courses as a methodological primer as well as an exemplary developmental study of control theory.

Controversial Issues Raised by This Work

Any study as rich as this one should stimulate debate about the controversial issues in its domain. In this discussion, I focus on three: links to other motivational theories, difficulties with studying complex, dynamic systems, and where and what is context.

Links to Other Motivational Theories

Allan Wigfield, Uli Schiefele, and I just completed a chapter for new *Handbook of Child Psychology* (Eccles et al., 1998). One thing that was clear in our review was the need to begin directly to compare various motivational theories to each other. There has been a tremendous proliferation over the last 15 years in both the theories and the key constructs linked to a social cognitive perspective on motivation. The control action approach guiding the work presented in this *Monograph* is one of the most important and well developed of these social cognitive perspectives. At the measurement level, it is most similar to Weiner's attribution and Bandura's self-efficacy theories. As the authors note, their approach also shares similarities with expectancy-value approaches and with the work by Dweck and her colleagues (e.g., Dweck & Elliott, 1983) on the meaning of ability. The authors do a very nice job of integrating their approach with Weiner's (1979); they provide a less complete analysis of the overlap between their approach and Bandura's (1996). Finally, like most of the researchers in the field of academic motivation, they provide very little analysis of the relation of their approach to other, more affective-based motivational theories, including the value component of expectancy-value models. Yet all these approaches seek to explain engagement and performance, and most of them include hypotheses regarding the mediating role of self-beliefs between context and engagement/performance. At present there is very little attempt within the broader community of motivational researchers directly to compare these various approaches in order to find out which are the most powerful influences on engagement/performance.

I believe that it is time to pit these various motivational models against each other. As both these authors and many others in the field point out, there are now many similar constructs linked to capacity and control beliefs (e.g., personal efficacy, outcome efficacy, expectancies, locus of control, attribution theory, etc.). And, as noted above, the models from which these constructs are derived make similar predictions about the general influences on engagement and performance. Like so many of the rest of us, Skinner et al. discuss some of these overlaps but then proceed to explore only those predictions derived from their model. Such an approach is quite acceptable if the goal is to test a specific set of hypotheses derived from one theory. It is less useful if the goal is either to move toward a more comprehensive theoretical understanding of academic motivation or to make policy and practice recommendations to school personnel about the best way to improve children's academic motivation. In my opinion, this field is now ready to move beyond this fractionated approach to a more comparative approach so that we can begin to understand the relative power of all these various constructs.

Effective intervention recommendations also require this type of work because we need to know which are the most economical and powerful points to target for intervention. Skinner et al. do a very nice job of discussing the types of interventions that one might consider on the basis of their findings. But they say little about other powerful variables such as affect/emotions and values/goals precisely because their study has no implications for these types of potential mediators. This will continue to be the state of our ability to make policy recommendations until all of us interested in academic motivation begin to do more direct comparative work. In addition, although the findings presented here are consistent with their theoretical model, these constructs actually explained very little of the variance in either engagement or performance—suggesting that belief in control may be necessary but not sufficient to produce engagement. We need to know which factors are most predictive of engagement in order to design the most effective intervention programs.

There are two additional important issues related to the relation of this report to other work in this field: general beliefs versus domain-specific beliefs and beliefs about the nature of ability. Skinner et al. have chosen quite general measures of control beliefs. Other motivational psychologists (e.g., Bandura, 1996; Marsh, 1984; Eccles et al., 1998) have argued that academic motivation is much more domain specific. Several of us have also designed domain-specific indicators of constructs quite similar to the constructs used in this report. Perhaps the amount of variance accounted for in engagement and performance would have been higher had Skinner et al. used more domain-specific indicators of their constructs.

Second, I have always been intrigued by the relations among theories of ability, perceived control, performance, and engagement. Most social cognitive motivational theorists assume that a strong belief in one's control and a belief that ability is modifiable are optimal—a strong sense of personal efficacy and belief in one's ability to master challenging tasks is good. I basically agree. But we need to consider the possibility that not all things are under our control and some individual differences in aptitudes contain an element of stability that is very likely to influence final possible levels of competence. Is it the case that children are born totally pliable with regard to aptitudes and interests, or are there genetic predispositions? Can any child become an Olympic champion in swimming, or are there innate differences that will make it much easier for some children to achieve this goal than others? And if, as evidence from behavioral genetics suggests (e.g., Loehlin, 1992; Rowe, 1994), the later is the case, then what are the implications for our social cognitive models of achievement motivation?

225

It seems to me that one important developmental task for each person is to discover which aptitudes and interests are most relevant to oneself. In other words, it is critical to discover either when one has control (that is when effort will matter) and when one does not or exactly how much control one has in each situation or domain. Within this model of development, one optimal adaptation strategy would be to identify those situations and/or domains in which one has maximal control or potential and then to focus much of one's energies on perfecting these potentials or situations.

Individuals have to focus their energies to some degree—they do not have sufficient time or energy to excel at everything. This focusing can be guided either by the individuals themselves through personal selection, or by the individuals' social context, or by some mix of both these influences. It is undoubtedly critical for optimal motivation in any specific context that individuals feel in control of their ability to master the demands of that situation. Work by a wide variety of motivational theorists has demonstrated this fact repeatedly. But it is probably also useful for individuals to be able to select themselves into settings in which they, in fact, have maximal control over their outcomes.

From this prospective, motivational problems are most likely to arise when there is not a good match between the demands of the situation and the individual's unique aptitudes and interests. For example, schools may be a risky setting for some children if there is no provision in that setting for them to demonstrate and develop competence in those areas most closely linked to their personal pattern of aptitudes and interests.

Several motivational psychologists have paid some attention to this dilemma. As noted by the authors, people like Nicholls (e.g., 1984) and Schunk (e.g., Schunk & Cox, 1986) have argued that retraining children's attributions or feelings of control without providing them with the skills necessary to succeed in the school setting is counterproductive. Furthermore, the launching effect of early school achievement on control beliefs demonstrated in this study suggests that children do adjust their control beliefs in response to academic feedback in a manner quite consistent to the adaptive model suggested above. But the full implications of this perspective for maintaining motivation in school settings and for providing children with a greater diversity in the types of skill areas in which they could focus their energies have not been adequately considered by motivational psychologists, particularly those with a social cognitive/control/personal efficacy orientation.

Studying Dynamic Systems of Influence and Behavior

Skinner et al. note that their model is dynamic. They include this dynamic perspective by including early grades as a launching factor in their longitudinal models and by including feedback loops in their LISREL models. In both instances, performance emerged as an important influence on, as well as an outcome of, control beliefs. But for the most part, and as is done in most developmental research, the analyses performed reflected a linear, unidirectional flow of influence. Developmental psychologists are very good at hypothesizing complex, dynamic models. We are much less adept at testing such models. To simplify our task in such situations, we typically generate linear models of causal influence. Although this is done by everyone, it is not clear that such empirical models are the best way to capture highly interactive, dynamic processes.

Skinner et al. are to be applauded for going beyond simple linear models in some of their analyses. I wish that they had extended these efforts further. For example, with the exception of including previous grades as a launch variable in some of their modeling of slopes and intercepts of control beliefs, their HLM and related regression analyses are quite unidirectional; and, to the extent that they did consider bidirectional effects, they focused only on the potential feedback relation of performance to control beliefs. Other feedback loops and bidirectional influences are also quite probable. For example, I suspect that early grades also have a launch type of influence on individual differences in perceptions of the teacher context. Similarly, I suspect that performance influenced teachers' ratings of their students' engagement. Finally, it is quite likely that control beliefs influenced perceptions of the context. All these bidirectional influences are theoretically feasible within various models of human perception.

Testing such hypotheses would have required more extensive use of either cross-lagged structural equation modeling or HLM analyses with time-varying covariates. The latter strategy would have been an especially good way to assess change-to-change models, particularly if the authors had tested both the predicted and the alternative causal relations using varying lagged patterns. For example, the authors could have used perceived teacher context in one set of analyses as the time-varying covariate to assess whether changes in perceived teacher context predicted changes in perceived control. They could then compare this with a model in which changes in perceived control predicted changes in perceived teacher context. A simplified version of such a comparison could have been done with more extensive cross-lagged structural equation modeling.

Let me reiterate—this concern, like the ones raised earlier, are more a comment on the current best practices in our field than a comment on this specific project. These authors have gone far beyond the level of longitudinal analyses usually used in longitudinal studies. As such, this study will be a strong stimulus to the field to move forward in its analytic sophistication.

Nonetheless, there is still much to be done to better specify and test dynamic psychological models.

Another important methodological issue raised by this study is the need to be very careful about inferences we draw when we compare within- and between-informant measures. As is true in all such studies, the relations between within-informant measures were much stronger than the relations between across-informant measures. For example, in this case, the links between perceived teacher context and perceived control were stronger than the links between perceived control and former grades. Does this mean that teacher context is a stronger influence on perceived control than grades? I do not think that the findings presented in this *Monograph* provide an answer to this question, precisely because the students provided the data for both perceived context and perceived control while the teacher provided the grades. The authors provide a very strong rationale for getting their measures from the specific sources that they selected. But we also need to recognize the methodological limitations that such choices place on our ability to draw strong inferences about differential relations in the data.

This brings me to my last methodological/theoretical concern: How should we operationalize engagement? At the simplest level, this is solely a methodological issue. Can teachers assess engagement? To the extent that engagement includes an emotional and motivational component (which it does in these authors' conceptualization), how good are observers at inferring these internal psychological states? Evidence from personality and social psychology suggests not very good. In addition, my colleagues and I have found that junior high school teachers, in particular, are not very accurate in their ratings of their students' adjustment to junior high school (Lord, Eccles, & McCarthy, 1994). Instead, we found that the teachers used the students' academic performance to assess the students' motivation and adjustment. Given these findings, we need to be cautious in interpreting the causal relation between teachers' ratings of their students' engagement and the grades that these same teachers give the students at the end of the year. Having an independent indicator of performance, such as a score on a standardized test in addition to teachers' grades, would have provided stronger evidence in support of the authors' causal prediction.

At a higher level, the issue of what is engagement is fundamentally theoretical. Skinner et al. operationalize the construct in one way. Other operationalizations are quite feasible. There is an emerging consensus that engagement is likely to be the most powerful mediator of the link between motivation and performance (see Eccles et al., 1998). We now need more extended discussion in the field about what engagement actually is and how it is best operationalized and measured.

Where Is Context?

As our field gets more engaged in research on context, we will need to develop much better theories about what context is and how it is best measured. In this *Monograph,* the authors treat this issue primarily as a methodological problem. They carefully point out, and discuss, the pros and cons of using student reports of classroom context, and, although they acknowledge a need for multiple methods, they argue quite persuasively for both the accuracy and the theoretical validity of student perceptions. I fully agree with their argument. I also think that there is a more fundamental issue here: Where and what is context? Is it outside or inside the individual or both? And, if the latter, as suggested by the classic works in perceptual psychology, what are the critical components of the perceiver and the context, and how do these components interact with each other to influence both perception and behavior? Although this has been a classic problem in perception, it has received relatively little theoretical attention in social and motivational psychology.

A Gibsonian analysis leads to the conclusion that the world external to the individual has affordances that restrict or bound the range of possible internal perceptions. Likewise, the perceiver has certain properties, both mechanical and psychological, that restrict or influence perception. Although some social and personality psychologists have studied the "eye of the beholder," little of this work has informed motivational psychologists' speculations about the influence of context on motivation. Many of us fall back on the assumption that the context is outside the individual and more real than the individuals' perceptions. Such an assumption leads us to focus on prediction regarding the influence of context on beliefs. Consequently, we miss opportunities to study equally compelling hypotheses regarding the influence of beliefs on perceptions of the context. The authors have a perfect data set in which to explore these types of hypotheses.

The problem of where is the context is further highlighted by an increasing number of studies of contexts at a variety of levels, ranging from the family to the neighborhood or school building, that find greater within-context variations in perceptions of the context than average between-context mean differences. For example, studies of classroom effects typically report that less than 10 percent of the variation in perceptions of the classroom context reflects between-classroom effects (Bryk & Raudenbush, 1992). Studies of neighborhood effects are finding similar patterns (e.g., Furstenberg, Cook, Eccles, Elder, & Sameroff, in press). Finally, the findings regarding shared and nonshared family environment influences also suggest a relatively weak influence of the shared properties of the family context on human development (Plomin & Daniels, 1987; Rowe, 1994).

So what are we to conclude about individual differences in perceptions of context? These patterns of results are consistent with several interpretations—ranging from the strength of differential treatment effects within a context to the kinds of individual differences in the perceiver discussed above. The point is that we need to think much harder about these variations for both theoretical and methodological reasons.

In summary, this is a wonderful *Monograph*. As noted earlier, the authors set our their goals very clearly and did an excellent job of carrying them out. The *Monograph* is a model of solid, tight theoretical and methodological rigor. It provides compelling evidence for the authors' control-action theory. But, even more important, both the methods and the results reinforce the importance of several critical issues that motivational psychologists need to consider very carefully if this field is to move forward in substantively important ways. The field can be grateful to these authors for providing such an excellent stimulus for this important future work.

References

Baltes, P. B., Lindenberger, U., & Staudinger, U. M. 1998. Life-span theory in developmental psychology. In R. M. Lerner (Ed.), W. Damon (Series Ed.), *Handbook of child psychology: Vol. 1. Theoretical models of human development.* New York: Wiley.

Bandura, A. (1996). *Self-efficacy: The exercise of control.* New York: Freeman.

Bronfenbrenner, U., & Morris, P. A. (1998). The ecology of developmental processes. In R. M. Lerner (Ed.), W. Damon (Series Ed.), *Handbook of child psychology: Vol. 1. Theoretical models of human development.* New York: Wiley.

Bryk, A. S., & Raudenbush, S. W. (1992). *Hierarchical linear models: Applications and data analysis methods.* Newbury Park, CA: Sage.

Dweck, C. S., & Elliott, E. S. (1983). Achievement motivation. In E. M. Hetherington (Ed.), P. H. Mussen (Series Ed.), *Handbook of child psychology: Vol. 4. Social and personality development.* New York: Wiley.

Eccles, J. S., Wigfield, A., & Schiefele, U. (1998). Motivation. In N. Eisenberg (Ed.), W. Damon (Series Ed.), *Handbook of child psychology: Vol. 3. Social and personality development.* New York: Wiley.

Elder, G. (1998). The life course and human development. In R. M. Lerner (Ed.), W. Damon (Series Ed.), *Handbook of child psychology: Vol. 1. Theoretical models of human development.* New York: Wiley.

Furstenberg, F., Cook, T., Eccles, J. S., Elder, G., & Sameroff, A. (in press). *Managing to make it.* Chicago: University of Chicago Press.

Loehlin, J. C. (1992). *Genes and environment in personality development.* Newbury Park, CA: Sage.

Lord, S., Eccles, J. S., & McCarthy, K. (1994). Risk and protective factors in the transition into junior high school. *Journal of Early Adolescence, 14,* 162–199.

Marsh, H. W. (1984). Relationships among dimensions of self-attribution, dimensions of self-concept, and academic achievements. *Journal of Educational Psychology, 76,* 1291–1308.

Nicholls, J. G. (1984). Achievement motivation: Conceptions of ability, subjective experience, task choice, and performance. *Psychological Review, 91,* 328–346.

Plomin, R., & Daniels, D. (1987). Why are children in the same family so different from one another? *Behavioral and Brain Sciences*, **10**, 1–16.

Rowe, D. C. (1994). *The limits of family influence: Genes, experience, and behavior*. New York: Guilford.

Schunk, D. H., & Cox, P. D. (1986). Strategy training and attributional feedback with learning-disabled students. *Journal of Educational Psychology*, **78**, 201–209.

Weiner, B. (1979). A theory of motivation for some classroom experiences. *Journal of Educational Psychology*, **71**, 3–25.

CONTRIBUTORS

Ellen A. Skinner (Ph.D. 1981, Pennsylvania State University) is professor of psychology and human development at Portland State University in Portland, Oregon. She was formerly at the Graduate School of Human Development and the Department of Psychology at the University of Rochester, where the data for this project were collected. Her research focuses on the development of perceived control and its influence on children's motivation and coping. She recently published the book *Perceived Control, Motivation, and Coping*. She received the Distinguished Researcher of the Year Award from the Western Psychological Association in 1996.

Melanie J. Zimmer-Gembeck (Ph.D. 1998, Portland State University) is a senior data analyst with the Multnomah County Health Department. Her current methodological interests center on methods for analyzing differential change. Substantively, she has focused on adolescent and women's health, stress, coping, and social development. Her dissertation examined the development of romantic relationships and changes in friendships among females during middle adolescence.

James P. Connell (Ph.D. 1981, University of Colorado at Denver) is president of the Institute of Educational Research and Reform, based in Philadelphia. He was formerly at the Graduate School of Human Development and the Department of Psychology at the University of Rochester, where he worked with the Motivation Research Group. His research interests center on the development of the self and motivation, and he is currently working with school systems across the country. He is also interested in conceptual and statistical models for describing individual differences in development.

James G. Wellborn (Ph.D. 1991, University of Rochester) is the clinical director for outpatient behavioral services at Tennessee Christian Medical Center in Madison, Tennessee. He was formerly at the Psychology Department of the University of Rochester, where he worked with the Motivation

Research Group, and at Vanderbilt University, where he completed postdoctoral training in developmental psychopathology. His research interests center on the development of self, motivation, and coping in school and family contexts. He is especially interested in stress and coping during adolescence and in how adolescents develop identity and autonomy in relationships with their parents, peers, and teachers.

Jacquelynne S. Eccles (Ph.D. 1974, University of California, Los Angeles) is the William McKeachie Collegiate Professor of Psychology at the University of Michigan and director of the Combined Program in Education and Psychology. She is also a research scientist at the Institute for Social Research. Dr. Eccles directs the MacArthur Research Network on Successful Pathways through Middle Childhood.

STATEMENT OF EDITORIAL POLICY

The *Monographs* series is intended as an outlet for major reports of developmental research that generate authoritative new findings and use these to foster a fresh and/or better-integrated perspective on some conceptually significant issue or controversy. Submissions from programmatic research projects are particularly welcome; these may consist of individually or group-authored reports of findings from some single large-scale investigation or of a sequence of experiments centering on some particular question. Multiauthored sets of independent studies that center on the same underlying question can also be appropriate; a critical requirement in such instances is that the various authors address common issues and that the contribution arising from the set as a whole be both unique and substantial. In essence, irrespective of how it may be framed, any work that contributes significant data and/or extends developmental thinking will be taken under editorial consideration.

Submissions should contain a minimum of 80 manuscript pages (including tables and references); the upper limit of 150–175 pages is much more flexible (please submit four copies; a copy of every submission and associated correspondence is deposited eventually in the archives of the SRCD). Neither membership in the Society for Research in Child Development nor affiliation with the academic discipline of psychology are relevant; the significance of the work in extending developmental theory and in contributing new empirical information is by far the most crucial consideration. Because the aim of the series is not only to advance knowledge on specialized topics but also to enhance cross-fertilization among disciplines or subfields, it is important that the links between the specific issues under study and larger questions relating to developmental processes emerge as clearly to the general reader as to specialists on the given topic.

Potential authors who may be unsure whether the manuscript they are planning would make an appropriate submission are invited to draft an outline of what they propose and send it to the Editor for assessment. This mechanism, as well as a more detailed description of all editorial policies, evaluation processes, and format requirements, is given in the "Guidelines for the Preparation of *Monographs* Submissions," which can be obtained by writing to the Editor, Rachel K. Clifton, Department of Psychology, University of Massachusetts, Amherst MA 01003.